Readings on Diversity, Inclusion, and Music for All

The National Association for Music Education

CONTENTS

III   Teaching Special Learners

IV   Teaching Beyond the School Years

Appendix

SECTION I

Recruiting and Preparing Teachers

Recruiting minority teachers

Programs aim to balance quality and diversity in preparing teachers

By Dan Gursky

Johanie Hernandez was absolutely certain she didn't want to become a teacher. She had enrolled in the pre-teaching academy at Walton High School in the Bronx mostly because her friends were in it and they seemed to enjoy it. But when the time came to actually teach a lesson, "I thought I was going to die," Hernandez recalls. "You can't believe how shy I was."

When the dreaded day arrived, a nervous but confident Hernandez survived her initial teaching experience and went on to become an enthusiastic, successful graduate of the program. The academy is a cooperative venture with the City University of New York's Lehman College, located right down the street from Walton High. Hernandez's student-teaching debut was back in 1986, just a couple of years after the program started. Today, she not only is a full-fledged New York City teacher, with a decade of experience behind her, but she also coordinates the pre-teaching academy at Roosevelt High School. The United Federation of Teachers member sees herself in her young charges, such as junior Jessica Rivera, who says she's "really, really nervous" about the prospect of teaching an English lesson as part of the program.

"I see my story repeating itself," Hernandez says of the 33 students in the academy, virtually all Latinos like herself. "They're put in situations that they don't think they can do, and in the end, they feel so good about it when they succeed. Looking at them reinforces my commitment to this profession and assures me there's nothing else I would rather do."

In a small but vital way, Hernandez and the other teachers and faculty involved in the project are addressing one of the burning issues facing public schools across the country: the shortage of minority teachers. The numbers are stark. Nationally, according to Recruiting New Teachers (a Massachusetts-based non-profit organization devoted to improving teacher recruitment policies and practices nationwide), 14 percent of teachers are minorities, compared with a student population that is 36 percent minority and growing. In city school districts, the group reports, almost 70 percent of students are minorities, while the figure for teachers is about half that.

"Many students will complete their K-12 school without having been taught by a single teacher of color," Jacqueline Jordan Irvine, a professor of urban education at Emory University, told participants at a recent "National Summit on Diversity in the Teaching Force" held in Washington, D.C. Irvine added that the current traditional teacher pipeline--undergraduate teacher-education students--doesn't look much different; 85 percent of the students are white females.

Across the country, dozens of programs are producing teachers of color by tapping a range of sources--paraprofessionals and other non-teaching school staff, career changers, people with degrees in high-demand subjects such as math and science, and students at historically black colleges and other institutions serving mostly minority populations. But the same demographics and market conditions that make the overall teacher shortage so ominous are, if anything, stacked even higher against efforts to make the teaching force look more like the student population.

Historically, teaching and nursing were virtually the only professions open to women and to African-American females, in particular. But in today's world, qualified college graduates across the board have a vast number of career options. The black teachers who joined the profession in sizable numbers back in the 1960s are reaching retirement age, and they're not being replaced by a comparable number of new minority educators.

As she describes the situation in her own school district, Molly Drew of the Toledo (Ohio) Federation of Teachers could be talking about almost any place in the country. "Young minority men and women can walk out of college and choose an industry that pays twice as much as teaching," Drew points out. "Until people find education and teaching valuable, [the profession] won't attract young people." School districts can recruit aggressively across the country, but the teaching market is more regional than national, so not many prospective candidates are willing to relocate long distances. "People aren't going to move from Mississippi to teach here," Drew says.

Why it matters

No one claims that a teacher needs to be the same race or ethnicity as his or her students. But there are compelling social and educational reasons for a more diverse teaching force--and some notable recent research on the topic. As our society in general and our schools in particular become more and more diverse, there's an undeniable benefit in exposing students to all sorts of role models.

The need for positive role models is clearly on the minds of some recent entrants to the profession. Jannis Glover was a paraprofessional in the Chatham County-Savannah (Ga.) school system when she entered the Pathways to Teaching program at Armstrong Atlantic State University. (Pathways programs, financed in part through the DeWitt Wallace-Reader's Digest Fund, have been around for a decade or more in locations around the country. They aim to help non-teaching school staff--minorities in particular-- make the transition to the classroom.)

"It's critical for these children to see African Americans as role models," says Glover, a teacher at Mercer Middle School and a member of the Savannah Federation of Teachers. "That's not to say that someone else can't teach them; that's a given. But if they don't see their own kind in positions of leadership, they have no one to aspire to become like."

Glover is an inspiring testament to the fruits of dedication and hard work. Like virtually all students in Pathways to Teaching and similar paraprofessional-to-teacher programs, Glover continued to work full time while completing the necessary college courses. But she didn't stop with earning a degree and a teaching certificate. This summer, after her fifth year in a program affiliated with Breadloaf College in Vermont, Glover will earn a master's degree from Oxford University in England.

"Some of my students have never even been to the beach--and it's 18 miles from the city," Glover laments. "I'm always trying to show them there's a whole wide world out there, and they can go anywhere they want in it." In addition to weaving in her own travels to inspire the youngsters, she can point out that for her and other successful professionals, education is a never-ending process. "My message is there's a better future for them, but education is the key."

Despite the obvious power of such sentiments, improved student performance--especially on standardized tests--is the bottom line for policymakers from President Bush on down through local school board members. So a new working paper from Thomas Dee at the National Bureau of Economic Research is especially timely. Using data from Project STAR, the same landmark study in Tennessee that has boosted the case for smaller class sizes, Dee was able to analyze results of students assigned to teachers of their own race. He reports in "Teachers, Race and Student Achievement in a Randomized Experiment" that "exposure to an own-race teacher did generate substantive gains in student achievement for both black and white students." More specifically, he writes, a year with a same-race teacher increased students' math and reading scores by about 4 percentile points. Dee points out that his analysis can't pinpoint the reasons for the results, but it does confirm the need for further research on the topic.

Reaching them early

Programs like the pre-teaching academy in New York that reach down into high schools-- some even start in middle school--are an especially powerful approach to broadening the teaching pool because they do a couple of things. In addition to exposing students to the profession and to the foundations of teaching and learning, they provide excellent college preparation. Of the approximately 800 students who have enrolled in the Lehman College-affiliated program since it began in 1984, approximately 95 percent complete high school in four years and more than 90 percent attend college. About 200 have gone on to become teachers.

"We've always said that the skills they learn in studying teaching are the same skills they need to be successful in any business or career," says Lehman's Anne Rothstein, a member of the AFT-affiliated Professional Staff Congress who coordinates the program for the college. She reports that the graduates include lawyers, social workers, ministers and many others in addition to educators. Adds teacher Johanie Hernandez, "Our goal is not for them to become teachers, although that's a great benefit. Our goal is to get them ready for college. If they want to be teachers, that's a plus."

Although many in the high school programs already have their sights set on a teaching career, others come to the teaching profession later in their academic careers or after having worked in other occupations. Teach for America is one alternative-route program that has enjoyed significant success in attracting minority teachers from some of the nation's top colleges and universities. This year's group of teachers is about one-third minority, while the proportion in some past years has been closer to half.

One of these teachers is Chari Patterson, a Baltimore Teachers Union member. A psychology graduate of Xavier University in New Orleans, Patterson says she joined Teach for America in part as an alternative to graduate school. As it turned out, she didn't avoid graduate school: She not only finished the classes she needed to become certified, but she also earned a master's degree from Johns Hopkins University during her first two years of teaching; she's now in her third year. "I was a full-time student, a full-time teacher and full-time tired," says Patterson, who teaches fifth grade at Curtis Bay Elementary School. "It was definitely challenging.

"After my first year, I knew I was going to quit," she adds. But she stuck with it, and the growth she has seen in her students has helped keep her going. Although Patterson has already continued past the two years that Teach for America requires of its participants, she's unsure of her future in the profession. But if she does leave the classroom, she says it will probably be for something related to education, such as counseling or psychology. Although this program and others that train teachers through a few weeks of intensive preparation are not without their critics, Patterson believes Teach for America candidates "really are the best of the best" because the program attracts so many high-quality applicants.

Some university-based programs, such as one at Montclair State University in New Jersey, are similarly interested in finding promising recent graduates with math and science degrees and preparing them to teach in urban settings--the Newark and Paterson school districts, in this case. Teacher Recruitment for Urban Schools of Tomorrow (TRUST), one of a number of programs run by the university's Teacher Education Advocacy Center (TEAC), produced its first group of teachers for the start of this school year. Among them is Kevin Mason, a biology major in college who worked for 10 years at a Veterans Administration hospital in New Jersey before enrolling in the Montclair program.

Mason got his first exposure to teaching as a substitute in rural Pennsylvania, where he was the only minority teacher in the district. While that experience helped sway him toward a career change, "I couldn't see myself working there for 30 years and retiring," he comments. A product himself of the Newark public schools, Mason is now teaching at the city's Camden Middle School. "I feel good about teaching there," he says. Mason quickly has earned a reputation as a demanding but caring teacher who expects a lot of his students--something he says is new for many of them. That was driven home recently when he gave failing grades to 11 students in one of his classes. "They see now that I'm not going to give them a D if they don't do the work," he says, adding that getting an F seems to have stimulated harder work in some students.

Jennifer Robinson, a member of the AFT-affiliated Montclair State University faculty association who directs TEAC along with Wandalyn Enix, says, "We've gotten very positive responses from the Newark schools" about the TRUST teachers. "They're very committed and focused on the students." The teachers' biggest challenge is not necessarily their content knowledge or teaching skills, which are both strong, she says. "Teaching anywhere the first year is difficult," Robinson adds. "Teaching in an urban district, however, has built-in challenges, such as high staff turnover and limited resources."

While their numbers are small, Mason is proud of the impact that he and his peers in the program are already making. "Even though there are only eight of us, these are eight people who are really concerned about the issues of urban schools," he says. "We really do care about what we're doing."

Underfunded minority colleges face big challenges

By far the biggest source of minority teachers, especially in the South, are minority-serving institutions (MSIs)--historically black colleges and universities, tribal colleges and Hispanic-serving institutions. According to the Alliance for Equity in Higher Education, a coalition of MSIs, these institutions award close to half of the bachelor's degrees in education earned by African Americans and Latinos and 12 percent earned by Native Americans.

A report the alliance released in September 2000 outlines the ongoing challenges these institutions face. "For programs dealing specifically with teacher education, funding not only has been inadequate but also now is being dangerously linked to narrow measures of outcomes of all teacher education programs at colleges and universities," the authors write in "Educating the Emerging Majority: The Role of Minority-Serving Colleges and Universities in Confronting America's Teacher Crisis." The report is referring to new amendments to Title II of the federal Higher Education Act, which eventually will tie federal funds to institutions' success in preparing students to pass teacher licensing exams.

These schools are already chronically underfunded compared to the national average, the alliance notes, so any further reduction in revenues would spell disaster. The lack of resources makes it even harder to prepare teachers adequately, which, in turn, could bring federal sanctions under the new higher ed amendments.

The Educational Testing Service in 1999 reported a distressing gap in passing rates on its PRAXIS exam, which teachers in many states must pass before they can be certified. Passing rates nationwide for white candidates were 82 percent vs. 46 percent for African Americans.

Virginia has set the highest required passing rates of any state. While the responsibility for preparing future teachers to pass the exam rests largely with the higher education institutions, the Norfolk Federation of Teachers in Virginia has tried to help increase the passing rate by offering its own PRAXIS prep classes. The math portion is particularly troublesome, says federation president Marian Flickinger, especially for candidates who haven't taken a lot of math and aren't planning to become math teachers. One of her own executive board members, a former paraprofessional who went through the Norfolk-area Pathways to Teaching program, taught for three years and was by all accounts a success in the classroom. But when she was unable to pass PRAXIS and earn her permanent certification, she had to return to being a paraprofessional, at least until she can raise her PRAXIS score.

The challenge for teacher ed institutions, Flickinger says, is to adequately prepare students to pass licensing exams without shortchanging them in vital areas, such as how to teach reading.

This article originally appeared in the Fall 2001 issue of *Journal for Music Teacher Education*.

PREPARATION FOR TEACHING SPECIAL LEARNERS:
TWENTY YEARS OF PRACTICE

BY ALICE MAXINE HAMMEL

Our first teacher-education experiences take place at the preservice level. It is here that many music-teacher competencies are acquired through course work and school field experiences. Competencies obtained during preservice classroom and field experiences guide beginning music teachers as they enter school classrooms. When the increase of special learners in music classrooms (National Center for Education Statistics, 1997) is considered, the need to acquire teacher competencies necessary to include special learners becomes apparent. It is imperative that preservice teachers have experiences that allow them to acquire the competencies necessary to meet the needs of special learners.

Several researchers have conducted studies on effective methods of preparing preservice students to meet special learners' needs. Wilson (1996) concluded that preservice music-education programs would be more effective if course work and field experience with special learners were included as part of the curriculum. Campbell (1995) designed a curriculum that included information about special learners throughout course work and field experiences. One goal of this infused curriculum was to provide preservice teachers with the ability to think of creative solutions to classroom situations.

Field experience with special learners prior to student teaching is necessary (Wilczenski, 1994) for future teaching success. Wilczenski suggests that having more field experience prior to student teaching can lead to more realistic expectations and, ultimately, more accepting attitudes toward the inclusion of special learners. Askamit and Alcorn (1988) showed that less than 50% of preservice teachers had field experiences with special learners prior to graduation. Preservice teacher participants in the study indicated that more course work and field experiences with special learners are needed prior to graduation. Askamit and Alcorn (1988) assert that preservice teachers need consistent experiences with special learners and that these experiences are necessary to practice techniques used with special learners.

Researchers have also investigated specific characteristics suggested by practicing teachers for preservice field experiences. Lyon, Vaassen, and Toomey (1989) surveyed practicing

Alice Maxine Hammel is assistant professor of music at University of Richmond in Richmond, Virginia.

teachers and recommended multiple preservice field experiences that include a representative range of classroom situations and students. Teachers and principals noted a lack of special-learner field experiences during preservice education (Brown, 1981). Specifically lacking were experiences with IEP (Individualized Education Program) conferences, diagnostic tools, strategies for learning, and structured field experiences with special learners prior to the student-teaching experience. Teachers who had such experiences perceived themselves to be more confident and willing to integrate special learners into the music classroom.

Moore (1995) conducted a study to determine the perception of beginning teachers about their preservice education. Results confirmed that preservice field experiences planned to illustrate specific situations and techniques were perceived as superior by respondents. Moore (1995) concluded that preservice students who are provided course work and field experiences that introduce competencies necessary to teach students in classrooms will be better prepared for students and situations they will encounter during their teaching career.

Williams (1988) studied the relationship between perception of teacher competencies and actual preservice preparation when including special learners in classrooms. Fifty-four percent of teacher respondents reported that, as a preservice teacher, they observed a special learner for one to five hours. According to respondents, the average amount of instructional time devoted to inclusion of special learners was approximately five hours during their preservice education.

Respondents recommended that preservice teachers receive an increased amount of course work and field experience prior to graduation.

Researchers (Ansuini, 1979; Atterbury, 1993; Dalrymple, 1993; Gfeller, Darrow, & Hedden, 1990; Gilbert & Asmus, 1981; Heller, 1994; Williams, 1988) have shown that additional course work, field experiences, and the identification of specific teacher competencies will increase teaching competence with special learners. The purpose of the present research was to examine preservice course work and field experiences of practicing elementary music teachers over a 20-year period to aid in the identification of current and prior practice among college and university music education faculty members.

Method

It was hypothesized that although preservice music teachers are being prepared to include special learners in music classrooms, current methods courses do not always contain the most appropriate teacher competencies necessary to effectively teach these learners. While field experiences are integral to preservice music-education curricula, it was also hypothesized that the extent, quality, and variety of these experiences are not always appropriate for acquiring these teacher competencies. A special-learner survey form was prepared and mailed to 653 Virginia elementary music teachers. Two-hundred-two forms were completed and returned. These practicing teachers, who had taught from one to more than twenty years, identified what course work and experiences they received that focused on special learners during their preservice education. Teachers indicated the types of special learners discussed during preservice classes as well as those observed and taught during preservice field experiences.

Results

Selected Responses. On the survey forms, teachers reported that, during preservice course work, special learners with educable mental retardation and learning disabilities were most frequently discussed.[1] Other types of special learners included were those with trainable mental retardation and those with hearing or visual impairments.[2]

When participating either as observers or teachers in preservice field experiences, music teachers indicated that they observed fewer special learners than they discussed in class and taught even fewer special learners than they observed (see Table 1). Exceptions to this were special learners with other

health impairments, learning disabilities, and emotional disabilities. These were encountered more often in field experiences than they were discussed in college and university classes. This may indicate a need for more discussion regarding these disabilities during course work in order to better prepare preservice teachers.

Respondents listed the approximate number of hours spent observing and teaching special learners during preservice field experiences (see Table 2). The vast majority of practicing teachers (76%) observed special learners from 0–5 hours prior to student teaching. A similar amount (64%) indicated that they taught classes that included special learners for between 0 –5 hours during preservice field experiences. These results support earlier research by Fender and Fiedler (1990) that 53% of students are required to have field experiences with special

Table 1

Practicing Music Teachers' Report of Preservice Preparation (*N* = 202)

Types of special learners	Discussed in class	Observed during field experience	Taught during field experience
Mentally disabled-educable	49	37	36
Mentally disabled-trainable	38	34	29
Mentally disabled-severe/profound	25	18	11
Visually impaired	36	18	14
Hearing impaired	30	21	15
Speech impaired	22	26	21
Deaf-blind	21	8	4
Orthopedically disabled	23	17	16
Multiply handicapped	24	22	17
Other health impaired	14	10	15
Learning disabled	63	73	77
Emotionally disabled	30	39	46

Table 2
Practicing Teachers' Report of Preservice Field Experience (*N* = 202)

Approximate number of hours	Observed during field experience	Taught during field experience
0–5	154	131
6–15	24	23
16–25	10	16
25+	4	21
No responses	10	11

learners during their preservice education. With the increasing number of special learners included in classrooms (National Center for Education Statistics, 1997), this is not adequate to prepare preservice teachers to teach these students.

Years of teaching experience were compared with types of special learners that had been discussed during preservice classes. Also paired were years of teaching experience with types of special learners observed and taught during preservice field experiences. Analysis of these comparisons reveals that practicing teachers with the least amount of teaching experience discussed special learners during courses more than those with the most teaching experience and also observed and taught special learners during preservice field experiences more than teachers with several years of teaching experience. These results indicate that preservice curricula are beginning to reflect the increase in numbers of special learners included in elementary classrooms.

Free Responses about Preservice Course Work. Many teachers responded to the final question on the survey requesting additional areas of study or experience thought to be beneficial in preservice music education programs. Several themes that recurred frequently are included below and have been analyzed accordingly.

A number of teachers spoke of the need for more course work regarding the inclusion of special learners in music classrooms. These teachers recommend that college and university faculty create courses that are "more real life and less ideal or perfect" and include methods and materials for adaptation in the music classroom. Several teachers even suggest that sign language classes would benefit future music teachers.

Frustration was apparent in many free-response answers received. Teachers expressed feelings of inadequacy when faced with special learners. One teacher stated:

I was never taught about special learners. My first year of teaching, I had a class of fifty that had every category from TMR (trainable mentally retarded) to the gifted in the same class. One child was prone to seizures, and no one informed me until after the fact. I was 21 and had no prior knowledge or training in this area. It was a horrible experience.

Some teachers are concerned about their ability to manage the behavior of special learners in the music classroom:

I wish I knew more on how to calm or pacify students who go into rages. I have found that these children relate very well to music, and I have to find certain pieces of music the teacher can use to calm the student and for her to gain control of their [sic] behavior.

Several teachers talked about the importance of support staff. Special education teachers and related support staff can provide music teachers with specific medical, behavioral, and instructional information regarding special learners. One teacher said:

The biggest challenge for elementary music teachers is the reality that we teach classes where all students are combined despite special needs. Adapting the music classes for all students, whether special needs or regular education, can be difficult without support staff.

Another teacher added, "We need to know what they can do. We need individual summaries on each student annually." Unfortunately, in some instances, support staff are unsupportive of music teachers:

Have tried for ten years to be actively involved with special education department. Am not consulted regarding IEP's, not included in placements, not asked to have opinions and to share with general teachers—just not encouraged to do so.

Free Responses about Preservice Field Experiences. Many teachers stressed the importance of field experiences that include special learners during preservice education. One teacher suggested, "Experience is the best teacher. Undergraduates need field experiences early on (at least by sophomore year) that are relevant and that the college or university recognize as valid." Another

teacher suggested, "Undergraduate programs must involve the observation of varied students and address appropriate strategies for teaching situations." One teacher indicated that preservice students needed "more hands-on and/or observation of how mainstreaming really functions on a day-to-day basis. How do you help the special learners without ignoring the needs of the other twenty students?"

Many teachers report having obtained much of their knowledge about inclusion through post-graduate course work and in-service opportunities. Others discuss ways they have learned about inclusion through other teachers in their schools. One teacher stated:

Many MENC publications and conventions have been helpful in this area—workshops by experts teaching music to special learners. I take the ideas and try various adaptations until a workable plan for each child is developed. Be creative, experiment, and keep trying. I work in a school system that consistently mainstreams all types of handicapped special learners, etc., at every grade level. We expect these children to adapt and become as independent as possible. Some children have their own "shadow" or aide; some can function without one in music. Consulting with the coordinator, the occupational therapist person, social worker, etc., is essential for me to adapt, plan, and facilitate an appropriate plan for each child to participate in class at the most effective level they are capable of. Observations of unified special learners in music, consulting with experts in the field, and creative adaptations of instruments come with experience teaching special learners.

Conclusions

In summary, practicing teachers expressed frustration about their preservice preparation and experiences with special learners. Their survey responses ask college and university faculty members to include more special learner course work and field experiences for preservice music-education students. They identified specific areas as deficient, including the ability to behaviorally manage the inclusion music classroom, to become involved in the IEP process, and to communicate with special education staff more or on an ongoing basis.

Music teachers perceive themselves as attempting to include special learners in music classrooms without necessary competencies. While the data indicate that preservice music education programs are including more special learner competencies, some teachers continue to indicate that they are unprepared to include special learners in their classrooms.

Lack of preservice field experience is a concern. Some practicing music educators received less than five hours of field experience with special learners during their preservice education. In addition, the quality of these field experiences, whether guided or unguided observations, student teaching, or model demonstrations, undoubtedly had some impact on the preservice teachers as they considered them very important to their preparation.

It is important to note, however, that preservice music education programs are including topics related to the inclusion of special learners more than at any time in the past. Graduates of the last five years report receiving more instruction and field experiences with special learners than teachers graduating fifteen years ago. College and university teacher-education programs are adapting curriculum to reflect the increased numbers of special learners in public-school classrooms.

In some cases, competencies needed by practicing music teachers are not taught during preservice education courses. The fact that music teachers do not perceive themselves as competent to include special learners, whether they have many years of experience or are new to the field, reveals a breakdown between the time of study and point of implementation. Music teachers are overcoming these perceived inadequacies by seeking competencies through workshops, graduate courses, in-service conferences, and collaboration with special-education support personnel. Although many teachers do not perceive themselves as well prepared to teach special learners, they are adapting methods and materials to the best of their ability. These teachers are committed to providing the best music education possible for all students.

Notes

1. Students with educable mental retardation are now sometimes referred to as mildy mentally disabled (MIMD).

2. Students with trainable mental retardation are now sometimes referred to as moderately mentally disabled (MOMD).

References

Askamit, D. L., & Alcorn, D. A. (1988). A preservice mainstream curriculum infusion model: Student teachers' perceptions of program effectiveness. *Teacher Education and Special Education, 11* (2), 52–58.

Ansuini, A. M. (1979). Identifying competencies for elementary school music teachers in planning learning experiences for children with learning disabilities (Doctoral dissertation, S.U.N.Y. at Buffalo, 1990). *Dissertation Abstracts International, 40–10A,* 5299.

Atterbury, B. W. (1993). Preparing teachers for mainstreaming. *Quarterly Journal of Music Teaching and Learning, 4* (1), 20–26.

Brown, M. C. (1981). Problems in mainstreaming programs in the L. A. Unified School District as perceived by junior high school music teachers (Doctoral dissertation, University of California at Los Angeles, 1981). *Dissertation Abstracts International, 41–12A,* 5017.

Campbell, D. M. (1995). *Reforming teacher education: The challenge of inclusive education.* (ERIC Document Reproduction Service No. ED 386 439)

Dalrymple, N. (1993). *Competencies for people teaching individuals with autism and other pervasive developmental disorders* (ERIC Document Reproduction Service No. ED 363 980)

National Center for Education Statistics. (1997). Enrollment, teachers, and schools. *Digest of Education Statistics.* [On-line]. Available: nces. ed.gov/ pubs/digest97/

Fender, M. J., & Fiedler, C. (1990). Preservice preparation of regular educators: A national survey of curricular content in introductory exceptional children and youth courses. *Teacher Education and Special Education, 13* (3–4), 203–09.

Gfeller, K., Darrow, A. A., & Hedden, S. K. (1990). Perceived effectiveness of mainstreaming in Iowa and Kansas schools. *Journal of Research in Music Education, 58* (2), 90–101.

Gilbert, J., & Asmus, E. (1981). Mainstreaming: Music educators' participation and professional needs. *Journal of Research in Music Education, 29* (1), 31–37.

Heller, L. (1994). Undergraduate music teacher preparation for mainstreaming: A survey of music education teacher training institutions in the Great Lakes region of the United States (Doctoral dissertation, Michigan State University, 1994). *Dissertation Abstracts International, 56–03A,* 858.

Lyon, G., Vaassen, M., and Toomey, F. (1989). Teachers' perceptions of their undergraduate and graduate preparation. *Teacher Education and Special Education, 12* (4), 164–69.

Moore, P. (1995). Beginning teachers' perceptions of their preprofessional preparation program and their need for follow-up assistance (Doctoral dissertation, University of Alabama, 1995). *Dissertation Abstracts International, 56-06A,* 2205.

Wilczenski, F. (1994). Changes in attitudes toward mainstreaming among undergraduate education students. *Educational Research Quarterly, 17* (1), 5–17.

Williams, D. (1988). Regular classroom teachers' perceptions of their preparedness to work with mainstreamed students as a result of preservice course work (Doctoral dissertation, Indiana University, 1988). *Dissertation Abstracts International, 49–09A,* 2622.

Wilson, B. (1996). *Models of music therapy interventions in school settings: From institutions to inclusion.* Silver Spring, MD: National Association for Music Therapy.

Teacher Education for a New World of Musics

Kathy Robinson

*A*s a biracial child growing up in the heart of Pennsylvania's conservative Dutch country, the teachings of Martin Luther, German Baroque music traditions, and a loving, caring family laid the foundation for who I have come to be. God blessed me with a powerful voice and gifted fingers that allowed me to master the organ, piano, clarinet, and accordion. My musical talents carried me through the awkward teen years—the tumultuous 1960s and 1970s—into an outstanding music teacher education program at Lebanon Valley College, a small liberal arts college in the heart of the Dutch country. But what I learned from this rich background and what I could share with my students in Central Pennsylvania was not all I was— personally and professionally.

Who I was extended beyond my Dutch interior to include the songs, stories, and feelings of those who shared my blackness—a part of me to which I had little access during my first two decades. When African-American perspectives, culture, and musics did find a way into my world, they were so marginalized that I was reluctant to claim them. The desire for advanced schooling took me out of the Dutch country to the big city of Chicago, where I met people and communities who valued and validated African-American culture—there I began to grow into my blackness.

To put my newfound personal and intellectual understandings into practice, I took a teaching position at Willard Elementary School— a center for Evanston's English as a Second Language Program and "home" to children who spoke more than twenty-six different languages. As I was preparing my students for the sights and sounds they would encounter in an upcoming theater presentation, I began to sing the Japanese rain song "Ame ame fure fure" to my first graders. One budding musician's eyes became wide as saucers—"That's my song," she said. I remember her beaming face as she sang the song for us; she told us about its meaning and how she had learned it in her native Japan. The passage of ten years has not faded the power of that moment. Daily I strive to teach in a way that honors a multiplicity of voices—including my own—and that roots music education in the reality of people's lives.

What Does Multicultural Music Education Look Like in the Elementary General Music Classroom?

Multicultural music education means many things to many people. Many educators disagree on its nature and value but do agree that in some form its curricula include "many" musics. Should these musics be studied on a daily basis or occasionally, such as during May Day, Black History Month, Hispanic Heritage Month, or the months of the Chinese, Vietnamese, and Korean New Years? Should the world's musics promote a connection to the lives of people from various cultures (like my Japanese student) or be studied in isolation for their pitch relationships, form, rhythmic content, and so forth? In U.S. schools, should these musics be sung in their indigenous language and learned as people of the culture would learn them, or sung in English from the printed page?

My recent study[1] of the practice of multicultural music education in public elementary schools was centered in Michigan—a state that mirrors the rest of the United States in many ways, including population distribution, ethnic breakdown, and teacher age, education, and experience. Based on self-reported data from elementary general music teachers in public schools, I determined that Michigan's most exemplary programs had at their core effective teachers with strong democratic attitudes, beliefs, and values, who have made a personal commitment to increasing competence in the teaching of multicultural music through continuing education, concern for authenticity, and understanding of the various uses and functions of music and its strong connections to culture. The following four profiles demonstrate four exemplary multicultural music education programs (the schools' names have been changed for purposes of confidentiality).

Washington Street Elementary (School A) is a PreK–5 elementary school in a diverse lower-class to lower-middle-class community in Detroit (Michigan's largest city) with a student population that is 65 percent Arabic, 20 percent African-American, and 15 percent Caucasian and an equally diverse teaching staff. Both the principal (in her late fifties) and music teacher (in her late twenties) are African-American female musicians with master's degrees who are committed personally and professionally to multiculturalism. The music teacher, in her sixth year at the school, is extremely well-organized; through her elegant teaching style and personal commitment to multiculturalism, she demonstrates great respect for each child she teaches.

Mitchell Bay (School B) is a K–5 elementary school in an upper-middle-class to upper-class monocultural suburb of Kalamazoo (Michigan's second largest city). The school's veteran music teacher is a European-American woman with more than twenty years' experience, a master's degree, and a dedication to continually gaining competence in world musics. The principal, a former vocal music teacher with ten years' administrative experience, believes that it is critical for Mitchell Bay students to develop global awareness and an understanding of and tolerance for others in this "small" world.

Kingwood Elementary (School C) is a K–5 elementary school in a middle-class to upper-middle-class suburban neighborhood bordering Detroit. The school community is very diverse—consisting of nearly equal numbers of Chaldean, Caucasian, and African-American students, plus students of other backgrounds. This diversity, however, is not reflected in Kingwood's teaching staff, which is 94% Caucasian. Multicultural education is critical to Kingwood School. The principal, an African-American woman and former music teacher, feels that the importance of and commitment to multicultural education should be communicated through her leadership. Of Middle Eastern heritage, the general music teacher holds a master's degree and has nearly twenty years' teaching experience. Interest in multiculturalism comes from her ethnicity, which she believes gives her a special sensitivity; she often thinks about her pride in her own background and wants that for her students.

Easterville Elementary (School D) is a PreK–6 elementary school with an attached special education center in a blue-collar, union-oriented suburban Detroit community. The school population and teaching staff are overwhelmingly Caucasian. Multicultural education is very important to the school; the European-American principal believes it to be the primary issue at Easterville. The African-American music teacher, with a master's degree in vocal performance, emphasizes singing, listening, theory, and music fundamentals in her classroom.

These exemplary programs vary greatly in location, school ethnicity, and classroom resources, yet they are closely aligned in their school and music-education philosophies. While of differing ethnicities, each of the teachers possesses a master's degree and a personal commitment to multiculturalism. While none of the teachers had multicultural content or perspectives in their preservice methods courses, they each enjoy and feel effective in teaching world musics in the classroom. To increase world musics competence, each teacher regularly seeks out workshops, conference presentations, multicultural music experts, and published materials. Two of the teachers have taken an ethnomusicology course, and two regularly consult teachers, students, parents, and community musicians in their quest to learn more about world musics.

Each of the teachers works in a school climate where multicultural education is very important and their work is supported by curricula that have specific multicultural goals. Musics from a wide variety of cultures are used in their classrooms; however, which musics are studied varies according to teacher preference, the heritages of students attending the schools, classroom teacher units, school themes, and proximity of each music to Western structure and function.

The "common elements" approach, in addition to separate multicultural units/lessons, is the primary means of multicultural music inclusion in each school. Singing and listening activities predominate, and teaching procedures usually involve the native language, English translation, and aural examples of authentic musics from the culture being studied. Teacher C notes that singing songs in their indigenous languages has become "second nature" for students whom she has taught since kindergarten.

These teachers identified the greatest challenges to multicultural music education: finding good quality materials that are interesting to the children; accurate pronunciation and translation of foreign language texts, developing curricula; and increasing world-musics performance skills, particularly in African rhythm patterns and the scale patterns of Asian musics.

Ultimate decisions regarding the musical content and perspectives taught in the classroom rest with the teacher—decisions for which a teacher often has had little training or support. While these teachers have administrative and curricular support and the motivation to seek out some world musics knowledge and skill, they have had limited opportunities to question individual beliefs and values and to develop musical and cultural competence beyond the Western European perspective. Without these opportunities, teachers continue to transmit what has been taught to them—the narrow lens and perspective of the Western-European-art tradition—even when teaching a variety of world musics. Their background and education have not provided them with a full knowledge of the range of issues surrounding teaching music with multicultural content and perspectives.

The following seven questions and challenges are at the core of today's music education practice.[2] Each music teacher makes decisions about these issues on a daily basis. While there are no easy solutions to these challenges, a comprehensive understanding of each is central to moving the practice of multicultural music education forward.

Musical content (form) and context: which to emphasize and when? how to balance the time available while resisting superficiality and tokenism in each area?

Folk and classical traditions: which to begin with? which to emphasize? how to achieve balance and resist superficiality? how to sequence experiences? how to honor both aural and written traditions?

Transmission and transformation: how to transmit musics of the past, present, and future? how to build bridges between tradi-

tions while removing barriers to understanding?

In-school and out-of-school music (continuity and interaction): how to connect the in-school and out-of-school musical lives of students? how to move from the student's world to another's world?

Making and receiving music: which to emphasize and when? how to balance the roles of composer, performer, and listener? how to embrace technology while experiencing music as a vehicle of personal expression?

Understanding and pleasure: how to relate understanding the structure and meaning of music to its pleasurable, sensual, and emotional dimensions?

Philosophy and practice: how to balance the ideas, tools, and methods that are inherent in each musical system with teacher and students' personal philosophical belief systems and with curricular goals? how to honor multiple beliefs and perspectives about music-making?

While these exemplary teachers struggle daily to balance musical content and context, folk and classical traditions, and in-school and out-of-school musics, the challenge of synthesizing philosophy and practice often proves most difficult. A substantially wide gulf existed between Teacher D's self-reported beliefs and her classroom practices. If Michigan's most exemplary teachers are struggling to understand some of these questions and to translate their beliefs into classroom practice, what does this mean for the majority of teachers?

Difficulties encountered by teachers in exemplary programs (e.g., deficits in education in world musics, language skills, clear-cut multicultural classroom goals, support, instructional techniques and strategies, and awareness of published world musics materials and of the full range of multicultural music education issues) were magnified in other Michigan elementary programs. The quality most noticeably absent from other teacher reports was the willingness to actively seek out world music resources (print and personal) and thus increase teacher competence.

In general, the interpretations and practices of multicultural music education in Michigan were "widely varied," ranging from curricular inclusion of multicultural content during holidays or month-long celebrations, to year-long infusion of diverse musics in a variety of instructional strategies, with concern for issues of authenticity and representativeness, inter/intracultural understanding, and context. Most Michigan teachers' commitment to multicultural music education tended toward the narrow, interpretive end, and thus their practice was superficial. Understanding the issues and challenges of teaching music with multicultural content and perspectives is crucial to moving the practice of multicultural music education forward. The key to improving the practice is music teacher education.

School-Level Issues in Teaching Elementary General Music with Multicultural Content and Perspectives

Superficial treatment of multicultural content and perspectives pervades our nation's public school music programs, as evidenced in the widespread use of the "heroes and holiday" curricular approach. Using musics similar to Western music,

rejecting indigenous languages in favor of English, teaching aural traditions by note-reading, and favoring Western tone colors are practices typically used in a superficial program.

While many teachers truly believe in the value of multicultural experiences for their students and in teaching from a multicultural perspective, a wide gulf exists between what teachers say they believe and the manifestation of those beliefs in their curricula and instructional practices. For the most part, the gulf between philosophy and practice is probably unintentional but may be the result of several factors: lack of training in multicultural education and multicultural music education; lack of opportunity and guidance to fully explore beliefs, values, and attitudes about multiculturalism; lack of time in an already crowded curriculum (coupled with reduced contact hours); lack of appropriate instructional materials, and of guidance and support from school administration; and confusion regarding the goals and possible strategies of implementing multicultural music education.[3]

Goals and Definition

Lack of agreement on the definition of multicultural music education, its goals, and strategies for implementation is a major obstacle to effective practice. Most music educators and scholars agree that multicultural music education in its various forms involves curricular inclusion of "foreign" or non-Western music materials. The term "multicultural" (i.e., many cultures) is one that characterizes U.S. society, often used interchangeably with the term "culturally pluralistic." According to Horace Kallen, however, a culturally pluralistic society has many cultures whose members enjoy *equal* access to the wealth of that society.[4]

In the United States, the Western European ideas and ideals upon which our country was founded still radiate from the country's every pore. Those people whose heritage falls outside of Western European strains may have some degree of limitation placed on their access to the "American dream." To fully embrace "cultural pluralism," those of Western European heritage who have traditionally enjoyed U.S. political, social, economic, and educational opportunities and resources need to make room for those of other cultural heritages who have not. What might a nation that wholeheartedly embraces and celebrates diversity look like?

"Culture" in almost every concept of multicultural music education has tended to refer to ethnicity (i.e., the music of a specific ethnic group or country). In general education, a much broader definition of culture exists—a definition that includes ethnicity but also encompasses gender, race, social class, religion, lifestyle, exceptionality, and age—all dimensions of multiculturalism that are beginning to garner more attention in music education. Gender issues involving women composers, performers, and conductors have found a louder voice in music education within the last ten years; however, their consideration has been primarily in the context of equity rather than multicultural music education as we now know it. What might a musical education that embraces diversity and the multiplicity of musics found in the U.S. look like?

The cornerstone upon which U.S. formal music education is built was note reading and singing—the study of which aided Protestant forebearers to more fully worship God. From these beginnings, music education grew into a way to elevate (and standardize) the "culture" of students whose heritages lay outside the influence of Western Europe. Does teaching multicultural music education or music from a multicultural perspective imply giving up curricular inclusion of Western art music? Does it imply, rather, that Western art music is one of many musics that should be included in the musical education of our nation's children? If the latter is true, and multiple musics are to be present in curricula, then we must also: (1) recognize the pervasiveness of the Western lens and develop other lenses allowing us to "see" clearly in a variety of contexts; (2) emphasize musical and contextual qualities that are critical to and valued by the culture being studied rather than those relevant to Western contexts; (3) respect the means of transmission of each music; (4) judge each music tradition on its own terms from an in-depth understanding of that specific tradition; and (5) understand that the role of music in people's lives varies greatly across cultures and that the ways people interact with music are rooted in the ways that their culture functions (e.g., means of socialization into society, symbolic representation, aesthetic enjoyment, etc.). Consideration of these issues requires a depth of understanding not adequately present in Michigan's exemplary music educators nor the majority of U.S. music teachers.

If one goal of education is to transmit the heritages of a society's peoples, our music education curriculum needs to reflect the reality of our diverse society.

How do we honor music and the music-making of the past, present, and future in our music curricula? Honoring the past means continuing the presence of Bach, Beethoven, and Mozart, as well as offering singing, reading notation, guided listening, and performance opportunities in wind ensembles, choirs, and string orchestras in U.S. music curricula.

This Western European tradition is part of who we are but not *all* of who we have been or are today. "We" includes peoples whose roots or heritage lies in Africa, Eastern Europe, Latin and South America, Asia and Southeast Asia, and other corners of the world. Honoring the past and present means honoring, valuing, and giving voice to multiple traditions rooted in geographical regions, gender, age, and styles, such as popular, classical and folk musics. Music education must be transformed and must encompass a broader way of viewing music—its transmittal, roles, and uses—using a new structure born of this new perspective. This is the challenge. To transform requires fundamental change—not just adding onto or adjusting existing curricula—but new ways of thinking and acting.

Issues at the heart of curricular transformation include selecting and balancing the variety of music traditions, which fall into two main categories—classical ("art") and folk—both found throughout the world. Most of the world's musics are transmitted orally (by watching, listening, and/or imitating, both formally and informally). Western classical music and many other classical traditions are not; these require specialized training and performance, often by professionals, and sometimes specialized notation as well. Works within this tradition are most often "set" and beloved of those within and outside the culture. Folk traditions, which may not be as well-known outside their regional base, are of the people (not elitist), perhaps "simpler" in structure, and transmitted orally. As such, one would think that classical and folk traditions are natural complements, but in U.S. society, they are very separate, as is their study.

Their separation is mirrored in our society, where the "cultural capital" (e.g., behaviors, skills, language, and meaning) of Western Europe has prevailed since our country's inception. What does the predominance of this "cultural capital" mean for the arts—for music in particular? The Western European art tradition is so strong that it has almost become an international musical "language," cutting across continents, languages, ethnicities, and social classes. What it has meant to be musically literate has been firmly grounded in the classical tradition: the ability to read and write music within the Western European tradition, the emphasis on the re-creation of music, and the entire Western European aesthetic have been highly legitimized and have long been thought of as the "right" way. It is only in the last thirty years that our African-American-rooted jazz tradition (an "aural" tradition) has been deemed appropriate for curricular inclusion. This incredibly strong legacy of Western European cultural domination makes curricular transformation quite challenging for music educators.

Conceptual approaches to multicultural teaching that place musics in the broadest possible context are known as "music-as-culture" approaches. Some scholars believe that a concept of multicultural music education that includes gender and other facets of culture is too broad, unwieldy, and confusing. Can we ignore issues such as age, gender, and race in the teaching of world musics? Should we teach world musics from a "music-as-culture" approach or with a musical, rather than cultural, focus?

While the "music-as-culture" curricular approach focuses on rooting music in context, comparative approaches, such as the "world musics education" approach of Anthony Palmer[5] and Jacqueline Yudkin,[6] focus on musical understanding and, as such, include a wider range of musical styles than the former. The "world-musics" approach isolates specific qualities of music and music making. However, the intent is to view those qualities through the eyes of the culture. While the practice of multicultural music education in Michigan does include a music-as-culture approach, the "common elements" approach is the most predominant; it isolates musical qualities but views them through a Western lens, placing a high value on analysis and structure and little value on context. The widespread popularity of this "conceptual" approach calls into question a teacher's depth of understanding of musics presented in "music-as-culture" units.

Beyond an emphasis on the "musical" or "cultural" approaches, there are few clear objectives to any concept of multicultural music education. To further obscure seemingly clear goals, teachers at times blend these two approaches in their classrooms. Should students "know about" world musics, or "know" the music itself, of which the latter seems to indicate some degree of multimusicality? Do music educators emphasize skill or appreciation when teaching multicultural content and perspectives? Each teacher will probably have a different response to the question, "What do we want our students to know and be able to do regarding the world's musics?" This language—"know and be able to do"—is reminiscent of the National Standards for Music Education, which were crafted to "guide reform of PreK–12 music as America moves toward the 21st century."[7] The National Standards advocate the classroom use of musics of diverse genres and styles in order to reflect the multimusical diversity of America's pluralistic culture, avoid musical stereotyping, cultivate understandings about relationships between music and other subjects, equalize opportunities to learn music, and increase utilization of community resources to enhance and strengthen the music program. Specifically, the National Standards call for students to sing, play, listen to, and describe musics of diverse cultures, in addition to distinguishing different characteristics of a variety of musics and recognizing the functions, roles, and contexts in which music-making occurs in different cultures.[8]

Most teachers successfully pass on what they themselves know or are able to do; while these broad goals are excellent for focus, their realization in the classroom will be filtered through the teacher's lens, which is often Western. Until teachers are provided with opportunities to understand and affirm multiple traditions and perspectives, our nation's music curricula will change only minimally. Multicultural music education's definitions, goals, and strategies for implementation are of utmost importance to successful practice. Michigan's four exemplary teachers each had different curricular goals and objectives with differing degrees of clarity in the teaching of multicultural music education. Many teachers around the United States, unfortunately, are less focused on what the outcomes of their teaching with multicultural content and perspectives should or could be.

Lack of Time

In addition to the confusion surrounding definitions and goals, another barrier to the successful practice of multicultural music education is limited student contact time. Many of our nation's schoolchildren have music classes only once a week. Some elementary general music teachers in my Michigan study reported seeing each child in their school(s) as little as eleven times in one year.[9] While lack of instructional time is any educator's nemesis, its widespread citation among these teachers also illustrates that they view multicultural music education as a content "add on"—an extra that is not valued as an integral part of the curriculum and thus not infused, along with perspectives, on a day-to-day basis within the music classroom. An add-on, content-driven multicultural music education, often approached through a Western lens, is likely to produce incomplete and inadequate understandings about music.

Materials

The exemplary teachers profiled at the beginning of this chapter indicated that finding quality multicultural materials was a challenge; for many others, it is a primary barrier to teaching multicultural music.

Instructional materials are essential tools for incorporating world musics in the elementary general music classroom. At no time in our history as a profession have there been more world musics materials (e.g., books, recordings, films, videos, CD-ROMs) available to music teachers. This proliferation of materials brings new and often unfamiliar traditions to music educators.

In addition to culture-specific materials, current music series textbooks, such as those published by Silver Burdett Ginn and Macmillan, include more songs and instrumental pieces of various world cultures presented in a more authentic manner than ever before. Many of these publications feature pieces to sing, dance, or play, with explicit directions, pronunciation, recordings of indigenous music-makers, and contextual information. While these materials are fine "starters," moving deeper musically into the culture requires additional education and experience.

Herein lies another challenge. How do teachers with little to no experience with world musics determine what is critical and valued by multiple cultures? Should not the qualities and characteristics of a culture's music and its role and transmission determine how we must teach the music of that culture? Attendance at world musics workshops and seminars; listening to recordings and performances; studying books, articles, videos, and films; attending festivals and celebrations; taking lessons, dance instruction, or college coursework; and going into communities to meet and talk with people are various means that increase knowledge and skills in multiple traditions. While these vital experiences require much time and effort, teachers must value others' music enough to seek out these cultures and then thoughtfully transmit what they learn to their students.

Several guidelines (including Tucker's checklist[10] for world musics choral literature) and annotated bibliographies and reviews (including those found in *Music in Cultural Context*[11] and *General Music Today*[12]) have been published to aid teachers in choosing appropriate materials for classroom use. While a proliferation of materials and a support system that helps identify appropriate materials exists, accessibility to the full range of instructional materials still depends on the mindset, experience, and perspective of the individual teacher.

This "lack of materials" barrier suggests that one of the greatest challenges to the successful practice of multicultural music education is not *what* is taught but *how*— the teacher's perspectives and instructional strategies. We do not adequately prepare teachers to relate to their students the combined social and cultural values that surround and underpin different musics in the course of instruction, yet this is an essential component of multicultural music education. Musical knowledge without cultural competence is ineffective and incomplete. Perhaps music teachers are charged with doing more than their education allows.

Teacher Beliefs and Attitudes

Teachers' beliefs, values, and attitudes about multiculturalism and diversity affect curricular content and perspective and also have a major impact on their students. The Michigan teachers indicated a strong value for multiculturalism. However, in interpreting their statement, we must remember that teachers, like the children that they teach, have been reared in a climate that places varying significances on racial, ethnic, linguistic, religious, gender, and socioeconomic differences. Teachers are human beings who bring their own cultural perspectives, values, hopes, and dreams to the classroom. They also bring their prejudices, stereotypes, and misconceptions to the classroom, despite any disclaimer to the contrary.[13]

"Teachers' values and perspectives mediate and interact with what they teach and influence the way that messages are communicated and perceived by their students."[14] Because students in teacher education programs often receive knowledge without time to analyze concomitant assumptions and/or values or engage in the construction of their own knowledge, they often leave teacher education programs with many misconceptions about people of diverse cultural, ethnic, and racial groups.[15] Current and prospective teachers need opportunities to explore their attitudes and biases in order to gain knowledge about people who are different from themselves.

Teacher Training

Lack of instructional time and/or quality materials, confusion surrounding definitions and goals, and other barriers contribute to a wide gulf between what teachers say they believe and the manifestation of those beliefs in classroom multicultural music education practices. The presence of these barriers also reveals a teacher's inability to fully grapple with the seven interrelated issues listed above. The key to increasing understanding of these interrelated issues, and thus fostering improvement in the practice, lies in music teacher education.

Many of today's teachers completed music education degree programs prior to the current emphasis on teaching multicultural content and perspectives. U.S. public school teachers are overwhelmingly female, in their early forties, have taught for approximately ten years, and are of a Western European background.[16] They are products of their home environments, schooling, and formal college and university training. Teachers with this background—predominantly monocultural education and heavily Western European socialization—may create a learning environment far removed from the students' world, where public schools are increasingly minority dominated.

Today, while many acknowledge the importance of moving beyond Eurocentric curricula and Western art music in college music education programs, many teacher education institutions still do not embrace that initiative. If twenty-first-century teachers are to adopt a broader perspective about music and music-making, how will they balance folk and classical traditions in their curricula? How will they reconcile note-reading and a certain level of technical proficiency in Western classical music with the languages, scales, and rhythmic/harmonic/textural qualities found in other musics? How do they teach using perspectives that they may not know? How do they obliterate class distinctions in music—distinctions that marginalize some musics and allow others to be emphasized by assuming they are of more value? Many music teacher education programs do not prepare teachers to answer these questions at more than a superficial level, if at all.

Until recently, few music teacher education programs required students to take coursework in world musics, or even popular music or jazz. When multicultural content and perspectives were present in music teacher education programs, Michigan teachers often indicated that what they did learn was overgeneralized, inaccurate, and not of much use in today's music classrooms. Poor quality or inadequate multicultural music instruction in teacher education curricula was also coupled with the presence of few in-service models or mentors in student teaching and initial teaching positions. Little value for multicultural content and perspectives in teacher education programs may translate to little value in teachers' classrooms.

The barriers to effective multicultural music education practice are substantial. The most powerful and pervasive barrier is that of teacher education. Music educators are expected to teach musical and cultural content and perspectives for which they have little to no education. What it means to be musically educated and prepared to teach our nation's children has clearly changed as we begin the twenty-first century.

Vehicles of Teacher Preparation

Western European musics and perspectives comprise ninety-eight percent of the courses and eighty percent of the scholarships found in U.S. public university schools of music, according to a recent *Chronicle of Education* article.[17] American music and jazz typically comprise less than four percent of course offerings, and ethnomusicology offerings, while present, seem to propagate elite foreign classical musics (e.g., traditions from India, Japan, and Indonesia) rather than folk traditions. The majority of the world's music traditions are currently left out in the training of musicians and music teachers, providing a monocultural music education in a multicultural world.

While most of these institutions of music learning were founded to propagate the Western European canon, that singular body of principles, standards, and norms is no longer solely valid in our multimusical nation. American music education curricula have changed little since the early 1900s. Prior to 1930, music education's guiding concept was to promote music literacy, performance competency, and educated taste through Western art music. Ethnic, folk, and popular musics were rejected in favor of music which would "elevate" and "uplift" all students—including students of color and immigrants whose heritage was not Western European. Music from "exotic" lands began to appear in the late 1930s, but the strongest support for curricular inclusion of music representing a broad range of genres, styles, periods, and cultures came in the final declaration of the 1967 Tanglewood Symposium report.[18] More than thirty years later, American music educators have only begun to heed the call. The musics and concomitant perspectives studied in most of our nation's music classrooms do not reflect the multimusical diversity in our multicultural society; music education is daily moving farther away from the worlds of our students. What it means to be musically educated in colleges and public schools has clearly changed since the 1930s; the institutions of musical learning have not kept pace.

What does it mean to be musically educated as we enter the twenty-first century? I believe that it means to view music as a universal human expression. The world of musical styles and genres and their creators who used to be found in the far corners of the world are now found in the centers of our communities. These diverse traditions and the ones that were always present in our communities have a voice that can no longer be muted, a voice that calls for us to view them as valuable forms of human musical expression that are valid in their own right. Barbara Reeder Lundquist calls this the "ethnomusicological perspective" about music and music-making.[19] In a nation where the musical traditions valued by an ever-increasing segment of society lie outside Western European traditions, we can no longer afford to invalidate or devalue multiple perspectives of music and music-making. When diverse musics and perspectives are not present in institutions of higher learning, these musics appear to be devalued and invalidated; this practice sends the message to people whose roots are not Western European that their music and their voice are not valued on the same level.

The celebration of our multiplicity of voices has taken many forms in our society. On just one weekend in the greater Philadelphia community, people were keeping their traditions alive and sharing with others through music and dance at a Native American Indian Arts Festival, Ecuadorian Andes music at local gardens, Brazilian Pop music at a downtown club, a Latin fiesta, a reggae festival, international folk and country line-dancing parties, the Gospel Jam at the year's first riverfront festival, and various orchestral and choral concerts in more traditional venues. In our multicultural society, music of nearly every region of the world is easily available, providing a fertile ground for rich musical exchanges and boundless new creations.

Earlier in the year, I witnessed such a creation—a piece by African-American composer Hannibal—that fused a symphony orchestra, West African *griot*, jazz trio, gospel choir, and Caribbean drummers. Tuxedoed string players and brightly clad, barefoot drummers sitting next to them on the stage of Philadelphia's Academy of Music all applauded the composer at the end of this extraordinary offering. However, the collaboration of a British madrigal ensemble, I Fagiolini, and Sadasa, a South African gospel choir from Soweto, which I witnessed at the 1998 International Society for Music Education (ISME) conference in Pretoria, was the most incredible. I cannot put into words the visual and sonic beauty created by the intertwining of these two disparate traditions, as two worlds became one. How much richer and more real a musical education would be if this multiplicity of voices were heard in our school music classrooms.

The vast array of musics resulting from the mixing of stylistic and conceptual elements found in traditional and Western cultures constitutes the bulk of most people's non-Western music experiences. Music teachers, who are almost universally concerned with issues of authenticity, have difficulty conceptualizing these musical hybrids. Authentic music refers to music that is "real" or "true." Traditional music is not the only vehicle of this. Whatever a group says is their music—the music practiced within their society—is their music and, as such, is authentic. Authentic music, then, can be traditional, a hybrid, or more popular—"world beat" musics. Interestingly enough, authenticity appears to be an issue of much greater concern for the music educator than for the indigenous musician.[20]

A musical education for today's U.S. society should consider technological advancements, along with burgeoning diversity. With the aid of technology, we can bring people and music together more rapidly and easily than ever before. The world's people and their musics are only the turn of a dial, a voice command, or a "mouse-click" away. With growing diversity and technological advancements, the learning needs of our nation's children have also changed. In our world, students have an unprecedented variety of stimulating activities and experiences from which to choose on a daily basis. Students' inability to differentiate between work, play, and learning, coupled with the need for instant gratification and a lack of focus and study skills, requires more and different teacher knowledge and skills than ever before.

How do we craft a musical education for the children of this century? Wherein does its value lie? The cultural, social, economic, technological, and political changes in our society warrant a change in philosophical position. Music must be taught from the perspective that music is a powerful factor in human society and cultural practice, a fact that *all* teachers must respect and represent. To "respect and represent" the teaching of a South African folk tune means to transmit it orally in the indigenous language with movement; a wide open vocal sound; limited involvement of the conductor; the large half-steps found in indigenous scales; an understanding of the text, meaning, and context; and an omnipresent vision of honoring those to whom the song "belongs." A twenty-first-century musical education should employ a multiplicity of musics presented through strategies that, according to James Standifer, "intellectualize and humanize."[21] Preservice music education should provide the necessary experiences, foci, perspectives, and possible processes to start student teachers on the path to giving such a musical education to today's children in today's world.

Prospective teachers should be prepared to respond to varied teaching situations—urban or rural, monocultural or multicultural, empowered or impoverished, oral or written, popular or classical, and countless others. To do so, they need a firsthand knowledge of several musical styles and systems and need to assimilate multiple approaches to music teaching and learning. Development of skills for effective crosscultural communication, whether face-to-face, written, or on-line, is essential. Teachers need the ability to look beyond their personal "cultural packages" and to develop strategies to connect with people, communities, and social and educational institutions that are different from their own points of reference. Technological skills to facilitate on-line learning, compositional and creative activity, and personal record-keeping must also be a required component of preservice teacher training. Computer and multimedia skills that are used in creating instructional materials and strategies are also primary.

A broad understanding of the various conceptions of "education," formal and informal, and the roles that they play in the lives of their students is essential for prospective teachers. Twenty-first-century teachers must learn how to honor the child whose musical knowledge and skills has developed in a variety of ways, from hearing and singing childhood songs that introduce fictional characters or instruct them how to "be" and act within their society, to singing plagal Amen cadences or gospel tunes every week in church, to watching and imitating family members who play the fiddle or congas at weekly dance parties, to spending time with grandparents enamored of Nelson Eddy and Jeanette McDonald, to imitating adult musicians with friends, to taking weekly private lessons in addition to participating in general music classes, band, orchestra, and/or chorus in school.

Prospective teachers must also be prepared to make daily decisions regarding the seven questions listed above and regarding challenges inherent in current music education practice: musical content (form) and context, folk and classical traditions, transmission and transformation, in-school and out-of-school music (continuity and interaction), making and receiving music, understanding and pleasure, and philosophy and practice.

The challenges to the teaching of world or multicultural musics are not easily solved; they need to be continually revisited. These and other dialectics surrounding the teaching of world musics are discussed in greater depth in Estelle Jorgensen's *In Search of Music Education*.[22] Many of these challenges, however, can be addressed within music teacher education programs in our colleges and universities. The following section offers some suggestions to help equip our future teachers with more skills, knowledge, and broader perspectives for teaching multicultural music in our nation's schools.

Music Teacher Education for Our Multimusical World: Experiences to Gain

While addressing the many challenges surrounding teaching multicultural content and perspectives may not bring immediate gains, it may be the best avenue for long-term growth. Giving prospective teachers the knowledge and skills of multiple traditions, along with opportunities to develop broader perspectives, are excellent ways to start addressing these challenges. Pre-service teachers need experiences that lead them to understand the impact of their background and biases on the classroom: teach *with* culture, not *about* it; know culturally specific dimensions of music with attention to representativeness; develop strategies to deal effectively with languages; soften the boundaries between student and teacher to develop a community of learners; experience the power of music-making and -receiving across cultures; and use technology to connect with people and their musical traditions.

Prospective teachers need to understand the powerful impact that their own backgrounds—socialization and formal schooling—have on all that they do and understand. The ability to question, look beyond the norm, and acknowledge the existence of diverse ways of seeing, hearing, and making music is essential to teaching music with multicultural content and perspectives. When linked with knowledge about a variety of peoples, this ability becomes a powerful tool in the classroom, which

affords more opportunities to connect with and respect diverse students and school communities.

Knowing culture-specific and universal dimensions of multiple traditions offers a warehouse of possibilities for teaching multicultural content and perspectives. Understanding the various roles, functions, and compositional processes of musics broadens possibilities for creative/compositional classroom experiences. The ability to link to scholars, ethnomusicologists, and indigenous musicians in person, on-line, in communities, and through writings and music-making can foster continual growth long after an undergraduate music education program ends.

The fastest and perhaps most critical way to move into a significant understanding of a tradition is through direct involvement. Performance opportunities in non-Western traditions bring students face-to-face with issues of authenticity. Building a repertoire of pieces and experiences will allow prospective teachers to share from their own knowledge bases, giving more power to their instruction. Experiences in receiving aurally transmitted music can strengthen and broaden aural skills and provide models upon which to base classroom instruction. The power of learning another tradition firsthand is undeniable.

Skills for effective interaction across cultural and ethnic boundaries can be developed through participating in performance ensembles and community music/cultural events and through making personal contacts with "culture-bearers" in familiar and unfamiliar settings. Knowing how to access resources available through social and educational institutions at the community,

Table 1. A Twenty-First-Century Undergraduate Music Education Curriculum

1. Social Foundations of Education, Psychology, and Sociology
   A. Exploration of the realities of multicultural society and education for twenty-first-century America
   B. Examination of cultural specifics and universals and the magnitude and pervasiveness of the Western lens

2. Foreign Language
   A. Minimum of two years of study, including exploration of cultural/linguistic differences among peoples
   B. Learning the International Phonetic Alphabet (IPA)
   C. Complement-to-Diction classes for singers

3. Music History: Multicourse sequence that includes a variety of styles, forms, and traditions and that links music to culture

4. Ethnomusicology
   A. Two courses: Survey of World Musics and a culture-specific class for in-depth knowledge
   B. Emphasis on listening, performing, creating
   C. Required attendance at non-Western music events

5. Music Theory and Composition
   A. Inclusion of non-Western scales, melodies, rhythms, harmonies (textures), and forms in aural, written, and creative experiences

6. Performance groups
   A. Western and non-Western groups utilizing aural and written transmission
   B. Western groups incorporating world musics repertoire, voicings, instruments, and melodies; variety of timbres (instrumental and vocal); and associations with traditional musicians

7. Music Technology
   A. Combination of classes (Notation, Sequencing, Multimedia, Web Page Construction, etc.) and Competencies (Word Processing, CD-ROM, Spreadsheets, etc.)
   B. Opportunities to use skills in preparing instructional materials and in instructing students

8. Music Education Classes (Methods and Instrument Skill Classes)
   A. Inclusion of diverse content and perspectives, including model lessons in all classes
   B. Inclusion of multicultural instructional materials and means for their evaluation as representations of specific tradition
   C. Inclusion of opportunities to become facilitators and approach differences as opportunities and challenges
   D. Capitalization on learnings in other course-work (language, education theory, etc.)
   E. Non-Western instrumental competency in skill classes
   F. Field experiences including observation and pre-student teaching that culminate in student teaching with a cooperative teacher who models strategies for curricular inclusion of multicultural content and perspectives
   G. Coursework in or extended experiences with teaching world musics in the schools

9. World Musics Workshops/Demonstrations/Concerts: Attendance at a prescribed number of events for edification beyond what the school or university offers in world musics

regional, and national levels is also an invaluable skill. Developing skills in on-line communication and linking through the Internet to communities and schools the world over can bring world musics to one's doorstep. Thus, the development of technological skills is critical to multicultural teaching and learning.

In order to access the information/resources necessary for multicultural teaching, the boundaries between teacher and student/culture-bearer need to be de-emphasized in order to foster a sense of the class as a community of learners. Knowing how to set the stage for students or outside-of-school culture-bearers to share their musics and cultures firsthand is critical to multicultural teaching and learning. Teachers must learn how, and when, to be the "guide on the side" as well as the "sage on the stage."

The experiences put forth in this section are more powerful if suffused into every facet of the undergraduate music education curriculum, including coursework in music (theory, history, and composition), foreign languages, and education. How do these experiences translate into undergraduate teacher-training curricula? Table 1 includes the aforementioned experiences and forms the basis for a twenty-first-century undergraduate music education curriculum that, while not a complete list, serves as an example of some ways to provide these experiences. Coursework that includes these experiences will greatly enhance the knowledge, skill, and mindset that music educators must develop for effective multicultural music teaching in the twenty-first century. Had the teachers mentioned above been privy to these experiences, they could be bringing a more real, more powerful world of musics and music-making to their students. Teacher education is the key.

Notes

1. Kathy M. Robinson, "Multicultural General Music Education: An Investigation and Analysis in Michigan's Public Elementary Schools, K–6" (Ph.D. diss., University of Michigan, 1996).

2. Estelle R. Jorgensen, *In Search of Music Education* (Urbana, IL: University of Illinois Press, 1997).

3. Robinson, "Multicultural General Music Education."

4. Horace Kallen, *Culture and Democracy in the United States* (New York: Boni and Liveright, 1928).

5. Anthony J. Palmer, "World Musics in Elementary and Secondary Music Education: A Critical Analysis" (Ph.D. diss., University of California–Los Angeles, 1975).

6. Jacqueline J. Yudkin, "An Investigation and Analysis of World Music Education in California's Public Schools, K–6" (Ph. D. diss., University of California–Los Angeles, 1990).

7. MENC, *The School Music Program: A New Vision, The K–12 National Standards, PreK Standards, and What They Mean to Music Educators* (Reston, VA: MENC, 1994), 3.

8. Ibid.

9. Robinson, "Multicultural General Music Education."

10. Judith Cook Tucker, "Circling the Globe: Multicultural Resources," *Music Educators Journal* 78, no. 9 (May 1992): 37–40.

11. Patricia Shehan Campbell, *Music in Cultural Context: Eight Views on World Music Education* (Reston, VA: MENC, 1996).

12. Bryan Burton and Rosella DiLiberto, "Resources for Teaching: Music of Africa," *General Music Today* 12, no. 3 (Spring 1999): 24–30.

13. Donna M. Gollnick, "Multicultural Education," *Viewpoints in Teaching and Learning* 56 (Winter 1980): 1–17.

14. James A. Banks, "A Curriculum for Empowerment, Action and Change," in *Empowerment through Multicultural Education*, ed. Christine E. Sleeter (Albany, NY: State University of New York Press, 1991), 139.

15. Ibid., 125–41.

16. National Education Association, *Status of the American Public School Teacher, 1990–91* (Washington, DC: National Education Association, 1992).

17. Sammie A. Wicks, "The Monocultural Perspective of Music Education," *The Chronicle of Education* (January 9, 1998): A72.

18. Robert A. Choate, *Music in American Society: Documentary Report of the Tanglewood Symposium* (Washington, DC: MENC, 1968).

19. Barbara Reeder Lundquist, "A Music Education Perspective," in *Musics of the World's Cultures: A Source Book for Music Educators*, ed. Barbara Reeder Lundquist and C. K. Szego (Nedlands, Australia: Callaway International Resource Centre for Music Education, 1998): 38–46.

20. Anthony J. Palmer, "World Musics in Music Education: The Matter of Authenticity," *International Journal of Music Education* 19 (1992):

32–40. See this article for a more detailed discussion of the issues of authenticity.

21. James A. Standifer, "Multicultural Education in Action" (unpublished paper, 1982). Photocopy.

22. Jorgensen, *In Search of Music Education.*

KATHY ROBINSON, assistant professor of music education at the Eastman School of Music in Rochester, New York, and co-director of Umculo: The Kimberley Project (a music teaching/learning/cultural exchange program sending experienced educators to teach in Kimberley, South Africa, schools), presents workshops frequently throughout the United States and abroad on the topics of world musics and general music education.

This article originally appeared in the July 1999 issue of *Music Educators Journal.*

DEVELOPING TEACHERS FOR EARLY CHILDHOOD PROGRAMS

Research about the impact of music on brain development highlights the need to prepare teachers to provide effective music instruction in day-care and preschool settings.

BY CAROL SCOTT-KASSNER

The public is developing a new awareness of the importance of children's early years to their learning—including their learning about music. The media has proclaimed what early childhood educators and researchers have known for years—that what happens before birth and through the preschool years significantly affects a person for life. On a nationally televised program about the importance of parenting to children's psychosocial and cognitive growth, Oprah Winfrey made a plea for parents to sing to their children. Cover stories about emerging research on brain development in *Time* (February 8, 1997) and *Newsweek* (February 19, 1996) made special reference to the role that music plays in the developmental process and discussed implications for day-care and early childhood programs. National Public Radio aired a segment (April 1997) on music and the developing brain, focusing on a music program for at-risk kindergarteners.

Carol Scott-Kassner, formerly professor of music education at Seattle Pacific University and the University of Central Florida, helped establish the ISME Early Childhood Commission and writes and speaks regularly on the subject of music and young children.

Young students and their teacher prepare to sing "Hush, Little Baby."

Photo courtesy of the author

The 1997 conference of the Music Teachers National Association (MTNA) in Dallas sponsored a "presession" on what it means to help children learn the language of music. Panelists came from the memberships of both MTNA and MENC and included studio teachers, early childhood specialists, and university experts in pedagogy and early childhood music education. They offered a wealth of suggestions and directions for further research, many of which were published in the August/September 1997 *American Music Teacher.* MTNA has continued to address these concerns at subsequent conferences.

Beyond the Sound Bites

Clearly, the time is ripe for reinforcing the importance of reaching children through music in the early years. The discussion needs to move beyond the evidence of the neurological impact of music to focus on the multiplicity of reasons *why* music is crucial to the development of the whole child. Moreover, we need to determine *how* to reach children through music. This inquiry leads us to ask some very practical questions. How can we identify—and how do we train—caring adults to create child-centered programs that offer music experiences of high quality? All who desire to bring music into the lives of young children in significant ways need to address these concerns in a thoughtful manner.

Certainly, parents are the first and most important teachers. Parents can reach their children through music while they are still in the womb. Later, they can comfort their newborns with lullabies. Then they can spontaneously sing to their toddlers, dance with them, and engage them in simple rhyming games. Parents are key to creating musically rich environments in which young children can explore sound and improvise with it. When parents take their children to musical events, expose them to high-quality recordings, and—eventually—provide them with music lessons and encourage their participation in school music programs, they model their own valuing of music. These ingredients are essential to a solid music foundation and cannot be replaced by any day-care or preschool program in music. However, at a time when many parents work outside the home during their children's early years, the desirability of reaching children musically in early childhood programs has increased.

Programs for Young Children

There are approximately fifteen million children under the age of five in day-care and preschool settings in the United States. Studies of what happens musically in these environments reveal a wide range of practices. Singing in large groups is the most frequently reported musical activity, followed by activities that involve moving in rhythm, playing instruments, listening to music, and using creative

dramatics. Recordings are often used as stimuli for activities. Typically, a small percentage of time is devoted to having children explore or create music on their own.[1] Overall, time spent on music can range from 15 to 120 minutes per week.[2]

■ ■ ■ ■ ■ ■

Clearly, the time is ripe for reinforcing the importance of reaching children through music in the early years.

■ ■ ■ ■ ■ ■

Close examination reveals that day-care and early childhood programs are often lacking in musical direction. What are called "listening" periods may simply be intervals when music is playing in the background rather than sessions devoted to focused or guided listening activities of the type included in structured music programs. Moreover, the songs that children sing or hear rarely reflect the multicultural nature of American society. Often, there is no music curriculum or planned music lessons. Instead, music is inserted into the curriculum to teach various "themes of the week" or to provide general enrichment. Although the infusion of music and the other arts into the curriculum can provide children with varied and creative ways of knowing, this use of music does not constitute music-centered learning. The musical practice that Susan M. Tarnowski and Janet R. Barrett found "most disturbing" in their study of Wisconsin preschools was teachers' use of music "to enhance other aspects of the early childhood program" instead of structuring musical activities to help children "learn about music through direct teaching and free play-time experimentation."[3]

Rachel L. Nardo extensively studied early childhood music practices in California. She found that two-thirds of the preschool teachers designed their own curricula, and she made the encouraging discovery that the same percentage of centers "provided direct music instruction with planned lessons one or more times per week."[4] Her finding that "80% of children were allowed free play time with musical materials at least once per week" also gave evidence of an enlightened approach to music for young children.[5] In addition, she found that about half the preschool teachers in California appeared to be prepared to use multicultural song materials with the children in their care.

In general, however, people involved in early childhood programs seem less well prepared to use music. Although many day-care providers and preschool teachers seem to be keenly aware that music is important for young children as a means of self-expression, they often have far less understanding of what a high-quality early childhood program in music involves. Many early childhood educators and caretakers feel inadequate as musicians or music teachers. Because they lack sufficient training to implement a music-focused program, they frequently rely on commercial materials that reinforce basic skills in non-music areas. Often, only the largest day-care centers in the most populous areas can afford to have a musician on the faculty whose job is to implement varied musical activities and a music curriculum. Rose Dwiggins Daniels found that most center directors did not consider screening prospective teachers on the basis of their music backgrounds.[6] Nardo found the opposite to be true in her study of California preschools.[7]

Other early childhood settings, such as community music schools and private studios, sometimes employ highly trained musicians who assume that they can easily teach young children by simply "watering down" music material. Some of these teachers are so focused on having young students "perform the music accurately" that they lose all sense of them as children. They will do such things as

Course content. Courses that prepare teachers of young children to use music in their instruction should include the following subjects:

- The musical world and musical nature of the young child, including the role of musical play
- The impact (intellectual, physical, social, emotional, and spiritual) of music on the whole child
- The musical growth of the young child through singing, moving, listening, creating, playing instruments, and thinking about sound
- Techniques for reaching all children through music, including at-risk children and those with special needs
- Music materials for young children, with opportunities for:

  (a) building a repertoire of songs, including multicultural materials, movement activities, rhymes, and singing games

  (b) becoming familiar with recordings, instruments, literature about music, and musical toys that are appropriate for young children at various developmental stages

- The role of the teacher, focusing on:

  (a) integrating music across the curriculum, infusing it into play, daily activities, and nonmusic subjects, while focusing on musical learning and development

  (b) creating music centers and selecting materials for musical play

  (c) helping children find their singing voices

  (d) interacting musically and discussing music

  (e) encouraging "musical parenting"

  (f) observing musical behaviors and documenting musical growth

  (g) modeling musical behaviors, including a valuing of music.

Key experiences. Activities and assignments should involve teachers of young children in experiences that give them critical information and skills. Teachers should be engaged in:

- Documenting and expanding their repertoires of age-appropriate songs, games, and rhymes
- Learning to critique and select materials for their age-appropriateness
- Observing and documenting children's mastery of songs, movement coordination, musical play, and informal music making at various stages of development
- Observing and documenting the musical development of a child over time and reporting it to parents
- Teaching music to young children (two or three experiences, minimum)
- Learning to adapt instruction to meet the special needs of at-risk children and children with disabilities
- Creating musical toys out of simple materials and evaluating commercial toys
- Planning an integrated unit in which music and the other arts play central roles, using the National Standards for Music Education[1] as a guide
- Gaining confidence in using their own singing voices and learning how to play simple instruments to accompany children
- Becoming familiar with the ways in which parents can help their children grow musically.

---

1. Consortium of National Arts Education Associations, *National Standards for Arts Education* (Reston, VA: MENC, 1994); see also Prekindergarten Standards in *The School Music Program: A New Vision* (Reston, VA: MENC, 1994).

hand a child a simple rhythm instrument and tell him or her exactly how to play it, warning that tapping it on the floor will make noise, which is not allowed in music. Such approaches are antithetical to the best practices in early childhood music.

Raising Standards

The MENC Position Statement on Early Childhood Education identifies developmentally and individually appropriate musical practices in the prekindergarten setting and suggests that certain characteristics are desirable in music teachers of young children.[8] MENC's list applies explicitly to everyone who works professionally with young children in the area of music but also has relevance for parents and care providers who are not trained in music. MENC recommends that early childhood music teachers

- like and respect young children
- value music and recognize that an early introduction to music is important in the lives of children
- model an interest in and use of music in daily life
- be confident in their own musicianship, realizing that the multiple facets of musical interaction afford many effective ways to affect children's musical growth
- be willing to enrich and seek improvement of personal musical and communication skills
- interact with children and music in a playful manner
- use developmentally appropriate music materials and teaching techniques
- find or create appropriate music resources or seek assistance in acquiring and using them
- work to create appropriate music learning environments
- be sensitive and flexible when children's interests are diverted from a planned activity.[9]

An informal survey of eight university-level experts in early childhood music elicited similar characteristics.[10] These specialists were asked to consider the case of individuals who are trained in music but may not be experts in early childhood education. Those surveyed recommended that such persons should

- have a love of young children that combines a respect for individual differences, a capacity to see music through the eyes of the child, patience, and kindness
- be adaptable in responding to the child, open to pursuing the direction he or she wants to take, playful in entertaining the ideas that he or she generates, and flexible in the use of musical resources
- have a solidly developed musicianship and possess abilities to hear well, sing well, and move well, in addition to knowledge of the instrument(s) they teach

■ ■ ■ ■ ■

Close examination reveals that day-care and early childhood programs are often lacking in musical direction.

■ ■ ■ ■ ■

- have an understanding of all areas of child development—social, emotional, physical, intellectual, and musical—that is not only theoretical but also informed by practice
- be genuinely spontaneous as music makers, capable of improvising, composing, and arranging music from a child's perspective
- be open to children's improvisations and compositions and sincerely value their input
- be keenly observant and thoughtful, reflecting on the growth of each child, as well as their own work with the child, and adjusting instruction accordingly rather than rigidly following a prescribed text or method

- know a broad repertoire of music for children, including songs from many cultures, and be able to use it spontaneously to suit the moment.
- value the process of documenting a child's growth, recognizing children's capacity to reflect meaningfully on their own progress from a very young age.[11]

Training in Early Childhood Music

These lists of characteristics give direction for identifying and training teachers for prekindergarten programs. Ideally, such training should occur through community-college- and university-level courses required for certification or degree programs. These courses should be taught by trained musicians who have expertise in the musical growth of young children. Review of the courses offered by such experts suggests a range of subject matter. The Training to Prepare Early Childhood Educators to Use Music sidebar lists content that such courses might cover. Some of this content is basic to the training of both early childhood teachers and music teachers, though the roles of these teachers are obviously different. Programs for music teachers will clearly require considerably more depth of musical expertise than those for early childhood teachers.

Examining the music training available to early childhood educators in community colleges in California, Nardo concluded that, because "the demands of learning music are highly complex …, music courses required of ECE [early childhood education] majors … should span no less than two semesters and include a breadth of knowledge concerning music teaching and learning."[12] Certainly, the early childhood educator is the adult most likely to introduce music into interactions with children. His or her musical training must be of high quality, as well as of sufficient depth.

Traditionally, music education majors in the United States have not received training to teach music to children under the age of five. In the past, most programs have prepared students for certification for K–12 programs in the public schools. However, many universities are now devel-

■ *Training to Prepare Music Educators to Use Music with Young Children* ■

Course Content. Courses that prepare music educators to teach music to young children should include the following subjects:

- The musical world and musical nature of the young child, including the role of musical play
- The impact (intellectual, physical, social, emotional, and spiritual) of music on the whole child
- The musical growth of the young child through singing, moving, listening, creating, playing instruments, and thinking about music, as well as the stages of musical play and symbolic representation of sounds
- Child development—social (including stages of play), emotional, physical, and intellectual
- Developmentally appropriate practice in music
- Methodologies and materials to accommodate students at different stages and with different abilities, including special learners and at-risk children
- Music materials for young children, with opportunities for:

    (a) building a repertoire of songs, including materials representing various cultural perspectives, movement activities, rhymes, and games, as well as a repertoire of age-appropriate listening experiences

    (b) becoming familiar with a range of recordings, instruments, literature about music, and musical toys that are appropriate for young children at various developmental stages

- The role of the teacher of music, focusing on:

    (a) creating and implementing a child-centered music curriculum related to the National Standards for Music Education[1]

    (b) creating and selecting materials for musical play

    (c) selecting and teaching age-appropriate materials in singing and listening sessions

    (d) interacting musically, discussing music, and inviting children to think musically

    (e) observing young children's musical behaviors and documenting their musical growth

    (f) encouraging "musical parenting"

    (g) collaborating with day-care providers or early childhood educators to help them broaden their curricula and grow in their ability to teach music.

Key experiences. Activities and assignments should involve music educators in experiences that give them critical information and skills. They should be engaged in:

- Collecting folk songs and rhymes for a variety of ages and from a variety of cultures and analyzing their melodic and rhythmic content
- Using sung and recorded music in order to develop visuals that will help children focus on some aspect of the music (e.g., picture puzzles to help children sequence song phrases, puppets or play mats to reinforce listening, and icons to represent rhythm or melody)
- Using sung and recorded music in order to develop activities involving movement or instruments that highlight various aspects of the music, adapting them for students with special needs
- Creating musical toys out of simple materials and evaluating commercial toys
- Observing and documenting children's mastery of songs, movement coordination, musical play (including children's responses to various instruments), informal music making, creative responses to music, and symbolic representation of sounds at various stages
- Observing and documenting the musical development of a child through a case study, engaging in a variety of musical interactions with the child over a period of time and reporting findings to parents
- Interning for one quarter or semester in a preschool music setting and thoughtfully observing students' growth
- Developing a series of strategies to educate parents about making music with their children.

---

1. Consortium of National Arts Education Associations, *National Standards for Arts Education* (Reston: VA, MENC, 1994); see also Prekindergarten Standards in *The School Music Program: A New Vision* (Reston, VA: MENC, 1994).

■ Selected Resources for Courses in Early ■ Childhood Music

The following materials may be useful to undergraduate students (U) or graduate students (G) in classes in early childhood music:

Andress, Barbara. *Music for Young Children.* Fort Worth: Harcourt Brace College Publishers, 1998. (U)

Bamberger, Jeanne. *The Mind behind the Musical Ear: How Children Develop Musical Intelligence.* Cambridge, MA: Harvard University Press, 1991. (G)

Bennett, Peggy D., and D. R. Bartholomew. *Song Works I: Singing in the Education of Children.* Belmont, CA: Wadsworth, 1997. (U)

Bruce, C. (ed.). *Young Children and the Arts: Making Creative Connections.* Washington, DC: Arts Education Partnership, 1998. (Developed by the Task Force on Children's Learning and the Arts: Birth to Age Eight.) (U)

Campbell, Patricia Shehan, and Carol Scott-Kassner. *Music in Childhood: From Preschool through the Elementary Years.* New York: Schirmer, 1995. (U/G)

Deliège, Irene, and John A. Sloboda (Eds.). *Musical Beginnings: Origins and Development of Musical Competence.* New York: Oxford University Press, 1996. (G)

Fox, Donna Brink. "MusicTIME and Music Times Two: The Eastman Infant-Toddler Music Programs." In Barbara Andress (ed.), *Promising Practices in Prekindergarten Music Education* (pp. 13–24). Reston, VA: Music Educators National Conference, 1990. (U)

Hargreaves, D. J. *The Developmental Psychology of Music.* Cambridge, MA: Cambridge University Press, 1986. (G)

Jalongo, Mary R., and Laurie N. Stamp. *The Arts in Children's Lives.* Boston: Allyn & Bacon, 1997. (U)

Music Educators National Conference. "Prekindergarten Music Education Standards." Reston, VA: Music Educators National Conference, 1995. (U)

Palmer, Mary, and Wendy L. Sims. *Music in Prekindergarten: Planning and Teaching.* Reston, VA: Music Educators National Conference, 1993. (U)

Scott-Kassner, Carol. "Research on Music in Early Childhood." In *Handbook of Research on Music Teaching and Learning* (chapter 45), edited by R. Colwell. New York: Schirmer Books, 1991. (G)

Sloboda, John A. *The Musical Mind.* Oxford: Clarendon Press, 1985. (G)

Wilson, F. R., and F. L. Roehmann. (eds.). *Music and Child Development: The Biology of Music Making* (Proceedings of the 1987 Denver Conference). St. Louis, MO: MMB Music, Inc., 1990. (G)

oping separate early childhood courses for music majors. Some of these courses are designed for undergraduates; others are intended for students at the master's level. Course content varies but has common components. The Training to Prepare Music Educators to Use Music with Young Children sidebar suggests key content for such courses, on the basis of a sample of ten such courses.

Other Approaches to Training

Early childhood educators are pursuing other avenues besides formal music instruction or certification as ways of learning how to enrich the music experiences of young children.

■ Organizations can set aside special time at conferences for local early childhood educators and day-care providers to come for training provided by music education professionals. MENC has devoted a day to such a program at its national conference for many years. This successful model could be implemented by MTNA and the Association of Community Music Schools, as well as by state and regional associations of music educators.

■ Trained music educators can visit day-care and early childhood centers, observing what is happening there musically and using interactive modeling to show other possibilities. By combining these experiences with training obtained in music workshops, providers can increase their confidence in their ability to notice and have a positive impact on the musical growth of children. Mary Lou Van Rysselberghe successfully implemented such training at a special music lab for children and parents at the University of Oregon in Eugene.[13]

■ Community music programs for early childhood, such as Kindermusik, Orff, Kodály, and Dalcroze programs, can offer training to early childhood educators as well as music educators.

■ Universities can collaborate with state early childhood organizations and state music associations to provide early childhood educators and day-care providers with ongoing in-service music training that is recognized through special certification. University students can be involved productively in such training. Barbara

Andress worked through a grant to develop an effective partnership of this type at Arizona State University.

■ State arts organizations can collaborate with universities, performing arts organizations, and music publishers to produce music materials or arrange events for early childhood teachers and parents of young children. The Arts for a Complete Education Project in Florida provides an excellent model for such collaborations. Public libraries can serve as convenient centers for distributing publications and disseminating information about upcoming events.

■ Community colleges can provide courses or programs leading to an associate of arts degree and dual certification in early childhood music and early childhood education. California has established a model that other states could usefully follow. A description of Pasadena City College's program leading to students' certification as "early childhood education preschool music specialists" is available on the World Wide Web at http: www.paccd.cc.ca.us.

Music educators need to make concerted efforts to develop or implement these and other innovative approaches. The more impact we have on parents and teachers, the more we will have on children.

Music education majors could benefit from exposure to a variety of models of early childhood music programs that music educators have established in university and community settings around the country, including parent-and-toddler sessions and other programs for parents and children. Examples include:

■ a program at the Oberlin Conservatory of Music (Ohio) that focuses on music listening. Contact: Catherine Jarjisian.

■ the MusicTIME program at the Eastman School of Music (Rochester, NY). Contact: Donna Brink Fox.

■ a program through the National Center for Music and Movement at the Hartt School (West Hartford, CT). Contact: John Feierabend.

■ the Preschoolers' Club at Bowling Green State University (Ohio) Contact: Joyce Gromko.

■ the Music Lab for Parents and Children at the University of Oregon Contact: Mary Lou Van Rysselberghe.

Music educators might also consider participating in MENC's Special Research Interest Group (SRIG) on Early Childhood. This SRIG publishes a newsletter (Web address: www. paccd.cc.ca.us/~menc) and sponsors a session at MENC's national conferences. Additional SRIG information can be obtained from MENC's Web site at www.menc.org.

■ ■ ■ ■ ■ ■

The more we understand the impact of music on crucial aspects of young children's development, the more clearly we will see our professional need to stretch to reach all children.

■ ■ ■ ■ ■ ■

Making It Happen

Finally, music educators at all levels and in all contexts—studio teachers, community music educators, church musicians, K–12 music educators, and community college and university music and education faculty—need to become aware of the relationship between children's early musical development and their development later in life. The more we understand the impact of music on crucial aspects of young children's development, the more clearly we will see our professional need to stretch to reach all children.

We will recognize our special responsibility to reach children whose families lack the economic resources to provide them with a head start in music.

We should not attempt to achieve this understanding all on our own. We must work through collaborative and thoughtful efforts, while honoring the desires of parents, early childhood educators, and day-care providers to deliver experiences that are rich and rewarding for every child.

Notes

1. Rose Dwiggins Daniels, "A Survey of Preschool Musical Education in Four Southeastern States," *Southeastern Journal of Music Education* 3 (1991): 20–31.

2. Kimberly Moody Golden, "An Examination of the Uses of Music in Selected Licensed Preschools in the State of Ohio" (Ph.D. diss., Ohio State University, 1989), University Microfilms No. 9011176.

3. Susan M. Tarnowski and Janet R. Barrett, "The Beginnings of Music for a Lifetime: Survey of Musical Practices in Wisconsin Preschools," *Update: Applications of Research in Music Education* 15, no. 2 (1997): 6.

4. Rachel L. Nardo, "California Survey of Music in Early Childhood Teacher Preparation and the Role of the Community College" (Ph.D. diss., University of Southern California, 1996), 4. University Microfilms No. 9720270.

5. Nardo, 5.

6. Daniels.

7. Nardo.

8. "MENC Position Statement on Early Childhood Education" (Appendix B), in Mary Palmer and Wendy L. Sims, *Music in Prekindergarten: Planning and Teaching* (Reston, VA: Music Educators National Conference, 1993).

9. Ibid.

10. Carol Scott-Kassner, "Learning the Language of Music" (paper presented at the national conference of the Music Teachers National Association, Dallas, Texas, March 1997).

11. Ibid.

12. Nardo, 10.

13. Mary Lou Van Rysselberghe, informal report of interactive modeling in music with early childhood educators undertaken at the University of Oregon in Eugene, 1990. ■

How Will Societal and Technological Changes Affect the Teaching of Music?

by Carlesta Elliott Spearman

(Excerpt)

Strategies for Minority Recruitment

While there are good reasons for recruiting minorities into the music teacher profession, increasing the number of minority music teachers will not be easy. There are many social and school factors that contribute to making the pool of minority college students and music education graduates small. Thus longer-term strategies must be implemented to help resolve larger issues such as institutional racism. While short-term things can be done to improve minority teacher representation, unless the larger more culturally based issues are addressed, little progress will be made.

Areas on which the music education profession can focus to begin to initiate change include:

- simplifying certification requirements
- avoiding the development of new barriers
- early recruitment of minority teachers
- providing support in undergraduate programs
- mentoring during the first years of teaching

Simplifying certification requirements. State music education certification requirements are based on the model of a four-or-more-year educational experience. For minority musicians with undergraduate degrees and an interest in teaching, a traditional route to certification typically would include a year or more of study, including student teaching. For experienced adults, these traditional paths to certification can constitute a difficult hurdle, having a negative impact on families and limiting financial resources.

Innovative certification routes, which require some additional study, possibly over a summer with immediate entry into a teaching position in the fall, with close supervision and mentoring may help limit the expense and disruption to families that such a transition into teaching might cause. In some states where the bar to provisional certification has been lowered, the requirements for permanent certification have been raised; thus the combination of coursework and teaching experience required for permanent certification has not changed dramatically. Alternative certification requirements that insure quality should be vigorously pursued.

Avoiding the development of new barriers. One new barrier some states have initiated is the expectation that prospective music teachers will have a five-year college experience (awarding both a bachelor's and master's degree) prior to entry into the profession. Five years of study does not necessarily make better music teachers, and it places additional burdens on minority candi-

dates for music teaching as it requires an additional year of financial expenditure before income can be realized. While the profession should continue to advocate additional professional study culminating in a master's degree, an approach that integrates teaching experience with graduate study can be more beneficial to the development of the music teacher, allowing the teacher to mature and integrate the knowledge and skills from courses with the experience of the classroom.

Another new barrier many states are placing in the paths of prospective teachers is competency testing. Fraser states, "There is virtually no correlation between success in tests and success in the classroom."[13] In addition, he states that it is a "clearly documented fact that any test available today has considerable race, class, and gender bias in it,"[14] thus making such testing inappropriate and contributing to the difficulty in finding minority teachers. While it is important to advocate for high standards, the challenge is to produce enough minority candidates who can meet high standards that meaningfully measure a prospective music teacher's fitness for the job.

Early recruitment of minority teachers. Rather than placing barriers, the music education profession must seek innovative ways of attracting minorities to music teaching. One approach may be to identify and recruit prospective music teachers at an early age. This might be as early as middle or high school. By identifying minority students with potential at that age and providing support and mentoring, one may begin to limit the dramatic dropout rates that plague the high schools with large enrollments of students, consequently limiting the pool of potential minority applicants for undergraduate programs. Such efforts have been undertaken in Boston by the teacher's union, which has proposed a program in which area colleges, in cooperation with public school teachers, would work with middle school students to help them complete high school, find college placement and scholarship support, and ultimately find jobs as teachers in the Boston Public Schools. New York City is also supporting this notion with the establishment of a High School for Teaching, which gives its students early experiences in tutoring younger students.

Providing support in undergraduate programs. Undergraduate music teacher programs are often organized with a series of "hurdles" instituted with the notion of insuring the quality of graduates. The first clearly identifiable hurdle is the admissions process. Many undergraduate music programs look for prospective students in traditional sites and with traditional backgrounds (e.g., played in the high school concert band). If undergraduate programs are going to increase the presence of minority students, they need to institute affirmative action programs that pursue prospective minority musicians in nontraditional venues. Some potential

minority students may have extensive music backgrounds comprising primarily informal music experiences, such as playing in a "rock band." While these atypical experiences may not provide prospective music teachers with the skills and understanding, such as reading music, that undergraduate music programs often expect of their entering students, they may still provide the students opportunities to develop very high levels of musicianship.

In addition to the admissions process, music teacher education programs often include other hurdles, such as a second admissions process into a specific education major at the end of the sophomore year. For a music education program, this screening may require a particular grade-point average, an audition, an interview, and additional recommendations. Faculty must monitor such hurdles to make sure they do not constitute a special barrier to minority students. Other affirmative actions can be taken to help students succeed in preservice music education programs. These include the presence of minority faculty in music teacher education programs and the mentoring of younger minority undergraduates by more senior minority teacher education students.

Mentoring during the first years of teaching. As many educators involved in teacher education realize, the development of career professional music educators does not end with undergraduate education. The first several years of teaching are often difficult and may be especially challenging for some teachers, particularly if they find themselves isolated within teaching environments that do not include models with whom they can identify. Several strategies can be employed to help the novice minority music teacher.

College teacher education programs can provide support and mentoring for their graduates, efforts that include both on-site visits to new teachers and on-campus seminars to help minority teachers with the transition to the professional world. Teachers' unions and professional groups such as the National Association for the Study and Performance of African American Music (NASPAAM) can also provide support for new teachers. School systems should also make efforts to hire a core of minority teachers so that isolation will be less of a problem.

Conclusions. Increasing the number of minority music teachers requires multiple efforts at different stages in the development of career professional music educators. With the profession's best efforts, it will still likely take a generation before significant numbers of minority music educators will be present in the nation's schools. Therefore, a continuing effort needs to be made to improve prospective music educators' understanding of diversity issues. A token course in music from other cultures is not sufficient to develop the depth of understanding required.

Music teacher education programs in colleges and universities must provide a well-structured and culturally inclusive core-curriculum representative of (a) traditional areas of music study that have undergirded the competencies and standards required to complete high-quality degree programs, and (b) ethno-musicological perspectives and competencies in order to prepare well-trained graduates for the teaching profession. If music education is to survive and progress in the future, these two components must work in close partnership with one another. The significant rise in the minority population indicates a marked transformation of the workforce, with women showing the greatest increase by 2005. Institutions that begin to plan now for this growing social diversity will tap the largest talent pool and enjoy a competitive advantage throughout the next century.

Music education needs the best and brightest as much as any other profession. That must be one of our priority efforts beginning now. Music occupies a very important place in the cultural lives of most minorities outside of the school setting. Our challenge is to capitalize on that inherent interest as a conduit into the serious pursuit of musicianship and skills requisite to entry into higher education music programs. That effort will call for support systems that assure that all students will receive unbiased instruction, sincere counseling, and role model mentors, as well as cultural representation included within the teaching materials.

Transforming the classroom environment to develop the potential of all students, regardless of their ethnicity, will require music teachers with highly developed crosscultural sensitivities and social skills. Music teachers should realize that the social needs and concerns of minorities are often not the same as those of majority students. For example, the competitive mode of the teaching/learning environment so favored in our American style of instruction does not receive positive responses from minority students who react more favorably to a cooperative mode.[15] Hispanics tend to be more concerned with the quality of relationships over time, rather than with simply getting the job done. They have a strong sense of family loyalties. They tend to maintain closer physical contact in their personal space than many non-Hispanics.[16] Asian students value education and have a high regard for teachers and their role in the instructional process. They have been reared by their parents to show obedience and respect in the school setting. Their studiousness and strong work ethic often translates into high academic accomplishment. However, lack of communication skills may sometimes pose a language barrier that will be a challenge to overcome for both students and teachers. Communication skills are also a problem for Hispanic students. As for the new Asian students, each is striving to balance two cultures; the culture of their homelands and that of mainstream American societies.[17] Argyle suggests the presence of seven skills for engaging in social transactions such as those of instruction: perceptive skills, expressive skills, conversational skills, assertiveness, emotional expression, anxiety management, and affiliative skills.[18]

Effective music teachers will have to devise appropriate classroom strategies for defusing tensions that normally arise from social differences. Teachers will have to work harder at treating all students equally and respectfully, bearing in mind the vital importance of consistent verbal and nonverbal behaviors in the acculturation process. Moreover, before academic behaviors can be effective, these social behaviors must be firmly established.[19] Research in classroom discipline and subject-matter presentation, as well as in establishing music behavior within applied settings, offers music educators, regardless of specialty, a wealth of data addressing the teacher-training process for future music educators.[20] The issues involved in improving undergraduates' skills are of vital interest to all music educators throughout the profession. Madsen wrote: "Besides the obvious role of college professors, most music teachers who have even a few years of experience serve as models for observations, supervisors of student teachers, and members of peer-review committees. Just as we care deeply about teaching children music, we are all concerned with teaching those who will themselves teach children."[21]

(for excerpted text)

13. Fraser, 23.

14. Ibid.

15. Lawrence Lyman and Harvey C. Foyle, *Cooperative Grouping for Interactive Learning: Students, Teachers and Administrators* (Washington, DC: NEA Professional Library, 1990).

16. Gerardo Marin and Barbara Van Oss Marin, *Research with Hispanic Populations* (Newbury Park, CA: Sage, 1991).

17. Patricia Shehan Campbell, "Cultural Issues and School Music Participation: The New Asians in American Schools," *Journal of Music Teaching and Learning* (Summer 1993): 55.

18. M. Argyle, "New Developments in the Analysis of Social Skills," in *Non-Verbal Behavior,* ed. Aaron Wolfgang (London: Academic Press, 1979).

19. Carlesta Henderson, "The Effect of In-Service Training of Music Teachers in Contingent Verbal and Non-Verbal Behavior" (Ed. D. diss., Columbia University, 1972).

20. Charles H. Madsen and Clifford K. Madsen, *Teaching/Discipline* (Boston: Allyn and Bacon, Inc., 1970); Clifford K. Madsen, Douglas R. Greer, and Charles H. Madsen, Jr., *Research in Music Behavior* (New York: Columbia University Teachers College Press, 1977); Clifford K. Madsen and Terry Lee Kuhn, *Contemporary Music Education* (Arlington Heights, IL: AHM Publishing, 1978); Clifford K. Madsen and Carol A. Prickett, *Applications of Research in Music Behavior* (Tuscaloosa, AL: University of Alabama Press, 1997).

21. Madsen and Kuhn, see note above, 71.

Carlesta Elliott Spearman is professor emerita of music at Keene State College, University System of New Hampshire.

This article originally appeared in the December 1997 issue of *Teaching Music.*

In Step with Inclusion

"Veteran teachers can keep current by communicating regularly with the special education teachers in their school, by attending sessions at clinics and workshops, by enrolling in appropriate courses at nearby colleges and universities, and by reading professional journals."

For some of the first and second graders in Renee Forrest's general music class, marching to a steady beat demanded concentrated effort and several attempts to coordinate their feet with sound. Yet other children in the class stepped into the activity with ease.

So it has always been with this age-group. But this scene last year at Schenk Elementary in Madison, Wisconsin, portrayed more than young children learning to march to a beat. It showed a successful example of inclusion, the education model for including students with disabilities in regular classrooms. Of the twenty children in Forrest's class, the four with disabilities were not necessarily the ones who found marching difficult. The class worked together so well that an observer would find it difficult to identify one of the children with disabilities, according to Forrest.

"Many in the class were struggling readers," said Forrest. "I taught by rote. I acted as if no one could read." When the class was familiar with the lesson, Forrest used printed material to teach the same lesson by a different method. "They (the children with disabilities) were able to do everything because of the struggling readers. There was nothing they were not able to do."

Yet inclusion doesn't always result in a positive experience. In another example, a child in a wheelchair attended one of Forrest's music classes once a week. The child, almost blind and nearly deaf, was at the school only a half day a week. This single class period was the child's only contact with the other children in the room, perhaps highlighting rather than downplaying this child's disabilities. "It wasn't positive. It didn't seem positive for the kids. It was basically a neutral experience," said Forrest.

Many general music teachers have experienced two sides of inclusion: the side where learning is enhanced for children with disabilities and their classmates, and the other side where the music class, at its worst, is in danger of becoming a dumping ground with little cooperative effort given to appropriate placement.

In the first example, the four children with disabilities were placed by the special education teacher, working with Forrest, for the best situation to meet the goals of the children's Individual Education Plans (IEPs). In the second example, an administrator scheduled the child after asking only about class schedules and grade levels. What made the difference? Forrest, along with other music teachers, emphatically said communication.

"Number one, communication," said Forrest, who also teaches adaptive music methods to music education students at St. Norberg College in DePere, Wisconsin. "Teachers have to communicate with the special education teacher. Special ed teachers can be supportive. And, number two, access to the IEP. Music teachers may or may not be able to meet these goals. It ranges from very doable to impossible. But take time to look at the IEP," she said. "The rule of thumb is every child is an individual. Deal with them as individuals."

INCLUSION HAS BEEN THE PHILOSOPHY and intent of the law since Congress passed the Education for the Handicapped Act twenty-two years ago, calling for states to provide children with disabilities a "free appropriate public education." More recently, Congress passed an even more inclusive bill—the Individuals with Disabilities Education Act (IDEA). The new version of the bill, signed by President Clinton in June 1997, expanded the law by defining "related services" a school should provide, extending the ages of a developmental delay provision, expanding the use of paraprofessionals and teaching assistants when certified special education teachers are not available, requiring states to offer professional development programs, and more.

Does inclusion work? "Yes and no," said Janet Montgomery, associate professor of music education at the University of Colorado in Boulder and chair of MENC's Society for General Music. "Yes, when students with disabilities are learning in their least restrictive environments (LRE)—in other words, if teachers offer opportunities for these students to receive instruction and to respond in various ways. For example, a student with severe hearing loss would not be in the least restrictive environment if the teacher only lectures. However, this same student might be quite successful if the teacher uses many visual aids and demonstrates—through action—the concepts or principles being taught. Inclusion works when each student's learning needs are considered individually; inclusion doesn't work when several students with disabilities are included in a class without consideration of those individuals' learning needs."

Inclusion has enhanced the education of students with disabilities because they work on interpersonal skills, intellectual functioning, and learning in the least restrictive environment possible, according to Montgomery. "Not only are we doing the right thing legally, we're doing the right thing ethically," she said.

Diane Maclay, who teaches general music to first through fifth graders at Silver Spring Elementary and Green Ridge Elementary schools in the Cumberland Valley School District in Pennsylvania, agreed. "The power of music to reach these kids is wonder-

The inclusive classroom diminishes isolation of students with disabilities.

ful," said Maclay.

"Honestly, I think they [children with disabilities] get more out of music classes—and for all the reasons we have music," Maclay said. She cited an example of a student whose emotional disabilities resulted in large outbursts and temper tantrums. "It happened only once in my class, and I kept telling myself 'follow through,' and had the aide remove the child. And it never happened again because she [the child] absolutely, positively loved music. She loved it and did not want to miss it."

Forrest also spoke about the power music has for students with disabilities. In the early years of Forrest's career, one child classified as trainable mentally handicapped had perfect pitch. The inclusion model kept this student in choral classes, making it possible for her to sing in the school choir during her high school years.

Advocates of inclusion also point to it as a way to change attitudes about these students, to promote teamwork among teachers and staff, and to develop interpersonal skills among diverse groups of students, said Montgomery. It diminishes isolation of students with disabilities and provides a spillover effect, enhancing the education of the other students in the groups, she said. In Maclay's general music class, the spillover effect was evident last year. New skills blossomed in the children without disabilities, noted Maclay. The children were learning the "skill of being a helper—not superior, but useful," said Maclay. She relates how children, independent of her instructions, adapted their dance movements when a child with cerebral palsy was beating the rhythms. "The kids are lovely and kind," Maclay said.

What has been the most help to Maclay when teaching children with disabilities in an inclusive model? "Communication with the special education teacher," she said. "I visited her classroom to see adaptations. It took the scariness away—knowing what I'm dealing with." Maclay also mentioned the importance of taking the lead and saying "I need to know about this kid."

Some of the adaptations Maclay has used with her students include noting each child's motor skill level and finding appropriate percussion instruments for the students. She also enlarged printed materials for a child with visual impairments. Forrest made use of signing for the hearing impaired, slowing down or pacing, and presenting the same concept several ways. Also, she placed some students close to the front of the classroom and provided audiotapes for visually impaired students to listen to outside of class.

INCLUSION CALLS FOR SPECIALIZED training for both music education students as well as veteran music teachers. University and college professors need to provide emerging teachers with information about learning characteristics of students with physical, emotional, or intellectual disabilities, according to Montgomery. "We need to create opportunities for our college students to observe and work with small groups of students with disabilities. We need to demonstrate model lessons that provide students with various ways to show their understanding—visual, kinesthetic, tactile, auditory—not just answering the question orally or in writing," she said.

"Veteran teachers can keep current by communicating regularly with the special education teachers in their school, by attending sessions at clinics and workshops, by enrolling in appro-priate courses at nearby colleges and universities, and by reading professional journals." said Montgomery.

"Music educators who teach hundreds of students a week, including those with special needs, often find it difficult if not impossible to become involved in the planning and implementation of special education programs for individual students," said Montgomery. "However, involvement is crucial if our goal is to provide students with opportunities for success."

"Music teachers may need to use different approaches to help these children with disabilities, and yet not lose focus of the rest of the students in the class," she said. "We want administrators to understand the types of learning going on with all learners while the musical experience is happening. With this knowledge, administrators will be better informed to make decisions about the most appropriate place for students with disabilities to learn."

Music educators will have a chance to discuss inclusion further, along with related issues, at the 1998 MENC Conference in Phoenix, Arizona. Inclusion is the topic for one of several "power sessions." The session, which is being organized by Montgomery, will address communicating and interacting with paraprofessionals, inclusion from the parents' and music teachers' perspectives, technology for students with disabilities, and the role of the music teacher and the music therapist. ■

Ideas contributed by Renee Forrest, general music teacher at Schenk Elementary School in Madison, Wisconsin; Diane Maclay, general music teacher at Silver Spring Elementary and Green Ridge Elementary Schools in the Cumberland Valley School District in Pennsylvania; and Janet Montgomery, associate professor of music education at the University of Colorado in Boulder. Compiled by Christine Stinson, MENC staff.

SECTION II

Teaching Diverse Cultures and Communities

This article originally appeared in the March 1997 issue of *Music Educators Journal.*

FROM HERSCHER TO HARLEM

A SUBJECTIVE ACCOUNT

Altering traditional perspectives and expectations can help promote success in the urban music classroom.

BY RANDALL EVERETT ALLSUP

In a recent survey, researchers asked successful urban music teachers, "Do you feel that your undergraduate/graduate education courses prepared you to teach in the urban setting?" The majority of respondents "felt woefully unprepared." Most shared the criticism that "preservice education prepared them for teaching the 'ideal' student and left them unprepared for the reality of urban schools, where most of the students do not conform to the ideal."[1]

How does the urban music teacher sustain a program in the face of these problems? What teaching strategies work and under what conditions? During six years of teaching music in New York City's poorest neighborhood, I have gone from the traditional "master/apprentice" philosophy of music education to one focused on and designed around an understanding of my students' lives. This has not been an easy or evident process.

I grew up in the Herscher School District among the countless acres of Illinois cornfields. As a student, my perspective on music education included traditional marching bands, jazz bands, wind ensembles, and solo

■ ■ ■ ■ ■ ■

It was not possible to teach music in New York City the same way it was taught in Herscher, Illinois.

■ ■ ■ ■ ■ ■

and ensemble contests in a small farming community of 700. With a high school population equivalent to the size of the community, it is not surprising that the community took a great deal of interest in the schools and spent a good amount of money on them. As a student, athlete, or band member, young people were always proud to represent the Herscher Tigers, even though being in the

Herscher band could mean twenty hours a week in practice and rehearsals.

In 1990, I arrived in New York and accepted a job teaching instrumental music in an all-boys high school in the South Bronx. I discovered firsthand that discipline is the primary concern for the majority of city teachers. In my first year in the South Bronx, I couldn't do a lot of teaching; most of the class time was spent trying to control my students. As a result, the pace of learning was very slow. We would often have to stop for "heart-to-hearts" on the issues of respect and valuing class work. While these talks prevented many problems, I still had to deal with graffiti-painted cymbals and fistfights in the band room.

Relearning/Rethinking

As a result, I found out rapidly that it was not possible to teach music in New York City the same way it was taught in Herscher, Illinois. In my early teaching experiences in New York, I failed most often when I assumed that my own personal educational experience could dictate the making of music within my classroom. Everything about teaching in New York was different. Compared to Herscher students, my students looked, dressed, and spoke differently. School organizations, from debate teams to track teams, were underattended. The

Randall Everett Allsup is a music teacher at the Our Children's Foundation in Harlem and a graduate of Northwestern University and Teachers College, Columbia University, in New York City.

Students can learn to play new instruments using melodies they already know.

Photo courtesy of author

students I have taught live lives free of commitment. Most are used to following their own impulses. With regard to music, they have radically different likes and dislikes. Because of that first experience, I can empathize with the new urban teacher. We are often prevented from doing what we were trained to do because of discipline problems in the classroom. Learning often becomes secondary.

I am currently creating an after-school performing arts program for Our Children's Foundation in Harlem. A community-based educational and cultural enrichment organization for students ages 7 to 20, the foundation is open after school, weekends, and all summer in order to provide a nonviolent and drug-free alternative to the streets.

The experience I've gained has taught me that to keep a student involved in music, every teaching consideration must be student-focused. Teaching strategies must be designed not only around the learner's interest, but must also take into account the student's culture and values, along with the student's relationship to learning and self-discipline. It is difficult to get the students to practice or even attend a minimum of rehearsals, say two hours a week. Therefore, for

each student I make a diagnosis. What is motivating this student to learn a musical instrument? Is it to play what he hears on the radio? Is it so she can have fun? Is it to be with a group? (Most have no idea what they're getting into.) I realized that I must capture my students' feelings; their likes and dislikes must be central to each strategy.

So I began to experiment, improvise, and research. What follows are suggestions for the urban teacher based on informal research from daily experience over the past six years teaching in an environment that is difficult and rewarding for students and teachers alike.

What Works

■ *Expect commitment.* Many students have not had positive experiences with school. In order for them to care about music, becoming involved with it must be a decision they freely elect to make. Students should be responsible for one thing: commitment—in effect, showing up regularly. If a student wants to take the clarinet, do not require an audition. Have only one requirement: attendance at weekly lessons. Allow the student to quit, if necessary, or to choose another musical activity at any time.

■ *Use nontraditional class groupings.* Group students by ability and personality type, not by instrument. Allow students to learn at their own pace. Some will be more relaxed, even casual, in their approach to music, and others will be more serious. If you know certain students can't get along with each other, why set them up for failure by placing them in the same group? If they make it past the first year, special arrangements will no longer be necessary.

■ *Start with what they know.* Incorporating popular idioms within a lesson is a very successful technique. It can maintain interest during the most difficult period of learning an instrument—the first year. For students, rap is the first room they enter in the house of music. It is a room they may stay in or return to visit later. From rap, invite them to try the blues, then jazz or classical music. Once they are intrigued, they may have little resistance to moving beyond and trying another room. Students and teacher will learn to respect the unfamiliar while creating commonalities.

■ *Teach through rap.* Tailor every lesson to the individual player or small group. Look for openings. For example, for those students who like rap music, focus learning around rap. Teaching "hip-hop" beginner instrumental methods is not the most comfortable approach for many teachers, but for students whose only musical experience is listening to rap, it is the only logical place to start.

■ *Use keyboards.* Structure lessons around a multifaceted keyboard.[2] This instrument is an invaluable tool for integrating what students hear on the radio with any musical element or fundamental the teacher wishes to focus on. Take, for example, a lesson that concentrates on tonguing. Choose a beat and a matching chord progression. For a trombone lesson, program the repeating progression in F and ask the trombone player to stick to first and third position. The lesson will take off from there. Insist on proper breathing and tonguing. The student will take ownership of the process by reproducing the popular rhythms and melodies of the day.

Teach students the basics of counting and playing whole notes and half notes by choosing a popular beat and accompanying chord progressions.[3] Learning these simple fundamentals with a back beat parallels the student's conception of what music is and could be. Any beginner melody sounds much better when accompanied, for example, by a salsa beat. It is more fun to play, and the electronic beat provides the perfect metronome. The simple chord changes underneath help with intonation.

Players get to perform in front of their friends, many of whom have never seen a clarinet or trombone before.

The electronic keyboard is also a successful tool for helping young instrumentalists establish a repertoire of songs. Try takeoffs on such tunes as "Hot Cross Buns (with Honey and Jam)," "Mary Had a Little Jam Session," and "Jinga Bellz." Sometimes you can introduce a song by rote, such as Coltrane's "Blue Train" or the theme from *The Simpsons*.

Other songs can be composed by the students. For example, the Foundation Flute Club created a piece called "Tropical Rainforest." Helping students create rap is much easier than it sounds, even if you are an urban music teacher who considers yourself an inexperienced rap artist. Let your

students start at the keyboard. (Make sure they are composing in a key that is good for the instrument they usually play.) Be there to assist and encourage, especially when they get stuck. Keep an open mind and let them have final approval. You will definitely improve the more you do it, and so will they.

■ *Record and play back.* It is not difficult to extend the exercise described above. After playing back a recorded improvisation, start with general questions, like "What did you hear? Did it work?" Next, find material from the improvisation and segue to new concepts. For example, ask your players, "Can you repeat an idea exactly the same twice?" "Can you copy something the person next to you played?" "Can we make a song out of this?" "Would you play differently if we chose another beat?" Record the lesson and play it back. Ask technical questions. "What were you doing with your lips when the sound was good?" If the sound wasn't right, ask, "What happened?" Do not focus solely on technique. Try asking, "What did you like about your solo?" "What would you do differently a second time?" "Can we make a song out of this?" "Where do we go from here?"

■ *Defer notation.* Do not teach music reading to beginning instrumentalists right away. Teaching the fundamentals of notation outside the context of what students know as music can be an exercise in irrelevance. Most of the students who experience frustration early in the learning process will not return to class. It is important that no one is *required* to read music. However, students who have demonstrated a proficiency on their instrument and want to be in a band will discover that they need to learn to read music in order to make progress.

Counting rhythms doesn't have to be complicated. Try using car names: Say "Jeep" for a quarter note, "Lexus" for two eighth notes, "Cadillac" for two sixteenth notes and an eighth note, "Volkswagen" for an eighth note and two sixteenth notes, and "Mazerati" for four sixteenth notes. Extend the exercise by collectively creating your own version. This is a big help to students for remembering difficult rhythms.[4]

■ *Perform regularly.* Because their success is tied to peer approval, the more students perform, the better they feel about themselves. Encourage students to be visible with their instruments. Celebrate birthday parties monthly, which are perfect opportunities for small-group or solo performances. Players get to perform in front of their friends, many of whom have never seen a clarinet or trombone before. The experience then becomes educational for everyone. In the future, larger concerts may become necessary as young musicians and your band become more sophisticated and polished.

Since I have lost several potentially great musicians to the streets, I am continually looking all around for answers.

■ *Stay current.* It is important to keep up with the latest theories, trends, and community values. On a personal note, since I have lost several potentially great musicians to the streets, I am continually looking all around for answers to my questions on how to reduce or prevent recurrences. Ironically, broad-based books and articles on social policy can often be as helpful to me as periodicals strictly devoted to music education. I recently saw the Spike Lee film, *Clockers*. I have read books by Maxine Greene,

By encouraging every effort early on, the teacher can help students build toward later success.

back in Herscher, but he is engaged and thinking critically, and therefore an "ideal" student.

Studying how children develop, whether through course work or observation, is invaluable. But in the classroom, success hinges on one's ability to be empathetic, even in the midst of chaos. As valuable as objective research may be in certain settings, it would be a mistake for urban educators to view their students too clinically. Such a perspective reinforces the us/them paradigms already in place within the school community. As with Troy, there are plenty of intelligent and talented students whose gifts are hidden. Whether we are from Herscher or Harlem, we should all grow up with the chance to create a song, play the flute, or sing in a choir.

Bell Hooks, and Jonathan Kozol.[5] On the radio, I listen to Hot 97.[6] And above all, I try to listen to the kids I teach. We all need to know what is important to them in order to fight against the violence and apathy that may debilitate their potential. "What is going on in their world? How can I help?" These are vital questions, and answers may change daily or even hourly.

■ *Interact with other teachers.* Does your organization or school work together and think like a family? I have observed that successful urban schools are decompartmentalized. Try to break out of the traditional music teacher role. Be a community activist, help with homework, or get a group of teachers and student leaders to organize a voter registration drive. Be seen as someone who cares about your organization and its community and get to know kids outside the music program. "Respect" is the word in the city, and you will get it if you are seen as caring for everyone.

■ *Establish links within the community.* For example, organize a concert around a charity, such as a food drive for the homeless. Ask as many different departments as possible to contribute by sharing a common theme,

such as "giving thanks." I helped to establish this type of event while teaching in the Bronx. Afterward, it became the springboard for interdisciplinary projects. Your students will often come up with great ideas, but they must also see and hear what others are doing.

Seeking Success

Failure is easy to find in the city. It is everywhere, inside and outside the classroom. In order to keep going, it is essential to look for success daily in small places. I am happy when a student is curious and asks questions. Success is watching my players believe in themselves or seeing them identify themselves as trumpet or flute players. We are lucky that in music we can see the best sides of our students. I'm thinking of a sax player I'll call Troy. Troy is a thirteen-year-old who doesn't allow many adults to get close to him. He has had a lot of trouble in and out of school, but always shows up for his saxophone lessons. By focusing on his musical talent, we have made his street reputation irrelevant. Troy loves to improvise, and I have found him to be a sensitive and intuitive musician. Maybe he doesn't approach the sax with the same rigor as the students

Notes

1. Richard K. Fiese and Nicholas J. DeCarbo, "Urban Music Education: The Teachers' Perspective," *Music Educators Journal* 81 (May 1995): 27–31.

2. A typical $300 keyboard can contain hundreds of popular beats from techno to salsa, just as many synthesized sounds, and gives chord progressions that can be programmed in any key. I use the Casio CTK-650.

3. There are several good beginner method books: *Band Plus,* by J. Swearingen and B. Buehlman, Heritage Music Press (501 E. Third Street, Dayton, OH 45401); *Yamaha Band Student* by S. Feldstein/J. O'Reilly, Alfred Music Publishing (16380 Roscoe Blvd., Van Nuys, CA 91406); and *Standard of Excellence* by B. Pearson, Neil A. Kjos Music (PO Box 178270, San Diego, CA 92117).

4. This strategy was created by Dr. Nathalie Robinson, arts administrator, Creative Arts Library, Teachers College, New York City.

5. Maxine Greene, *Releasing the Imagination* (San Francisco: Jossey-Bass Publishers, 1995); Bell Hooks, *Teaching to Transgress* (New York: Routledge, 1994); and Jonathan Kozol, *Savage Inequalities* (New York: Harper Perennial, 1991).

6. A New York hip-hop radio station. ■

This article originally appeared in the February 2002 issue of *Teaching Music*.

Mariachi

Ethnic Music as a Teaching Tool

According to a recent newspaper article in the San Diego *Union Tribune* (January 2, 2001), the U.S. national *Census 2000* reports that the Hispanic population is growing faster than anticipated. The article's headline—"Future Growth: San Diego County's Fate Linked to Success of Hispanics"—could easily be adapted to report similar trends in other cities throughout the American West and Southwest. In California, the Hispanic population is increasing at record rates; whites are no longer the majority, making up only 47 percent of the state's population. In Arizona, the Hispanic population increased by 88 percent over the last decade. States like Iowa, Colorado, Nebraska, Maine, New York, and Illinois have seen double-digit increases in their Hispanic populations. Hispanics are the fastest growing ethnic group in America, and the trend shows no sign of slowing down for the next fifty years. Hispanics are now considered the largest minority in America. Even California's signature rock group, the Beach Boys, is riding the Latin wave with its release of the Spanish-language album *Acapulco Girls*, recorded with the group Mariachi Sol de Mexico.

Unfortunately, current statistics quoted from the *Census 2000* report in the *Union Tribute* article mentioned above also reveal that one of two Hispanics does not graduate from high school, and only 8 percent have college or advanced degrees. Hispanic boys and girls drop out of school at a rate 400 percent higher than their white counterparts.

Many studies have shown that music can connect students to school, cutting down the drop-out rate. Data from the Educational Testing Service show that students involved in music for four years or more score 84 points higher on the SAT test than students not involved in music. Music also helps improve a student's self-esteem. In spite of these benefits, the advancement of popular music and the ethnic diversification taking place in many schools may make it more difficult to lure students into traditional music programs like band, choir, and orchestra. One solution for music directors who teach in schools with high Hispanic populations is to change with the times. Adding a mariachi ensemble to the music program is one way to make this change and accomplish the goal of keeping students in school.

ILLUSTRATION BY LARRY MILAM

History

The history of mariachi falls into three time periods: colonial, evolutionary, and modern. The roots of mariachi music can be traced to the late 1700s. Mariachi first appeared in the western region of the Mexican state Jalisco; the music was rustic and the musicians generally rural people. Instruments of the day included violins, a guitar or guitar variant, and an *arpa grande* (big harp). Songs were happy, reflecting life in the region. The *son* form, with the unique features of a meter that alternates between 3/4 and 6/8, fluid use of grace notes, whimsical lyrics, and heavily syncopated melodies, evolved as the signature form of the mariachi group. Groups were very informal and always present at local celebrations. The most common mariachi group consisted of two combinations of four musicians: the Cocula-style group, with two violins, *guitarrón,* and *vihuela,* and the Tecalitlan version, with two violins, *arpa grande* and *guitarra de golpe.*

Between the years 1920 and 1950, mariachi music changed dramatically as a result of the invention of radio and the appearance of mariachi groups in Mexico City (beginning in the 1900s). An early well-known group was the Mariachi Coculense de Cirilo Marmolejo. The general public accepted mariachi first as a novelty, but the demand for a more sophisticated, urban sound grew, effecting a drastic change in the makeup of the traditional group. Changes in instrumentation made mariachi more versatile and easier to market commercially. The most drastic and important change was the addition of the trumpet. One of the first known trumpet players to contribute to this development was Miguel Martinez. His unique style of staccato tonguing and melodic flourishes paved the way for two trumpets to find a permanent place in the mariachi group.

The modern period of mariachi began in 1988. Linda Ronstadt's "Canciones de Mi Padre" tour inspired an entire young generation of Mexican-Americans to explore their ancestral culture. The music also reached the masses in America and created many mariachi fans—ironically, mariachi's popularity has grown in the U.S. but not in Mexico. In 1966, with the introduction of bilingual education and desegregation in the schools of San Antonio, Texas, music educator Belle San Miguel Ortiz started teaching choir in Spanish at a local elementary school, naming her ensemble, which was very popular throughout the community, "Los Tejanitos." The success of this program led her to start a mariachi ensemble in 1970 at Lanier High School in San Antonio, the first mariachi to be introduced into public schools. From this seed, others began to study mariachi music, which encouraged more schools and communities to teach the music to young and old alike. Mariachi has bridged the gap for Mexican-Americans across generations, races, social classes, historical differences, and cultural tastes. Young people especially have become involved in mariachi music, making it commonplace in hundreds of schools nationwide.

Mariachi Instruments

A modern traditional mariachi group consists of the following instruments: violin, trumpet, guitar, *vihuela* (a small, five-stringed guitar with a convex back) and *guitarrón* (a large six-stringed bass played in octaves). The harp and *guitarra de golpe* (an instrument similar to the *vihuela* with a flat back and a unique tuning) are also considered traditional instruments, although few mariachi groups have them. Other instruments used but not considered proper are the flute, *requinto* (a type of small guitar), and accordion. To be considered complete, a group should have a minimum of eight musicians in the following combination: three violins, two trumpets, one *vihuela,* one guitar, and one *guitarrón.* Additional violins may be added, up to three. Next, a harp, guitar, and/or *guitarra de golpe* may be added. Lastly, a third trumpet may be used, but this is rare. Groups in competition usually have no more than one *guitarrón* or *vihuela* and no more than fifteen pieces total. Although this is the recommended size, many school groups, especially at the middle school level, exceed this number, with as many as forty players.

Getting Started

It is best to attend one of the seventeen mariachi conferences offered throughout the Western and Southwestern United States before starting a school mariachi program (see sidebar on Major Mariachi Conferences). Some of the best mariachi conferences are held in Wenatchee, Washington; San Jose, California; Las Cruces and Albuquerque, New Mexico; and San Antonio, Texas. Their primary mis-

Major Mariachi Conferences

Albuquerque Mariachi Spectacular! in Albuquerque, New Mexico: University of New Mexico; contact Norberta Fresquez at fresquez @unm.edu; 505-272-6440/1 or 505-277-1990 (fax).

American Airlines Mariachi Spectacular International Music Festival in Kansas City, MO; contact David Chavez at dchavez@mlcr.org; 816-531-5669, ext. 202.

Arizona Christmas Mariachi Festival in Tucson, Arizona: Los Ninos Productions, PO Box 11146, Casa Grande, AZ 85230-1146; 800-637-1006.

Bank One Tucson International Mariachi Conference in Tucson, Arizona: PO Box 3053, Tucson, AZ 85702; www.tusconmariachi.org; contact Lolie Gomez at timc@azstarnet.com; 520-884-9920, ext. 243, or 520-792-9854 (fax).

Belles Artes Mexicanas Mariachi Festival in Omaha, Nebraska: South High School, 24th & J Sts., Omaha, NE.

Ford's Mariachi Concert and Extravaganza in San Antonio, Texas: Munoz Public Relations; 210-225-3353 or 210-414-8409.

Encuentro Internacional del Mariachi in Guadalajara, Jalisco, Mexico: Canaco Av. Vallarta 4095, C.P. 45000, Guadalajara, Jalisco, MX; contact José at josecardiaz@mexis.com.

Las Cruces International Mariachi Festival in Los Cruces, New Mexico: www.lascrucesmariachi.org; contact lcmariachi@zianet.com, workshop registration; 505-525-1735 or 505-528-1738 (fax).

Las Vegas International Mariachi Festival in Las Vegas, Nevada: Elias Entertainment Group, PO Box 10485, Casa Grande, AZ 85230-0485; 800-637-1006.

Mariachi Extravaganza in Lubbock, Texas: Texas Tech University, School of Music, PO Box 42033, Lubbock, TX 79409-2033; contact Louis Constancio at louisconstancio@hotmail.com; 806-832-5375.

Mariachi Northwest in Wenatchee, Washington: 920 Westchester Dr., Wenatchee, WA 98801; www.mariachinorthwest.org, contact Mark Fogelquist at huenachi@yahoo.com; 509-662-3616 or 509-663-1985.

Mariachi USA Festival in Hollywood, California: 11684 Ventura Blvd., #671, Studio City, CA 91604; www.mariachiusa.com.

Oxnard Mariachi Festival in Oxnard, California: 805-983-1377.

Radio Lingüe's ¡Viva El Mariachi! Festival in Fresno, California: www. radiobilingue.org; 559-455-5760.

San José International Mariachi Festival & Conference in San José, California: Mexican Heritage Corp., 1700 Alum Rock Ave., San José, CA 95116; 408-928-5500.

sion is exchanging ideas as well as educating teachers and students about mariachi. The conferences generally last from two to three days and are filled with clinics and hands-on workshops for beginner and intermediate players. Many conferences conclude with a competition and concert, featuring several headliner ensembles. Arriving several days before the conference provides opportunities to visit schools in the area that have successful mariachi programs—the conference coordinator should be able to provide this information.

Several models for mariachi programs can work within the music curriculum:

• The best approach involves a full-time mariachi teacher. If the school has a large Hispanic population (60 percent or more), enough students are likely to participate to ensure the dedication of a full-time teacher. Successful examples of schools that use this model are Irving Middle School in San Antonio, Texas (180 students in grades 6, 7, and 8, with two full-time teachers) and Montgomery Middle School in San Diego, California (130 students in grades 7 and 8, with one full-time teacher). These schools offer separate mariachi classes in beginning *guitarrón*, guitar/*vihuela*, trumpet, and violin. Classes should have no more than a 1:20 teacher-to-student ratio. Beginning-level students practice one to two days a week after school so that they can meet as a full mariachi ensemble. The intermediate (second-year) mariachi ensemble can be taught together, but at least one assistant is optimal.

• Beginning ensemble, which contains all the mariachi instruments in one class, could be offered during the school day or after school (students should still receive credit). This model can be a problem for the teacher and frustrating for the student, because it is impossible to teach the mariachi instruments together. Unlike concert band—where all the instruments are wind, except for percussion—the violin, trumpet, guitar/*vihuela,* and *guitarrón* have few techniques in common. Students learn at a much slower rate, and the teacher is forced to separate the different sections to give each group effective instruction. Keeping students on task becomes a challenge, making student dropout rates likely to be high. Of course, this model works better if several assistants help the teacher during class.

• A mariachi ensemble can be established using existing trumpets from the band and violins from the orchestra. Encourage bass/cello players in the orchestra or tuba players in the band to learn *guitarrón*. Other students in band and orchestra can be encouraged to learn guitar and *vihuela*. The learning curve is far easier on the *guitarrón*, guitar, and *vihuela* than on the violin or trumpet. This class could be offered during or after school. The downside is finding enough students from the band or orchestra who are interested in learning mariachi also. Teachers who have used this model have found it difficult to recruit students from traditional music ensembles. In many cases, mariachi ensembles draw students who were not initially interested in traditional ensembles. Also, students interested in band or orchestra need to find time in their already crowded schedules to take an additional class each semester. With all of the newly mandated education requirements and emphasis on core subjects, this time consideration can present an even greater problem.

Mariachi ensembles by nature are relatively small and cannot be taught in the same manner as concert or marching band. It is absolutely imperative that administrators understand that mariachi classes be funded and set up as "out-of-ratio classes." The most difficult part of starting a school mariachi program is selling the idea to the decision makers—administrators and board members. However, the chances of success are much greater if the teachers proposing the idea have done their homework up-front and clearly articulate their ideas to decision makers. Be prepared to present a "business plan" or "program proposal" to anyone who can help the idea become a reality. Those with influence might include the principal, district music supervisor, assistant superintendent, superintendent, or the board of trustees. (If at all possible, invite a decision maker to attend a mariachi conference with you.) Although administrators might agree that the idea is good, the standard answer will be, "There is no money." The bottom line is this: if the school district is made to think that a mariachi ensem-

ble is a priority, it will be funded. Like someone in sales, be prepared to hear "no" many times while trying to gain support for the program. Remember that a tenacious person will in time receive a "yes."

It is appropriate to mention as well that school ensembles that perform, either gratis or for ticket receipts, should never displace or disadvantage professional musicians who would be remunerated for their services according to the norms of the music industry, either at concerts or other private functions where musicians would normally be paid.

Mariachi Sheet Music Sources

Mariachi Connection (100+ songs), www.mariachi connection.com; 2106 W. Commerce, San Antonio, TX 78207; 877-565-3222 or 210-271-3654 (fax).

Mariachi Publishing Company, www.mariachipublishing. com; 213-727-0783.

Marna Bowling Publishing, *Method Book for Teaching Mariachi + 6 Songs;* 480-641-1818.

Vargas Publishing, www. vargaspublications.com; 145 Cottonwood, Uvalde, TX 78801; 830-776-0129.

Selecting Folk Instruments

Consider these important factors when purchasing folk instruments:

• **Budget.** The price range can be divided into three categories: inexpensive ($200–350), medium-priced ($400–700), and high-end ($750–2000). As with any product, one gets what one pays for.

• **Materials.** Low-end instruments are made from inferior woods; medium-grade, generally of cedar and tacote; high-quality, of fine woods such as magnolia, *palo escrito*, rosewood, *ojo de pajaro*, maple, and *guardalagua*.

• **Craftsmanship.** A budget product shows obvious signs of poor workmanship, such as badly matched joints, rough surfaces and edges, uneven varnish, and so forth. Mid-price items are well-constructed, with occasional minor cosmetic defects. Top-quality instruments are outstanding in every detail. Ease of playing is

also a factor in judging craftsmanship.

• **Availability.** Most Mexican border towns with a *mercado* have budget instruments on hand. Medium-range instruments can be purchased from a reputable dealer. High-end products are custom-made and may take several months for delivery.

• **Acoustic Properties.** A good instrument in any price range should have a 'live' sound. The timbre should not be muted or muffled. A *vihuela* should be bright and percussive. A *guitarrón* should 'punch' through on the higher notes and be felt on the lower range. (See sidebar on Various Sources for Mariachi Instruments, Costumes, and Accessories.)

Selecting Sheet Music

Obtaining published mariachi music can be more challenging than music for band, orchestra, or choir. Availability has improved significantly over the last four years, with a growing list of composers and publishers throughout the United States (see the sidebar on Mariachi Sheet Music Sources). At least 150 of the most popular mariachi songs can be purchased without any difficulty. Most songs contain all parts, including vocals and a score, although some companies do not provide the vocals and a melodic line because of copyright infringements. This can be a real problem for the director who is unfamiliar with the repertoire or does not speak Spanish. It is best to ask before ordering. In any event, almost all published music has been recorded by professional mariachi ensembles and is readily available on CD.

One of the most important factors in choosing repertoire for a specific group is the capability of the members—success depends heavily upon its members having comparable ability levels. Groups can generally be classified as beginner, intermediate, and professional. Age is also important; musicians that are close in age (which is the norm in an academic or fine arts setting) usually develop musically with more success. A student's exposure to theory and aural training may also determine the selection of appropriate repertoire.

Beginner. First-year music students should concern themselves with instrument technique and music-reading skills. Songs should be very simple, consisting of the following elements: for violin (mostly open strings and first position), music with whole, half, and quarter notes and the keys of C, G, and D. For trumpets, the range between low C-sharp up to A on the staff challenges most beginners. Music should also be selected with the same basic time values as the violin.

Intermediate. These students can play the instruments and read basic music notation. Chord structure should mostly be limited to I–IV–V progressions and the basic rhythm patterns. Students should be introduced to bar chords, the keys of A and F, and sixteenth notes. Trumpets should increase their range to F on the top line and A below the staff.

Advanced. This group has mastered the basics and can play extended melodies from memory with no difficulty, with an extensive repertoire, including *sones* and *huapangos*.

Purchasing the Mariachi Outfit

No mariachi is complete without the *traje de charro* ("suit of the cowboy"). Nine factors should be considered when selecting a *traje*: (1) Budget/Terms: A set price-range is imperative when purchasing *trajes de charro*, which cost $150–$1,000 ($300 should provide something nice.); (2) Measurements: Proper fit is essential—a specially trained representative should measure for a custom fit; (3) Delivery: Individually handmade *trajes de charro* are produced on a "first-in, first-out" basis, requiring a minimum of three months. U.S. Customs makes shipping complex, adding up to two weeks to delivery; (4) Experience: Do business with a reputable dealer or tailor specializing in *trajes de charro*. Be wary of eager moms or business-suit tailors; (5) Style: Many factors are involved, including color combinations, fabric, *botonadura* design, and/or *greca* pattern; (6) Age: Growth patterns and weight fluctuations can have a significant impact on fit; (7) Durability: *Trajes* should be dry-cleaned by a knowledgeable professional using a nonpetroleum solvent; (8)Accessories: *Botines, sombrero, moño,* and *cinto* are needed to complete the outfit; (9) Warranty: A transaction based upon consideration of all these factors should be the most successful in ensuring good fit, good durability, and general satisfaction.

In summary, a school mariachi program is likely to bring many students into the school music program who might not have been drawn to more traditional music ensembles and will most certainly open many new doors for students and teachers alike.

By Keith R. Ballard, mariachi coordinator for the Sweetwater Union High School district in San Diego, California, who teaches five classes in mariachi ensemble and one in steel drum band, and by C. Rene Benavidez, founder and president of the Mariachi Connection, a mariachi and ballet folklorico retail business in San Antonio, Texas.

Various Sources for Mariachi Instruments, Costumes, and Accessories

Arte & Charro (Mariachi suits and accessories), www.411web.com/A/ARTEANDCHARRO; 2734 East Cesar Chavez Avenue, Los Angeles, CA 90033; 323-263-5814.

Candelas Guitars, 2716 Cesar Chavez Ave., Los Angeles, CA 90033; 213-261-2011.

La Casa Del Musico, 1850 E. 1st Street, Los Angeles, CA 90033; 213-262-9425.

El Charro (Mariachi suits), www.elcharro1.com/TRAJES.htm; 866-863-2623 or 800-878-5444 (fax).

Fiesta del Mariachi (discography), www.geocities.com/Broadway/2626/CDs.html; (list of suppliers), www.geocities.com/Broadway/2626/supplies.html.

Guitarras Ramirez, Oscar Ramirez, Calle Corregiodora #270, Cd. Juarez, Chihuahua 15-93-75.

Jerry Starr, Luthier, 411 61st Street SW, Albuquerque, NM 87121; 505-836-1369.

El Mariachi.com (extensive Mariachi links), www.elmariachi.com.

Mariachi Connection (comprehensive selection of uniforms and all other Mariachi accessories), www.mariachiconnection.com; 2106 W. Commerce, San Antonio, TX 78207; 877-565-3222 or 210-271-3654 (fax).

Mariachi Depot, San Diego, CA; 858-292-5800.

El Mariachi Suena, //members.tripod.com/~mariachimex/welcome.htm.

Southwest Strings, www.swstrings.com; 800-528-3430 or 800-528-3470.

This article originally appeared in the May 1995 issue of *Music Educators Journal*.

URBAN MUSIC EDUCATION
THE TEACHERS' PERSPECTIVE

Richard K. Fiese and Nicholas J. DeCarbo look at responses from twenty urban music teachers about the unique teaching situations they face.

BY RICHARD K. FIESE AND NICHOLAS J. DeCARBO

The subject of urban music education must be explored from various viewpoints in order to provide the clearest and most realistic vision of the state and future of music in our urban schools. To gather information on the attitudes and opinions of urban music teachers, we asked twenty-five state MEA presidents or executive secretaries representing large urban areas throughout the United States to provide the names and addresses of two or three established, successful urban music teachers in their region or state. We sent to these selected teachers a questionnaire that was designed to collect background information on their teaching experience and responses to four open-ended questions regarding different aspects of teaching music in the urban setting.

Twenty of the twenty-eight selected teachers responded, and their responses provide the basis for this article. (The participating teachers and their schools are identified at the end of the article.)

Richard K. Fiese is assistant professor of music education at the University of Houston School of Music, Houston, Texas; and Nicholas J. DeCarbo is assistant dean and associate professor of music education at the University of Miami School of Music, Coral Gables, Florida.

. . . . . .

The majority of the respondents felt woefully unprepared to teach in the urban setting.

. . . . . .

Our Urban Representatives

The teachers who responded, ten males and ten females, were from urban schools in California, Colorado, Georgia, Illinois, New York, Pennsylvania, and Tennessee. Eight had bachelor's degrees, eleven had master's degrees, and one had a doctorate. The ranges in teaching experience varied from seven to thirty-two years, with the average number of years taught being twenty-two; of the twenty respondents, thirteen had twenty or more years of teaching experience.

These teachers have assignments that span the spectrum of school music education from elementary to high school. Their work includes a variety of music teaching experiences providing a wide range of instructional foci, from traditional instrumental and vocal ensemble performance classes (band, orchestra, choir, and piano, for example) and traditional nonperformance classes (general music, music theory, and music history, for example) to selected specialty courses (music for foreign-born students and multicultural music, for example). The diversity of these individual assignments is staggering, with teacher responsibility sometimes limited to a single grade level and sometimes encompassing the entire K–12 instrumental and vocal music curriculum in a school.

What Teachers Said

Many of the actual responses from the teachers are found in the four sidebars accompanying this article. We attempted to summarize all of the responses to each of the questions to get an overall impression from teachers working in urban schools.

Our first question was "Do you feel that your undergraduate/graduate education courses prepared you to teach in the urban setting? If yes, what specific areas in your education prepared you? If no, what areas would you suggest need to be included?" Three

Do you feel that your undergraduate/graduate education courses prepared you to teach in the urban setting? If yes, what specific areas in your education prepared you? If no, what areas would you suggest need to be included?

"Even though I was educated at a college located inside New York City, the faculty were many years removed from the experience of the contemporary urban classroom setting. Professors who are training today's and tomorrow's teachers must go into the public schools to see what the needs are of the students in urban schools. They must also communicate with the people who are teachers presently teaching in these situations." —*Kenneth Jernigan*

"More of the knowledge that I use on a daily basis has been gleaned from workshops, convention sessions, and in-service classes offered in large urban systems in which I have worked. One of the most valuable courses that I have taken was designed for business managers and presented on a limited basis in our school system. It taught us how to work with people. ... Classes in general teaching strategies with an emphasis on the learner (as opposed to the material) have also been usable and valuable, but I have rarely found another music teacher who felt that this kind of class was designed for a specialist." —*Suzanne Shull*

teachers (one with a bachelor's, one with a master's, one with a doctorate) felt that their education had prepared them for teaching in the urban setting; twelve (four with bachelor's, eight with master's) felt that their education had clearly not prepared them for teaching in the urban setting; and four (two with bachelor's, two with master's) felt that while aspects of their education (especially performance, theory, and music history) were valuable, they were not prepared by their educational training for teaching in the urban setting. Among those who indicated they were prepared, most felt their musical training was both sufficiently extensive and intensive and had an impact on their preparedness for teaching in the urban setting.

The majority of the respondents felt woefully unprepared to teach in the urban setting. While several felt *musically* prepared, they said their pre-service education prepared them for teaching the "ideal" student and left them unprepared for the reality of urban schools, where most of the students do not conform to the ideal.

According to these urban teachers, more training is required to help prospective music teachers deal with some of the complex emotions of students from differing social and economic backgrounds. A particular concern is dealing with students affected by various types of family situations or crises such as single-parent or no-parent households, children having the responsibility for raising other siblings, teenage pregnancies, students ejected from their homes, and custody battles. Teachers who are in an urban situation have to be prepared to help mediate some of the effects of these events in students' lives.

Several teachers said that many of the teacher-education courses, and the professors who taught these courses, were many years removed from the reality of modern urban schools and consequently lacked relevancy. The teachers felt that increased contact between teacher-preparation institutions and the urban schools would help professors keep pace with the status of students and their needs. One teacher mentioned that her graduate

studies were more realistic and more practical than her undergraduate coursework; however, she felt that most of what was of value in her day-to-day teaching was the result of participating in a number of workshops and clinics. While one teacher noted that experience and maturity are the ultimate sources of help in dealing with the situations that urban music teachers encounter, several others agreed that prospective teachers would benefit from increased attention to student differences, differing life styles, classroom and rehearsal management, and methods for demonstrating to students and parents that they are valued as individuals irrespective of race, economic status, or other external conditions.

Our second question was "Can you describe one or two specific teaching techniques, strategies, or approaches that you found to be particularly effective for teaching music in the urban situation?" Generally, the teachers suggested that individual teachers should experiment and see which techniques work in a specific setting. It was noted, however, that before any teaching could take place, the teacher must have the respect of the students and control of the teaching/learning environment. Of particular importance is that all teachers should be well-informed regarding the materials and content in their subject areas, especially with regard to having knowledge of as many instruments and performing artists as possible. Familiarity with the application of current technology is also important, according to the respondents. Finally, they suggested that teachers must find a way to relate to the students initially and then adapt the curriculum with that in mind.

Many of the respondent teachers reported that one way to relate to students is to allow students to have input regarding their instruction. Small-group activities and cooperative learning were mentioned as ways of involving students in decision making. Another successful method was to use experienced students as tutors, section leaders, and peer teachers. This is particularly important because teachers in an urban situation are often teaching very musically inexperienced beginning students—so-called raw beginners.

The third question was "What factors have most contributed to your personal success as a music teacher in the urban setting?" Several teachers identified various types of support networks of teachers, supervisors, mentors, and others that helped them meet their goals as teachers. Some said that they have continued to study education through professional clinics and conferences on a regular basis. Others also mentioned that they have continued to be active consumers of the arts, and that opportunities to see performing groups should be increased for those teachers who live in large urban centers with access to thriving arts communities.

Many other factors that go beyond the music classroom were mentioned as contributors to the success of these urban music educators. These factors include developing relationships between the students and the parents; being a leader and contributing citizen in the school community; maintaining solid relationships with the guidance staff, other teachers, and administrators; and being supportive of students while consistently adhering to rules and policy, thereby developing a classroom discipline plan that really works. It is also necessary to have the use of facilities, equipment, and materials.

The final question the teachers were asked was "Do you have any general observations for ways to improve music education in the urban schools?" The responses reflected perceived teacher-training needs in management skills, knowledge of materials (particularly the selection of repertoire), and knowledge of the psychology of urban students. According to the respondents, the teacher trainers themselves have to be genuinely qualified, knowledgeable regarding the application of technology, and familiar with methods for developing and incorporating a multicultural curriculum. It was noted that due to the increasing diversity of the urban student population, multicultural education is uniquely suited to the urban environment. Some individuals also suggested that programs specifically aimed at reaching children

Questionnaire Item No. 2

Can you describe one or two specific teaching techniques, strategies, or approaches that you found to be particularly effective for teaching music in the urban setting?

"Nothing but experience and maturity can prepare you to handle some of the situations that you will confront."—*George DeGraffenreid*

"A good teacher bridges education gaps. Find out where students are, know where you want them to be, and build the bridge."—*Betty Link*

"You can only stop so many times and explain something. You have to go on. I can't save everyone. Treat everyone fairly, honestly, and with discipline even if it hurts sometimes. There have been disappointments, but the success for the program and the students has been great."—*George Paris*

"I stress performance—extensive use of the popular culture is used as a basis for performance in vocal, dance, and musical theater. Scheduling a performance every other month keeps students and the music specialist on their toes—'come see what we do!'"—*Virginia T. Lam*

"By teaching students skills, I sent the message that I cared about their education and growth; by letting them have some choices, I told them that I cared about them as individuals."—*Suzanne Shull*

"I try to use a variety of activities in each lesson in order to accommodate the various learning styles of the students within each class setting. This makes it possible for every child to succeed at something in my class. This increases their self-esteem and gives them something about which to feel positive. For many of these students, school is the only place that they can get any kind of positive reinforcement."—*Beth Henry*

"Since any background in music is woefully absent, any activity involving listening to, performing, or reading about music subjects seems to be effective. Most students particularly respond to performances by professional musicians brought into the school or going to an orchestra hall to hear professional performances."—*John C. Cina*

"Orff-Schulwerk is based on things children like to do: sing, chant, rhyme, clap, dance, and keep beat on anything near at hand. ... [It] is designed for all children, not just the privileged, talented, or select few. Each child contributes according to ability. The atmosphere is noncompetitive and children enjoy the pleasure of making music with others. ... Orff-Schulwerk provides a balance between emotional and intellectual stimulation to develop healthy human beings."—*Jo-Ann W. Kilton*

Questionnaire Item No. 3

What factors have most contributed to your personal success as a music teacher in the urban setting?

"The opportunity to share both joy and problems with my peers has been a factor in my success. ... I listen to recordings of college and professional bands and regularly attend Chicago Symphony concerts lest I lower my standard of musicianship. I subscribe to a number of professional journals, including *The Instrumentalist, Music Educators Journal,* and the *Journal of Research in Music Education*."—*Sue Glossop*

"I believe that students will give only as much as you ask. I make high demands on the students personally and musically. Mediocrity is not okay. Setting high goals, being a positive role model, and going the extra mile are characteristics that I work for."—*Richard K. Kusk*

"As a teacher in New York City, the keys [to success] are [that] you had better love teaching, be a strong disciplinarian, be organized and prepared, be creative, and be flexible. ... Most New York schools are undermanned, underequipped, underfinanced, and there is a lack of [suitable] learning space. For this reason, a teacher must be flexible and prepared. Creativity is also a must. You never know when your department will be severely changed due to budget cuts, administrative ignorance, or whim."—*Kenneth Jernigan*

"I take time to communicate with students during nonteaching periods. Sometimes it is more important to talk to students than only worrying about correct fingerings. My students are from the Cabrini-Green projects, the affluent Lincoln Park area, and from the entire city. They all have the common desire to be treated with respect, encouragement, and understanding."—*George Paris*

"School is, for many students, an oasis from the harshness of the urban environment. Because the school is an oasis, I set a standard of behavior in the classroom that I expect everyone in the classroom to abide by. They do! I have students from the most deplorable home/neighborhood situations who have been some of the most dedicated and "successful" students. Contrary to wisdom, most students, though at times they may appear to act otherwise, want to be related to as people, not as a member of some racial, ethnic, or socioeconomic group. Although I am very sensitive to where my students come from, when it comes to music, they are in my eyes just students interested in doing music."—*George DeGraffenreid*

of a low economic status need to be articulated and integrated in the school curriculum. Another suggestion was offering extracurricular programs to students and adults during the evening and summers.

Other responses focused on enhancing the relationships among music teachers, administrators, and music supervisors to provide the best environment to facilitate an inner-city program. Having all of the constituencies involved in dialogue, rather than parallel monologues, for the advancement of the students' music education is perhaps one of the central features of successful urban school music programs, according to the respondents.

Conclusions

The responses reflect some of the attitudes, beliefs, strategies, and techniques that these selected urban music teachers were willing to share with the rest of the profession in an effort to enhance the quality of urban music education. All of the teachers' responses reflect a genuine commitment to music, to music education, and to the students in their charge. Moreover, there is a commitment on the part of each of these teachers to overcome the unique set of challenges of the urban school, to take advantage of the unique rewards of such teaching, and to provide a quality music education to the young people in their classes as they begin to develop their lifelong relationship with music. While the information we have presented may not reflect a scientific sampling of urban music teachers' views, this does not diminish the importance of those views. We believe that both those who framed the responses to the questionnaire and those who read this article will gain new perspectives with respect to teaching music in urban America.

Note

We wish to recognize these teachers for their significant contribution to this article and their ongoing contribution to urban music education:

Bob R. Barnette, Central High School, Macon, Georgia; Grades 9–12; beginning band, intermediate band, marching band, symphonic band.

Grady Black, Jr., Brainerd High School, Chattanooga, Tennessee; Grades 9–11; secondary instrumental music, general music, varsity band (concert and marching).

John C. Cina, Lane Technical High School, Chicago, Illinois; Grades 9–12; beginning strings, intermediate strings, symphony orchestra (advanced strings).

George DeGraffenreid, Van Nuys High School, Van Nuys, California; Grades 9–12; orchestra, band (concert and marching), jazz ensemble, keyboard, song writing.

Sue Glossop, Beasley Academic Center, Chicago, Illinois; Grade 4; music literacy, music appreciation.

Beth Henry, Riverdale Elementary School, Jonesboro, Georgia; Grades K–5; elementary general music.

Kenneth Jernigan, Hastings High School, Hudson, New York; Grades 6–12; concert band (high school and middle school), general music (middle school), jazz ensemble (high school).

Jo-Ann W. Kilton, Hendrick Hudson School, Webster, New York; Grades 1–6; elementary general music, primary chorus, intermediate chorus.

Michele D. Kneer, Von Steuben and Longfellow Middle School, Peoria, Illinois; Grades 5–8; general music, chorus, beginning choir chimes, intermediate choir chimes, show choir.

Richard K. Kusk, Coronado High School, Colorado Springs, Colorado; Grades 9–12; orchestra, marching band, wind ensemble, concert band, jazz band, pep band.

Virginia T. Lam, Wanamaker Middle School, Philadelphia, Pennsylvania; Grades 6–7 and special education; general music, choir, dance, drama.

Betty Link, Herbert Hoover Middle School, San Francisco, California; Grades 6–8; chorus (grades 7–8), unified arts (grades 6–7), keyboard (grade 8), instrumental and vocal music (K–6), general music.

Charles Lute, Academy High School, Erie, Pennsylvania; Grades 9–12; music theory I & II, orchestra, percussion ensemble, jazz band, concert band.

Jack Martens, Benjamin Franklin Middle School, Pleasant Hill (San Francisco), California; Grades 6–8, band.

Andrea H. Morris, Franklin D. Roosevelt High School, Brooklyn, New York; Grades 9–12; music appreciation, beginning piano, intermediate piano, advanced piano (piano lab), music theory, music for foreign-born students (recorder, violin, piano—introduction; multicultural music).

Don Reginald Ogletree, Tri-Cities High School, East Point, Georgia; Grades 9–12; choral music.

Mary Jo Papich, Woodruff High School, Peoria, Illinois; Grades 9–12; instrumental music, music theory, music history.

George Paris, Lincoln Park High School, Chicago, Illinois; Grades 9–12; beginning band, intermediate band, advanced band, advanced concert band.

Nancy Shankman, Christopher Columbus High School, Staten Island, New York; Grades 9–10; combined chorus, ensemble (chamber singers).

Suzanne Shull, Ridgeview Middle School, Atlanta, Georgia; Grades 6–8; general music, chorus.

Questionnaire Item No. 4

Do you have any general observations for ways to improve music education in the urban schools?

"Music education in the inner city will not improve until we stop spoon-feeding our students, raise our expectations, and develop critical thinkers who will challenge us to improve our teaching skills. We, the teachers, are the ones who set limits on what children can learn."—*Sue Glossop*

"We need to know more about inner-city schools, students, discipline, etc. ... We need to learn how to better educate and control these students."—*Michele D. Kneer*

"It is not enough to fill a music [teaching] position with a qualified music instructor. The position must be filled with the "right" qualified music instructor. Students are too sensitive and aware to have anyone sent to them to teach them. Even if [the students] are totally unaware of a teacher's personal feelings for them, whether they be feelings of concern or the lack of, many times the students' personal circumstances are just too overwhelming for them to be 'turned on' to music education. The key is to have an instructor who can truly accept a position of challenge and meet it with expectation of great success despite the odds. He or she must look beyond what exists and be willing to create the right atmosphere and program based on a realistic analysis of the situation in which he or she will be teaching. In order to be a success in the business of music teaching, one must first be in the business of people."—*Don Reginald Ogletree*

"I am afraid that my outlook is very general, applicable to all teachers of urban children: small classes; more opportunities for successful performance and positive feedback; teachers who believe anything is possible; mentoring by successful adults in the community; and treating children as individuals rather than members of a particular group."—*Suzanne Shull*

"Develop programs that include performance/reward starting at the early grades through high school. Have the music program coordinated. ... Let high school students work as mentors for middle school students, one on one. Show by example. This works in [other academic subjects] and can work in music education."—*Charles Lute*

"Take every sincere student who wants to be involved in music into the music classes or ensembles. If the student is willing to work, let him. In an urban school, one does not have the luxury of turning anyone away. ... Although I am striving to produce the best music that the ensembles are capable of, the students know that I am far more interested in them being the best people they can be. The rehearsals are all music business, but I talk to them about many things, other than music, outside of the classroom."—*George DeGraffenreid*

This article originally appeared in the July 1995 issue of *Music Educators Journal.*

RATIONALES FOR TEACHING WORLD MUSICS

C. Victor Fung discusses the importance of introducing students to multicultural music by including it in school curricula.

C. VICTOR FUNG

The inclusion of world musics in music education programs in the United States has become increasingly important since the middle of the twentieth century. Since that time, American society has undergone major social changes, which are reflected in its attitudes toward various ethnic groups and their civil rights. Events related to these changes included the civil rights movement, the desegregation of schools, and an upswing in the melting-pot ideology.[1] In recent decades, there has been greater recognition of the value of maintaining various cultural traditions in America and of encouraging, rather than neglecting, a culturally diverse society.

The long-standing claim of the superiority of Western art music (referring to the Western European tradition) has been increasingly considered problematic, as has been the manifestation of this belief in the music curriculum.[2] The belief that Western art music is more natural, complex, expressive, and meaningful than other musics has come to be seen as both an intellectual and a moral problem. It is an intellectual problem because this belief is narrow-minded;

C. Victor Fung is assistant professor of music in the General College at the University of Minnesota in Minneapolis.

The United States has increasingly recognized the diversity of ethnicity and cultures within its borders.

it denies the naturalness, complexity, and meaningfulness of non-Western musics by ignoring the possibility of alternative aesthetics. It is a moral problem because it implies that non-Western musics and non-Western cultures are inferior. Today, through greater attention to and more research on non-Western musics, many have come to understand that the musics, like the societies, are based on different systems and philosophies. Musics from all cultures have begun to emerge in music programs as part of the ongoing debate on the inclusion of underrepresented groups in the musical canon and the curriculum of the nation's schools. These changes in music education parallel changes in other aspects of American society, such as its laws and its academic societies.

Ethnocentrism, the belief in the superiority of one's own ethnic group, is a phenomenon that exists across cultures and is by no means a problem limited to the United States or Western culture. However, the United States has increasingly recognized the diversity of ethnicity and cultures within its borders, and this has been reflected in various legislation, such as Public Law 88-352, Title VI, of 1964 and Public Law 92-318, Title IX, of 1972. Both laws acknowledge the value of the heterogeneous composition of the nation and were enacted to eliminate racial discrimination.

In education, the declaration of the American Association of Colleges for Teacher Education explicitly recognized the value of diversity in 1973.[3] In music education, both the Yale Seminar in 1963 and the Tanglewood Symposium in 1967 advocated the inclusion of musics of all cultures and styles in the schools. The establishment of the Society for Ethnomusicology in 1955 reflected the increased interest in and demand for knowledge about non-Western musics. Recent meetings of the Music Educators National Conference, the College Music Society, and the Society for Ethnomusicology include sessions concerning non-Western musics in music education contexts. Moreover, discussions concerning multicultural issues in the arts and education can be found frequently in daily publications such as newspapers, magazines, and journals.

Authors such as Maria Navarro, Terese Volk, and William Anderson have dealt with the history of the use of world musics in music education programs in depth. Navarro observed strong Austro-German influences since the inception of public school music education in the United States in 1838 and suggested that these influences are still evident in current music teacher training curricula.[4] Navarro concluded that three Germanic values prevailed throughout the history of American public school music education and teacher training: priority for Western art music as curricular content, emphasis on performance, and de-emphasis on the history of American music in curricula. Navarro suggested that the profession should be much more sensitive to the changes in culture and should rethink the suitability of imposing Austro-Germanic values in a multicultural American society.

Volk saw a gradual change of values within one of the most important publications in the music education profession, the *Music Educators Journal,* by studying the issues published between 1967 and 1992.[5] Documentation showed the growth of the use of world musics in music education in the United States. Volk concluded that a greater depth of interest in and knowledge about world musics developed during the 1970s. In the 1980s, there was a growing need for methods and materials for the implementation of multicultural music studies in the classrooms. Volk also identified the need for teacher training in world musics. Since 1990, according to Volk, a broader world perspective for music education emerged that viewed music education at all levels from a multicultural perspective and included the study of musics and of the relationship of those musics to their respective cultures. Volk's findings paralleled Anderson's finding that research in multicultural music educa-

tion grew following the Tanglewood Symposium in 1967.[6]

Constantly changing social demographics underlay these changes and events. According to the 1992 Statistical Abstract of the United States, between the years 1950 and 1990 the white population decreased from 89.3 percent to 83.9 percent and nonwhite ethnic groups increased from 10.6 percent to 16.1 percent.[7] The U.S. Bureau of the Census also projected in 1992 that, by the year 2050, the nonwhite population would continue to increase to 28.2 percent and the white population would continue to decrease to 71.8 percent.[8] These projections reflect the growing multicultural profile of American society.

■ ■ ■ ■ ■ ■

World music traditions brought into the country are worth studying and are worth being incorporated as part of the nation's musical life, including its education.

■ ■ ■ ■ ■ ■

Rationales

Due to these changes in society, some philosophers, ethnomusicologists, and music educators have identified three major rationales—social, musical, and global—for teaching world musics in the United States.

The Social Rationale. Some educators have suggested that the learning of world musics develops multicultural awareness, understanding, and tolerance; promotes a deeper understanding and acceptance of people from other cultures; cultivates open-mindedness and unbiased thinking; and eradicates racial resentments. These social functions of world music education were reiterated with slightly

different wordings by philosophers in music education,[9] ethnomusicologists,[10] and music educators.[11] Many have also suggested that the inclusion of world musics in music education programs would better reflect ethnic diversity, help students explore the rich culture of the United States, and prepare them to live in a global environment.

Based on this social function of music, some writers have discussed various concentric-circle models for the inclusion of world musics in education. James Banks suggests that students should develop clear, positive, and reflective self-identifications at three levels: ethnic, national, and global.[12] The ethnic identification is defined as the innermost level, with the global identification as the broadest level. According to Banks, the inner levels of this concentric-circle model are the prerequisites to the outer levels.

Estelle Jorgensen proposes that, as a form of education, enculturation involves a series of concentric circles, which represent progressively more inclusive understandings that extend outward from a particular culture to embrace a global view of humanity.[13] Although no specific levels of concentric circles are given, Jorgensen suggests that enculturation involves both the transmission of cultural traditions and the acculturation process, which is the acquisition of musical wisdom in situations of culture contact. Enculturation is common in modern multicultural societies.

This outreaching notion parallels to some extent Bennett Reimer's "selfness" and "otherness."[14] According to Reimer, "one must go beyond one's present self, through sounds encountered, to a self not yet known."[15] In other words, one reaches outward from the self to others. Reimer also points out that human beings are capable of being transcultural and transpersonal. This notion is related to the concepts of "egocentrism" and "allocentricism" in Piagetian developmental psychology theory.[16] As a child grows, there is a gradual change of focus from self to others in social cognition and communication. Banks, Jorgensen, and Reimer agree that

In recent decades, U.S. classrooms have begun to encourage an awareness of different cultures and their traditions, including music.

music is one of the disciplines that could help to achieve this outreaching goal.

World musics are especially important when we view education about culture as a series of concentric circles moving outward from ethnic identification (the innermost) to global identification (the outermost). In the United States, the music learned in the classrooms reflects the cultural diversity and ethnic content of the society. Since the United States claims to be a democratic and free society that seeks to achieve incorporative freedom—freedom that involves individual rights and the protection of rights for others—the freedom of musical expressions of diverse traditions must be ensured.[17] World music traditions brought into the country are worth studying and are worth being incorporated as part of the nation's musical life, including its education.

The Musical Rationale. Some writers are convinced that the inclusion of world musics in music education programs can provide opportunities to study musical concepts and reinforce the knowledge of musical elements;[18] refine aural skills, critical thinking, and psychomotor development;[19]

■ ■ ■ ■ ■ ■

To be a complete person in the modern world, one must be sensitive to culture in a global context.

■ ■ ■ ■ ■ ■

increase tolerance of unfamiliar music; and develop more sensitive perceptions of familiar music.[20] These results are possible because world musics provide a broader range of musical materials than any one musical style.

Since each musical tradition has its unique history and musical materials, the study of one musical tradition may not reveal the full spectrum of musical

possibilities available globally. For example, music has been considered more a product than a process in the Western art music tradition.[21] The roles of music participants—such as composer, performer, and listener—are more clearly demarcated in Western art music, while participants' roles in many other musical traditions are not differentiated.[22] In many African traditions, for instance, music participants are simultaneously composers, performers, and listeners. Moreover, the transmission of Western art music has a strong emphasis on notation, while many other musical traditions rely on oral transmission.[23] By exploring some qualities that are not emphasized in Western art music, one may gain a better understanding of the nature of music and how music relates to human life. This notion relates to David Elliott's inductive model—a dynamic multiculturalism from which students can induce the concepts of music, musical thought, and musical behavior from a palette of musical cultures.[24]

The Global Rationale. Another rationale involves a global view of humanity. Music is a global phenomenon, and no culture is without music.[25] To be a complete person in the modern world, one must be sensitive to culture in a global context. In Mark Slobin's discussion of a global view of music, he wrote:

> World music looks like a fluid, interlocking set of styles, repertoires, and practices which can expand or contract across wide or narrow stretches of the landscape. It no longer appears to be a catalogue of bounded entities of single, solid historical and geographical origins.[26]

Marshall McLuhan's concept of the "global village" has become a reality.[27] Every human being is a member of this global village. The technology of travel and communication has facilitated global interchange. Given this concept of a global village,

> Each [cultural] group is coming to be understood as another manifestation of the larger human community with similar basic needs and aspirations. As a

result of the intense activity, many musicians and scholars have come to realize that other music cultures could not be ignored; like next-door neighbors, even when the distances were thousands of miles, they were there.[28]

Alan Lomax was one of the first ethnomusicologists who studied musics on a global scale rather than studying a specific musical culture.[29] Despite Lomax's controversial classification of world musics, his project reflected the need for scholars to include a global perspective in their studies. Regardless of the common elements or discrete elements of musics across various cultures, knowledge of these musics can broaden one's view of humanities at the global level.

Estelle Jorgensen argued that music, through communication, could be used to enhance political understanding and international relations.[30] In light of the U. S. role as the leader of the world, the inclusion of world musics and their variants in music curricula seems essential.

■ ■ ■ ■ ■ ■

The last part of the twentieth century is certainly a world-music era.

■ ■ ■ ■ ■ ■

Assumptions

Educators must accept two important assumptions when music from various cultures is used for educational purposes. First, absolute authenticity of world musics is not achievable due to factors such as the sociocultural context of the classrooms and the equipment used (for example, videos

Music educators should try to introduce their students to world musics through authentic recordings or performances. Here a musician plays a Chinese mouth organ, or sheng.

and recordings).[31] Second, world musics in U.S. classrooms are set within the context of the U.S. music education scenario.[32] This scenario uses world musics to support music education and education in general, rather than to focus on the purpose of the music in its original culture. Including world musics in the classroom removes the music from its prior musical and cultural context and places it in a different context. Whatever style of world music is used, the musical and social context of the music naturally becomes a classroom context. This parallels Ulf Lundgren's point that the concept of any public education curriculum is typically "decontextualized."[33] Nevertheless, in creating music-listening experiences in the classroom, teachers should still try to use recordings made by indigenous people or recognized scholars with original traditional instruments.

Implications for Educators

The last part of the twentieth century is certainly a world-music era. The social, musical, and global rationales for world musics in music educa-

tion have been broadly established since the mid-century. More and more music educators have agreed on the value of including world musics in their classrooms. However, the study of world musics is such an extremely wide area that music educators need to constantly increase their knowledge about the world's musical cultures. Since it is impossible to learn about all musical cultures in a short period of time, students and educators are encouraged to start with the musical cultures that are closest to them. In other words, the sequence of learning world musical cultures varies widely depending on one's location and cultural identification. One suggestion is to apply the concentric circle models discussed previously.

Once music educators have the competence necessary to include world musics in their classrooms, they need to be conscious about the changing contexts of the musics, typically from the indigenous context to the classroom context. They must help students explore the questions of who, what, where, why, and how in regard to the music and the culture.

-68-

Although absolute authenticity is not achievable in a classroom context, music educators can still attempt to create the most authentic musical experience for students. As discussed earlier, teachers should try to use the most authentic recordings available. In addition, they should present materials about musical cultures based on authoritative and thorough research. To promote musical sensitivity, they can use student participation activities, such as actual music making. During all classroom activities, from discussions to using instruments to learning voice production, the teachers should try to make the musical experience as authentic as possible.

Notes

1. Mary J. Montague, "An Investigation of Teacher Training in Multicultural Music Education in Selected Universities and Colleges," *Dissertation Abstracts International* 49 (1988): 2142A (University Microfilms No. 88-21622); and Patricia K. Shehan, "Towards Tolerance and Taste: Preferences for World Musics," *British Journal of Music Education* 3, no. 2 (1986): 153–63.

2. Judith Becker, "Is Western-Art Music Superior?" *The Musical Quarterly* 72, no. 3 (1986): 341–59.

3. American Association of Colleges for Teacher Education, "No One Model American: A Statement on Multicultural Education," *Journal of Teacher Education* 24 (1973): 264.

4. Maria L. Navarro, "The Relationship between Culture, Society, and Music Teacher Education in 1838 and 1988" (Doctoral dissertation, Kent State University), *Dissertation Abstracts International* 50 (1989): 2866A.

5. Terese M. Volk, "The History and Development of Multicultural Music Education as Evidenced in the *Music Educators Journal,* 1967-1992," *Journal of Research in Music Education* 41, no. 2 (1993): 137–55.

6. William M. Anderson, "World Musics in American Education, 1916-1970," *Contributions to Music Education* 3 (1974): 23–42.

7. U. S. Bureau of the Census, *Statistical Abstract of the United States,* 112th ed. (Washington, DC: Author, 1992).

8. U. S. Bureau of the Census, *Population Projections of the United States by Age, Sex, Race, and Hispanic Origin: 1992 to 2050* (Washington, DC: Author, 1992).

9. Bennett Reimer, *A Philosophy of Music Education,* 2d ed. (Englewood Cliff, NJ: Prentice-Hall, 1989); and Keith Swanwick, "Music Education in a Pluralist Society," *International Journal of Music Education* 12 (1988): 3–8.

10. John Blacking, *A Commonsense View of All Music* (Cambridge: Cambridge University Press, 1987); and Anthony Seeger, "Celebrating the American Music Mosaic," *Music Educators Journal* 78, no. 9 (1992): 26–29.

11. William M. Anderson and Patricia Shehan Campbell, eds., *Multicultural Perspectives in Music Education* (Reston, VA: Music Educators National Conference, 1989); René Boyer-White, "Reflecting Cultural Diversity in the Music Classroom," *Music Educators Journal* 75, no. 4 (1988): 50–54; Patricia S. Campbell, "Cultural Consciousness in Teaching General Music," *Music Educators Journal* 78, no. 9 (1992): 30–36; Joan C. Conlon, "Explore the World in Song," *Music Educators Journal* 78, no. 9 (1992): 46–51; Karl Glenn, "Music Education in Tune with the Times," *Music Educators Journal* 77, no.1 (1990): 21–23; Egon Kraus, "The Contribution of Music Education to the Understanding of Foreign Cultures, Past and Present," *Music Educators Journal* 53, no. 5 (1967): 30–32, 91; Samuel D. Miller and Manny Brand, "Music of Other Cultures in the Classroom," *Social Studies* 74, no. 2 (1983): 62–64; and Patricia K. Shehan, "World Musics: Windows to Cross-Cultural Understanding," *Music Educators Journal* 75, no. 3 (1988) 22–26.

12. James A. Banks, *Multicultural Education: Theory and Practice,* 2d ed. (Boston: Allyn and Bacon, 1988).

13. Estelle R. Jorgenson, "In Search of Music Education" (Paper presented at the meeting of the College Music Society, Chicago, Illinois, October 1991).

14. Bennett Reimer, "Selfness and Otherness in Experiencing Music of Foreign Cultures," *The Quarterly Journal of Music Teaching and Learning* 2, no. 3 (1991): 4–13.

15. Reimer, "Selfness and Otherness," 5.

16. John H. Flavell, *Cognitive Development,* 2d ed. (Englewood Cliffs, NJ: Prentice-Hall, 1985).

17. Maxine Greene, *The Dialectics of Freedom* (New York: Teachers College Press, 1988).

18. Anderson and Campbell, *Multicultural Perspectives*; Miller and Brand, "Music of Other Cultures."

19. Shehan, 1988, "World Musics."

20. Patricia K. Shehan, "Transfer of Preference from Taught to Untaught Pieces of Non-Western Music Genres," *Journal of Research in Music Education* 33, no. 3 (1985): 149–58.

21. Christopher Small, *Music Society and Education* (London: John Calder, 1980).

22. Roger Sessions, *The Musical Experience of Composer, Performer, Listener* (Princeton, NJ: Princeton University Press, 1974).

23. Philip V. Bohlman, *The Study of Folk Music in the Modern World* (Bloomington, IN: Indiana University Press, 1988); Patricia S. Campbell, "Orality, Literacy and Music's Creative Potential: A Comparative Approach," *Bulletin of the Council for Research in Music Education,* no. 101 (1989): 30–40; Patricia S. Campbell, *Lessons from the World* (New York: Schirmer Books, 1991); and Small, *Music Society.*

24. David J. Elliott, "Key Concepts in Multicultural Music Education," *International Journal of Music Education* 13 (1989): 11–18.

25. John Blacking, *How Musical Is Man* (Seattle: University of Washington Press, 1973).

26. Mark Slobin, "Micromusics of the West: A Comparative Approach," *Ethnomusicology* 36, no. 1 (1992): 9–10.

27. Marshall McLuhan, *The Global Village: Transformations in World Life and Media in the 21st Century* (New York: Oxford University Press, 1989).

28. Anthony J. Palmer, "World Musics in Elementary and Secondary Music Education: A Critical Analysis" (Doctoral dissertation, University of California–Los Angeles), *Dissertation Abstracts International* 36 (1975): 118, 7266A.

29. Alan Lomax, *Folk Song Style and Culture* (Washington, DC: American Association for the Advancement of Science, 1968).

30. Estelle R. Jorgenson, "Music and International Relations," in *Culture and International Relations,* ed. J. Choy (New York: Praeger, 1990), 56–71.

31. Anthony J. Palmer, "World Musics in Music Education: The Matter of Authenticity," *International Journal of Music Education* 19 (1992): 32–40.

32. Barbara B. Smith, "Variability, Changes and the Learning of Music," *Ethnomusicology* 31, no. 2 (1987): 201–20.

33. Ulf P. Lundgren, "Curriculum from a Global Perspective," in *Current Thought on Curriculum,* ed. A. Molnar (Alexandria, VA: Association for Supervision and Curriculum Development, 1985), 119–36. ■

This article originally appeared in the July 2000 issue of *Music Educators Journal.*

CHALLENGES OF PERFORMING DIVERSE CULTURAL MUSIC

Although many ensembles perform multicultural music according to the Western musical system, there are ways to achieve multicultural performances on their own terms.

BY MARY GOETZE

Students can be shown how to imitate the visual aspects of a particular type of music, especially movement.

I t has become the norm to see children's choirs, all-state bands, and church choirs performing music that comes from such diverse sources as Serbia, Kenya, and Japan. The number of publications for ensembles focused on music from traditions beyond Western art or popular traditions has increased exponentially over the past ten years. At first glance, it appears that we are doing a fine job of addressing the multicultural interests of performance ensembles and meeting Standard 9 ("Understanding music in relation to history and culture") of the National Standards for Music Education.

However, according to Kazadi Wa Mukuna, "Errors that continue to be committed are those of transcribing music from different cultures into the Western system in order to teach it to Westerners. This practice is one of the most frequent mistakes, perhaps made unwillingly for the sake of convenience, or simply from ignorance. If a multicultural perspective in music is

to be successful, new methods must be designed with these dilemmas in mind."[1] If we are to achieve what I believe to be the true mission of multiculturalism in education—to acknowledge and validate the numerous cultures that are now represented in our school population and to foster

tolerance and appreciation of those who differ from ourselves—then we need to do more than sing a song or play a composition based on a non-Western melody or text.

In this article, I will challenge some of the assumptions held by Western-trained musicians that are apparent in

Mary Goetze is professor of music and director of the International Vocal Ensemble at the School of Music at Indiana University in Bloomington.

the way they typically present culturally diverse musical works and direct ensemble performances of these works. I will describe a general picture of performance practices that I have observed and participated in as a conductor, teacher, and arranger. Then, based on a recent exploration of an alternative approach, I will suggest ways in which students can more deeply interact with the music and develop an understanding of the culture from which it comes.

I am going to use the term *diverse music* to mean music that originates outside the Western art tradition. This term will refer to all music traditions—Western, as well as non-Western—that are not studied in a typical college music history course.

Western Adaptations

First, let's examine the literature that is performed by ensembles. Many publications of diverse musical works are, in fact, arrangements or compositions by a Western or Western-trained musician and are based on material from non-European sources. Regardless of the voicing of the individual or group that performs the music within the culture, the arrangements are typically written for a standard Western vocal or instrumental ensemble. While in recent years the amount of written documentation about the music has increased in some editions, many existing publications provide only a translation and pronunciation guide, with minimal or no background information about either the music or the culture.

Scores that are based on a transcription of a native performance attempt to be true to the model. However, Western notation focuses on pitch and duration in accordance with the way Westerners conceptualize, organize, and value these elements. The five-line staff was devised to represent subdivisions of an octave into eight pitches. Even the notation of chromatic music looks cumbersome on a staff. Clearly, the staff fails to accommodate the division of the octave into quarter tones and the complexities of Indian, Turkish, or other scales.

Similarly, Western symbolization of duration forces the rhythm into metric groupings of two, three, four, or more, whether the music was originally structured metrically or not. Furthermore, there are numerous essential elements for which there is no musical symbol, such as pulsations, surges, slides and ornaments, movement, or vocal timbre.

■ ■ ■ ■ ■ ■

Most publications of diverse musical works are, in fact, arrangements or compositions by a Western or Western-trained musician and are based on material from non-European sources.

■ ■ ■ ■ ■ ■

Typically, the score is presented to the ensemble like other scores in Western notation, according to the conductor's analysis of the musical structure and the skills needed to perform it. Some conductors meticulously investigate the source of the material and the culture, while others rely on the often sparse information accompanying the score.

Regardless of the vocal technique used in the native style, the choral ensemble will likely use traditional Western choral intonation, tone quality, and blend. Vocal timbres vary widely around the globe. For instance, music from Eastern European styles requires a high instead of a lowered larynx, and some African styles make extensive use of the chest voice instead of the head voice. While only in dire circumstances would we substitute a tenor for a soprano, an oboe for a clarinet, or a women's chorus for children,

we usually adjust vocal timbre to fit the bel canto style in singing and use any available rattle or drum when performing diverse music calling for percussion.

Western vocal pedagogues generally believe that singing in any other way than a European style will threaten students' singing technique and vocal health. Despite the fact that singers within diverse cultures have enjoyed singing in these styles for centuries, we operate on the assumption that singing in any way other than our own must be unhealthy or impossible.

These observations of Western musical practices led me to ask: Will our students sense the unique character of the music when we alter the style in such fundamental ways? Will they experience the qualities that make the music different from Western music—and make the music expressive and meaningful while learning about its culture of origin? And, lastly, is such an experience consistent with the goals of either music or multicultural education?

I believe the time has come to reexamine our methods and their consistency with our goals—time to update our thinking, to acknowledge the extent to which ethnocentricism underlies our educational and musical practices, and to explore alternatives. While there was a time when learning from notation was the only means by which we could access music of other traditions, this is not true today. Audio and video recordings of native models are available, and there is equipment in our schools to play them for students. We have only begun to explore the capacity of the Internet, distance education, and CD-ROM technology for teaching diverse music. There are also native artists living and performing within our communities who can bring the music and the culture to life for students.

Before making recommendations, let me clarify one point lest I be misinterpreted. I am not suggesting that it is inappropriate to arrange, compose, or perform published works based on diverse material. Such fusions and adaptations are an inevitable and exciting aspect of the global arts scene. However, I am asserting that, because this music is notated and approached in the same way as Western music, the experience that we provide our students is more of a Western art musical experience than one from a diverse culture.

Performing Multicultural Music

The following suggestions spring from an experimental vocal ensemble that I founded four years ago at the Indiana University School of Music. The ensemble's goal consists of re-creating music from outside the Western art tradition with integrity by learning about the culture and matching as many aspects of the model as possible. While these recommendations are based on a choral ensemble experience, I include some additional suggestions for instrumental ensembles.

■ Honor the culture by deferring to the experts—native musicians from that culture. If they are not available to you in person, then seek them out or make a recording—preferably a video recording—that can be presented repeatedly as a model for your students. When you make recordings, be certain to inform the musicians of your plans to use the video and get their permission in advance.

■ It is also essential to speak with a native artist or cultural representative to determine the appropriateness of the ensemble learning the music and performing it for others. Too often in our history, we have taken possession of and misused cultural musical treasures without being sensitive to the meaning and function they have for those from whom we have *borrowed* or claimed the music.

■ Learn as much as you can about the culture from written and video resources and share the information with your students. An increasing number of documentaries are available on video from public television sources or libraries. Students can explore the World Wide Web for information and resources. In your study, attempt to discover how the music reflects the culture, how and where music is learned and performed, and if it accompanies extramusical activities.

■ If at all possible, invite a native of the culture to meet the ensemble in

order to foster a personal connection with the group. In our high-tech world, it might be possible to arrange a satellite linkup with a distant site as a means of connecting your ensemble to a native performer.

■ ■ ■ ■ ■ ■

Regardless of the vocal technique used in the native style, the choral ensemble will likely employ traditional Western choral intonation, tone quality, and blend.

■ ■ ■ ■ ■ ■

■ Have the ensemble learn the music aurally—especially if it is transmitted that way within the culture. They will listen more intensely, knowing that they will be reproducing what they hear. (This heightened attention is perhaps the greatest value of oral transmission.) In addition to improving their aural acuity, the process contributes to memory, rhythm, and pitch perception. In vocal music, students are required to discriminate and match vocal timbre, vowel color, and minute differences of consonant production. I recommend listening and imitating the model first, even when you plan to use a score. Then, have the students compare the score to the model that they heard and lead them to recognize what is not symbolized. (For trained musicians, looking at a score first often limits perception; that is, they hear only what they see on the printed page.)

■ In leading students to explore unfamiliar methods of vocal production, educate them about their voices, but be sensitive to individual limitations. I have found that with careful conditioning and sensitivity to vocal

fatigue, the exploration of multiple vocal styles can be done without risk and may even contribute to vocal facility and endurance.

■ Have the students imitate the visual aspects of the performance carefully, especially any movement. Inquire as to the importance of the formation and spatial arrangement of the performers. Notice details such as posture and facial expressions. If possible and appropriate, consider costuming as part of the musical event. (Western musicians consider music to be only sound and thus downplay the visual aspects of a performance even though, in many cultures, dance, dress, and even context and community are inseparable from the sound.)

■ For vocal pieces, record a native performer who can pronounce and translate the text. Learning unfamiliar words is aided by viewing the words and translation while listening to the music. Works from languages with characters may also be written in the International Phonetic Alphabet.

■ Show your respect for the culture by re-creating the music with integrity; that is, match your performance as nearly as possible to the model. This requires listening to the model repeatedly, *especially after the group has learned to perform the music.* Upon reviewing the model, you will be amazed at the details that you and your students missed previously.

■ Explore performing music without a conductor, if appropriate to the tradition. Students take ownership of the music and benefit from the experience of being responsible for entrances and cues.

■ Share information about the music and culture with the audience through program notes or, if possible, spoken comments by the native performer. The video model can be shown, and the learning process can be described. Consider performances as educational sessions that broaden the musical horizons and cultural understanding of parents and the community.

Instrumental Ensembles

I realize the challenges that this approach holds for instrumental groups. Because of the obvious need for different instruments, accurate re-creation cannot be achieved. However, students can watch or listen to a native group performing the material on which a composed piece is based. If the model is a vocal group performing the melody that inspired the composition, students can learn to sing it and work toward fulfilling Standard 1 ("Singing, alone and with others, a varied repertoire of music"). Alternatively, conductors might consider a percussion experience, learned directly from an African or Latin American percussionist. Why couldn't students put down their Western instruments once in a while to drum, clap, sing, and move?

The essence of the approach that I am suggesting consists of (1) learning and performing diverse music the way it is learned and performed in the culture, and (2) developing an understanding of how the music functions within its original cultural context.

Value of Multicultural Music

The oral process of learning the music has educational and musical value for students' musical skill development. Through the experience of accurate re-creation, students can identify with the makers of the music; that is, they can sense the complexities and subtleties of the music and the means by which it is learned. Re-creation based on understanding makes it possible to experience diverse musical expressions on their own terms rather than in a Western context. The insights that students gain into cultures and humanity through making music with integrity and understanding are not attainable through scholarly learning or verbal expression alone. This knowledge is not only the goal of multicultural education, but the ultimate reason for educating our youth in music and in all arts.

Note

1. Kazadi Wa Mukuna, "The Universal Language of All Times?" *International Journal of Music Education* 29 (1997): 47–51. ■

This article originally appeared in the July 1995 issue of *Music Educators Journal.*

URBAN MUSIC EDUCATION
PROVIDING FOR STUDENTS

June Hinckley looks at music education in urban schools and at various curricula and program offerings.

BY JUNE HINCKLEY

The nature of urban life has created profound challenges for schools throughout America's growing number of urban centers. In the inner cities, these challenges are often intensified. Our urban schools are frequently underfunded, understaffed, and over-populated. The campuses are often located in economically depressed areas where hope has become little more than a word and where neglect, indifference, decay, and even hatred—toward others and toward oneself—are such daily realities that some might consider them to be part of a normal existence. Sometimes these urban areas are little more than incubators of indifference; they can scarcely be said to be an appropriate environment for children's education.

It is because of these challenges that urban schools and the education they provide are so critically important. In her book *The Measure of Our Success,* Marian Wright Edelman, founder and president of the Children's Defense Fund, writes:

> It is the responsibility of every adult—especially parents, educators, and religious leaders—to make sure that children

Students sing together at their desks in an urban classroom.

File photo

hear what we have learned from the lessons of life, and to hear over and over that we love them and that they are not alone.[1]

The chasm between the often bleak and forbidding urban world and a supportive and loving environment in which children inherit our shared heritage and knowledge must be bridged by the administrators and teachers in the urban schools. This is the challenge they face in designing and delivering music education to urban youth.

While recognizing and describing the existing problems in our urban schools is important, it does not offer much in the way of solutions. We who are concerned for and committed to the children in these schools must look beyond the problems to determine what is "right." We need to examine innovative trends in policy, programming, and curricula and determine how music in the schools can contribute to providing a better education and, concomitantly, a better quality of life for those in the urban schools.

We must also evaluate the potential

June Hinckley is music, fine arts, and instructional strategies specialist at the Florida Department of Education in Tallahassee.

long-term costs that may result from the absence of music instruction in the urban schools. The president of the National Academy of Recording Arts and Sciences, Inc., Michael Greene, cites findings of the Los Angeles Youth Summit (which followed the 1992 riots in that city) that indicate young people in Los Angeles expressed rage at being denied the opportunities that their older siblings had in band and chorus, since these programs had ceased to be offered in the majority of schools in the area.[2] These enraged young people saw the elimination of music programs as one more expression of a lack of caring on the part of the school leaders and the community at large. It would seem that while the adults, who are policymakers, cannot necessarily agree on the importance of the arts in education, the children in our cities have. Their opinion cannot, and should not, be easily disregarded.

What can music programs provide children in the urban school that will make a positive difference in their lives? Relevance, high expectations, and variety are part of the secret of the success and survival of music programs in many urban areas.

Relevance

A 1993 *New York Times* article described several classroom scenes in some of the Dade County schools in the greater Miami area.[3] In these schools, hands-on creative approaches to the arts make learning meaningful and fun and appeal to students who may have difficulty in learning in traditional ways. For example, in one elementary classroom in one of the poorest areas of the county, students were writing their version of "The Twelve Days of Christmas." The students' lyrics included "red roach spray, two dollar bills, three mouse traps, up to 10 food stamps, 11 neck bones, and no collard greens."[4] All of the students in the scene were engaged and involved in the process of writing this unorthodox version of the song and making the words relevant to the world in which they lived.

In Jacksonville, Atlanta, Washington, D.C., and Houston schools, gospel choirs, salsa bands, mariachi bands, and synthesizer ensembles cap-

ture and nurture the diverse interests of inner-city students. These nontraditional music experiences are often very important to urban children, who come from very diverse cultural backgrounds, because these experiences make a connection between their lives and school. This concept is supported by Barbara Means and Michael S. Knapp, who encourage teachers working with disadvantaged students to make connections with the students' out-of-school experiences and to use a variety of instructional strategies.[5]

■ ■ ■ ■ ■ ■

Our urban schools are frequently underfunded, understaffed, and overpopulated.

■ ■ ■ ■ ■ ■

Some of these programs may be viewed with reservations by traditionalists, particularly when they eclipse or replace regular band, chorus, and orchestra programs. Good music teachers, however, extend the learning opportunities within these less traditional or alternative ensembles to include sight-reading, notational skills, and eventually other types of music. In Dade County, the Liberty City Tri-Level String Ensemble, made up entirely of African American students, prides itself on playing the literature of Bach, Mozart, and Beethoven. Whether the students are playing Western art music or salsa, the fact that they have the opportunity to make and learn about music within the school day is the critical issue. It must be made clear that making music programs attractive and relevant should not make them less musically challenging. Irrespective of the school location or the demographics of the school population, teachers' expectations for students should be high.

High Expectations

The importance of teachers' having high expectations for students cannot be overemphasized. A recent study, *The Role of the Fine and Performing Arts in High School Dropout Prevention,* revealed that high expectations for all students is a key factor in building self-esteem and a desire to please and achieve.[6] It was also reported in this study that at-risk students felt demoralized if they received preferential treatment, but felt special pride when they knew that they were competing with everyone in their class and that their artistic accomplishments were "real."

These results would seem to correlate with the "Effective Schools" research that reports: "Teachers set high standards for learning and let students know they are all expected to meet them. Standards are set so they are both challenging and attainable."[7] "Effective Schools" research identifies schools where test scores are high, attendance is good, the community is involved, student self-esteem is high, and teacher morale is high. Means and Knapp further the "Effective Schools" contention by suggesting that, to make learning meaningful to educationally deprived students, schools must focus more on higher-order skills and less on minimums. They note, "Too often teachers underestimate what students are capable of doing and postpone more difficult, challenging work—sometimes forever."[8]

Variety

Teachers must also provide alternatives to large-ensemble, performance-oriented classes. So-called "academic" music classes, such as composition and theory, need to be made available, and it is the teacher's job to convince the decision makers that these and other courses are relevant to the urban students. This is particularly true since the reason most students give for wanting to study music is to write and perform their own music.[9] Readily available technology makes composition much more accessible to the student and belongs in the music room every bit as much as in the computer lab. The ability to immediately hear how a composition sounds gives important feedback to the at-risk learner.

Variety in music classrooms allows teachers to stimulate interest, infuse meaning, and develop cultural connections with other content areas. Disadvantaged students respond well to a sensory-laden instructional environment. All too often, however, teachers of other subject areas believe that having their students compose rap lyrics as part of a unit of study is integrating music into their content area. As with "The Twelve Days of Christmas" scenario cited earlier, this can be involving to the students, but it is musically shallow.

Music educators need to help teachers in other subject areas use music to breathe life into lectures and student seat work. For example, "The effects of technology on the recording industry in America from 1973 to 1993" is a potential research topic that urban students in social studies might want to pursue. Perhaps a science class could deal with the musical acoustics involved in making a guitar or violin, or a history class might explore how a particular time or event in the past was reflected in its music. A middle school language arts class could keep a record of the kinds of music various commercials use and discuss how the nonverbal musical messages contribute to the advertisement. Moreover, children who have come from other countries can share some of the culture from their homeland by teaching favorite songs to their classmates and later discussing how the songs of their land differ or are similar to American folk songs. In these ways, the concept of "the community as school" becomes more of a reality. The more open, inviting, and accepting the environment of the school becomes, the greater is the potential for the community to be more involved in the future of the school and its students.

Schools That Reach Out

Community involvement, so suggests the "Effective Schools" literature, is vital to creating successful, effective schools. Parental involvement is particularly important. Parents in the inner cities typically care about the education of their children. Often,

however, inner-city parents—many of whom are not English proficient—may feel unqualified to speak to school leaders. Frequently, due to work schedules or because some simply don't think they would feel comfortable, parents and guardians do not participate in school organizations or attend school functions. These parents easily accept the elimination of arts programs due to budget constraints because they have been forced to make similar compromises at home. Efforts to reduce the hesitancy these parents feel toward getting involved in their children's school require patience and persistence, but are well worth the effort.

■ ■ ■ ■ ■ ■

Parental involvement is particularly important.

■ ■ ■ ■ ■ ■

The music program in the schools offers a unique means of involving parents and community leaders. Parents, even with limited English proficiency, may be willing to share their music with the students in the school if invited. African American churches, which have been a traditional source of community activism and solidarity in many inner-city communities, can also be tapped as a resource. Asking an organist or a director of a choir in a local church to share his or her expertise with students is a wise use of local resources and helps to bridge the gap between the school and community.

Music in Special Schools

To meet the needs of urban students more effectively, there has been an increase in the inner city of several types of specialty schools: vocational, alternative, and magnet. Special

schools for gifted and talented students are often located in urban centers to encourage enrollment and a more balanced socioeconomic and racial mix of students. These schools frequently draw from the entire city. In some school districts, they have provided competition for the comprehensive high schools, and this competition has been both positive and negative. On the positive side, the comprehensive schools—schools with a full academic program as well as a varied elective program—in some districts began offering more diversified arts programs to entice students to stay in their regular high school. On the negative side, arts magnet schools have become the token arts program for an entire school district. In the latter situation, arts magnet schools have meant a reduction or elimination of music offerings in the comprehensive schools.

The inclusion of the arts in vocational and alternative schools has been prevalent in states that have a performing arts requirement for graduation. These schools focus on teaching technical skills to prepare students for the work force or provide alternatives for students who cannot or do not find success in the regular school settings. Some teachers in these settings are using the "real world" music making that students see on MTV and hear on recordings (such as MIDI, drum machines, and synthesizers) to create jazz ensembles, teach composition, and, in some cases, provide job training.

Teachers Helping Teachers

The difficulties of teaching in the urban environment are many and are readily recognized. Teachers, even after many years of integrated schools, still receive little real help in understanding students whose culture and learning styles may be different from their own. Ninety percent of teachers in America are white and members of the middle class, while more than 33 percent of America's students are minorities and disadvantaged.[10] Music teachers who are successful in the urban setting must share successful teaching strategies so that new teachers can benefit from their experience in spanning what is often a cultural void between teacher and learner.

Elementary music specialists can offer valuable insights and information regarding their students and the community to middle level and high school teachers. Mentoring of younger teachers by more experienced colleagues can enhance the probability of success of the initiate and can serve to energize the mentor. Supporting teachers who work in difficult situations is vital to improving their conditions of work and improving education.

The Ideal School

The current reform movements center around the need to do a better job of educating the lower one third of the student population, who for the most part are concentrated in America's largest cities. It is with these young people that American schools are failing. Schools are searching for ways to spark students' interest in learning and to offer them hope for a better life. Such efforts are viewed by many of our leaders as the only viable means of ending the cycle of poverty and purposelessness to which many of those in the inner cities have fallen victim.

If we were to imagine a music program that truly provided all the opportunities for disadvantaged students that we believe it can, what might we envision? Certainly the facility would be attractive and well equipped. The teachers would be the best available and would have a clear understanding of the various cultures present in their community. The school would be visited regularly by parents and community leaders, who would volunteer their time, offer their support, and demonstrate a genuine interest in their children and those of their extended school family.

In our ideal program, music making would be an ever-present aspect of the education process throughout the school and would serve as a bonding agent for the diverse interests and backgrounds of the students. Students would be curious and discuss their opinions about the music they heard at home, on television, on the radio, and in music class. They would select music from many styles and periods for their personal listening. School

performances would showcase an eclectic repertory. Performing ensembles might include diverse and alternative ensembles in addition to, and alongside of, traditional performing groups. Students would be composers, and their peers would perform their compositions. Course offerings would provide various options for exploring music, complete with technological support in all classrooms.

■ ■ ■ ■ ■ ■

The contrast in our urban schools between what should be and what is cannot be ignored.

■ ■ ■ ■ ■ ■

The music, theater, dance, language arts, and graphic and plastic arts classes would be involved in creating and executing collaborative productions. Teachers would have at least two hours of planning time so that they could visit other schools, collaborate with other faculty members, and have adequate time to plan individualized instruction for their students. Teachers would have the opportunity to participate in exciting professional-development opportunities, including the latest discoveries in successful instructional practice.

If it were a just world, all that has been described would be characteristic of all schools, since this is what all teachers and students deserve. However, in the world in which we all reside, few, if any, schools, regardless of location, would meet the standard of our "ideal" school.

The Real World

The contrast in our urban schools between what should be and what is cannot be ignored. No student should be deprived of an education in music because of circumstances of birth and residence. Music educators are not

absolved from speaking out against budget and program cuts in inner-city music programs because the local community does not openly challenge them. As Marian Wright Edelman writes, "All Americans must commit personally and as voters to a national crusade of conscience and action that will ensure that no child is left behind."[11]

Each of us has the responsibility to see that all children learn the lessons we have learned, are loved as we have been loved, and know the power of music as we do. Teachers, in place of the parents, must sometimes provide the voice for the inner-city children. It is often up to us to speak up for the children of poverty. If we don't, who will?

Notes

1. Marian Wright Edelman, *The Measure of Our Success: A Letter to My Children and Yours* (Boston: Beacon Press, 1992).

2. Michael Greene, speech given at the Getty Conference on the Arts, San Francisco, CA, February 1993.

3. Susan Chira, "Missing Muses," *New York Times,* 3 February 1993, A-1, B-8.

4. Ibid., A-1, B-8.

5. Barbara Means and Michael S. Knapp, "Cognitive Approaches to Teaching Advanced Skills to Educationally Disadvantaged Students," *Phi Delta Kappan* 73, no. 4 (December 1991): 282–89.

6. Nancy H. Barry, Jack A. Taylor, and Kim Walls, *The Role of the Fine and Performing Arts in High School Dropout Prevention* (Tallahassee, FL: Center for Music Research, Florida State University, 1990).

7. Northwest Regional Educational Laboratory, "Effective Schooling Practices: A Research Synthesis, 1990 Update," in *Onward to Excellence* (Portland, OR: Author, 1990).

8. Means and Knapp, "Cognitive Approaches," 282–89.

9. This information comes from a Yamaha Corporation of America study done by the Pelican Group. (The study was commissioned in preparation for developing the *Music in Education Program,* Los Angeles, CA, 1987).

10. Ana Maria Villegas, "Culturally Responsive Pedagogy for the 1990s and Beyond" (paper commissioned by Educational Testing Service, Princeton, NJ, 1990).

11. Edelman, *Measure of Our Success.* ■

This article originally appeared in the Spring 2000 issue of *General Music Today*.

SOCIAL CONTEXT AND MUSIC LEARNING

by Roy M. Legette

The effect of social context on learning has become an issue of growing importance in education. Social context influences how teachers teach and how children learn. Cognitive psychologists have shown that children spontaneously develop particular informal concepts outside of school that can often be related to academic knowledge obtained in school. This informal knowledge can serve as a scaffold or underpinning for what is taught in school (Vygotsky, 1978). Rogoff and Lave (1984) also believe that people are able to transfer existing knowledge, learned in informal (nonschool) settings, to formal school settings.

An Example

In teaching music in the public schools, more attention should be given to the social environments of children, including how they live and what kinds of music they listen to during the time they are

Roy M. Legette is assistant professor of music education in the School of Music at the University of Georgia in Athens.

■ ■ ■ ■ ■

Students must be able to relate what they learn in school to how they live and what they do outside of school.

■ ■ ■ ■ ■

not in school. For many poor and minority students, the social contexts in which they live and learn can be quite different from what they encounter in school. Inadequately addressing social context can result in serious problems. Consider the following scenario:

John is a recently graduated first-year music teacher. He accepts a job teaching band and general music at a junior high school situated in the inner city of a major west coast city of the United States. The junior high is located in a low-income, high-crime neighborhood. Most of the students who attend this junior high school are minorities (African-American, Hispanic-American, and Asian-American).

Most of John's college training centered around learning and embracing music of the European tradition—music of great masters like Bach, Beethoven, and Brahms.

John begins his first week of school with a series of listening activities for his students. He brings in recordings of classical composers and attempts to point out important features of the music—melody, rhythm, harmony, and form. John is quickly besieged by a plethora of discipline problems. Some students begin playing group games in the back of the classroom. Gradually, absences become more and more frequent, and John's class eventually turns into utter chaos.

John has fallen into a trap that many beginning educators succumb to—teaching exactly the way that they have been taught. There can be serious problems with this approach. We live in a multicultural, multiethnic society, and for learning to be most meaningful, students must feel that they have a stake in the learning process. That is, students must be able to relate what they learn in school to how they live and what they do outside of school. John failed to consider the ethnic composition of his class or their social backgrounds. The music of Bach, Beethoven, and Brahms was foreign to them and not a part of their everyday experiences.

Over thirty years ago, the Tanglewood Symposium gave the following admonishment to music educators (Mark, 1996): "Music of all periods, styles, forms, and cultures belongs in the curriculum. The musical repertory should be expanded to involve music of our time in its rich variety, including currently popular teenage music, avant-garde music, American folk music, and music of other cultures" (p. 44).

Had John heeded their admonishment, he might have spared himself a calamity. John and his students have different musical realities. For John as a music teacher, classical music was the music most real to him. For his students, the music that they listened to and identified with every day (pop, rock, rap, folksongs, and so on) was the music most real to them. Perhaps the same musical concepts that John was trying to teach could have been taught and would have been better received if he had started by using music from the students' own experiences.

Successful Learning

There is no doubt that students should be exposed to the rich body of the classical music repertoire and encouraged to reap its many benefits. Music educators would be remiss in their duties if they did otherwise. However, in many school music settings, classical music might not be the best point of entry. Prospective music teachers should be prepared to offer meaningful music experiences in contexts in which their students can be most successful.

What musical contexts could be more meaningful than the musics that students listen to every day?

Social context may also have an influence on learning styles (Purdie and Hattie, 1996). This point is illustrated by the following observation of a student over the course of six months:

Ben is a fourth-grade student. He does not have a father at home and consequently is often called upon by his mother to share the responsibility of running the household. Ben's involvement can range from helping to keep the house clean to helping his mother find solutions to problems that develop around the home. Ben's mother gives him a fair

■ ■ ■ ■ ■ ■

Prospective music teachers should be prepared to offer meaningful music experiences in contexts in which their students can be most successful.

■ ■ ■ ■ ■ ■

amount of freedom to express himself. As a matter of fact, at home Ben is outgoing and extremely talkative. At school, however, Ben is constantly reprimanded for unacceptable behavior like fighting and unruliness. Furthermore, Ben, who is failing most of his subjects, is repeating fourth grade.

Ben is a different person in music class. He is attentive, self-controlled, and genuinely interested in the subject matter. In this class, with minimal aid from the music teacher, Ben works on

complex music projects, listens critically, and revises his own work. With the aid of a computer-assisted keyboard program, Ben creates his own melodies, as well as accompaniments for pre-existing melodies.

Why is there such a marked difference in Ben's behavior and performance in music class compared to other classes? Perhaps it is because in music class, unlike other classes in the school, which tend to follow a more restricted and traditional format, the teacher creates an environment in which Ben is able to work independently. Instead of relying solely on the music teacher for information, Ben can create his own music problems and find his own solutions. Perhaps in music class, Ben feels a sense of responsibility and freedom similar to what he experiences at home.

More attention needs to be given to the Bens in our school systems. It is encouraging to note that, while the issue of social context as it relates to different learning styles is complex, some music educators agree that there are more and more students who, like Ben, have learning styles that are incompatible with the often rigid structure of traditional classroom settings (Scripp and Meyaard, 1991).

Learning Styles

This position is not without foundation. Emerging theories suggest that each student has a dominant learning style. Four learning styles widely accepted are sensing-thinking, sensing-feeling, intuitive-thinking, and intuitive-feeling (Hanson, Silver, and Strong, 1991). Traditionally, the sensing-thinking and intuitive-thinking categories are emphasized in school instruction. The other two categories, sensing-feeling and intuitive-feeling, are often neglected. Consequently, the needs of students who happen to fall into the latter two categories and respond better to a less traditional, less-structured classroom environment are often not met. These are the very students who may feel disillusioned with education because their preferred learning styles are neither encouraged nor invited in the traditional classroom (Hanson, Silver, and Strong, 1991).

Some research and education programs have begun to address the needs of those students who fall into the sensing-feeling or intuitive-feeling categories and have difficulty learning in more traditional and highly structured classroom environments. Educators involved in these programs are sensitive to and aware of the fact that learning style and social context influence how students learn. They recognize that "having a personal stake in one's work, creating multiple solutions to open-ended tasks, and interacting frequently with teachers and peers" are necessary learning ingredients for students like Ben (Scripp and Meyaard, 1991).

At Harvard Project Zero, for example, the learner is placed at the center of the educational process—a process that respects the different ways in which students learn, as well as differences among the ways in which individuals perceive the world and express their ideas. Students are encouraged to tackle open-ended problems and to trace the development of their work through each stage of the creative process. In this type of environment, students write poems, compose their own songs, and tackle other "real-life" projects as starting points for exploring future artistic endeavors (Gardner, 1989).

In a musical setting, students might work together in groups of various sizes at computer terminals. The notes of a simple melody such as "Twinkle, Twinkle, Little Star" are displayed on

∎ ∎ ∎ ∎ ∎

Social context is an integral part of teaching and learning that should not be ignored.

∎ ∎ ∎ ∎ ∎

the computer screen in conventional music notation. The computer plays the melody correctly except for the ending. The students are asked to determine what is wrong with the melody by pointing to incorrect notes on the screen as they hear them. Students are then asked to compose their own endings to the melody. The students approach solving this problem in different ways. Some may start by erasing the current ending and entering notes into the system. Others may sing the familiar tune aloud against the computer's playback of their on-screen revisions. Others may choose to play the tune over and over before acting. The approaches and solutions may vary, but all of the students are engaged in solving a musical problem.

What is most important is that children are presented an interesting task that allows them to be creative and to make choices. Harvard Project Zero has been successful, in part, because students can draw upon the storehouse of musical skills and knowl-

edge that they have accumulated both inside and outside of school. They are encouraged to build upon what they already know. In addition, students can bring into the classroom thinking processes that occur naturally to them in their own social settings and that they may have learned from others. This approach tends to help students develop and strengthen multiple ways of learning, rather than forcing them to adjust their learning to a particular teaching method.

Social context is an integral part of teaching and learning that should not be ignored. Similarly, teaching that respects the different learning styles of students can also help music educators tap the rich musical resources and contributions that many students have to offer.

Literature Cited

Gardner, H. 1989. Zero-based arts education: An introduction to Arts Propel. *Studies in Art Education: A Journal of Issues and Research*, 30 (2): 71–83.

Hanson, J., H. Silver, and R. Strong. 1991. Square pegs: Learning styles of at-risk students. *Music Educators Journal*, 78 (3): 30–35.

Mark, M. L. 1996. *Contemporary Music Education*. 3rd ed. New York: Schirmer.

Purdie, N., and J. Hattie. 1996. Cultural differences in the use of strategies for self-regulated learning. *American Educational Research Journal*, 33 (4): 845–71.

Rogoff, B., and J. Lave. 1984. *Everyday Cognition*. Cambridge: Harvard University Press.

Scripp, L., J. Meyaard, and L. Davidson. 1988. Discerning musical development: Using computers to discover what we know. *Journal of Aesthetic Education*, 22 (1): 75–88.

Scripp, L., and J. Meyaard. 1991. Encouraging musical risk for learning success. *Music Educators Journal*, 78 (3): 37–41.

Vygotsky, L. 1978. *Mind In Society: The Development of Higher Psychological Processes*, eds. M. Cole et al. Cambridge: Harvard University Press.

This article originally appeared in the Fall/Winter 2000 issue of *Update*.

INCREASING PROSPECTIVE MUSIC EDUCATORS' TOLERANCE FOR STUDENT DIVERSITY

JAYNE M. STANDLEY
Florida State University

Despite the pluralism that will cause ethnic and racial minorities to comprise 40% of our school population within the next 30 years, prejudice against non-white, non-European groups remains high (Cartledge & Milburn, 1996, p. 1). A survey in 1992 revealed that many Americans believe there are irreconcilable differences among ethnic and racial groups with blacks (46.2%) feeling more strongly about the issue than whites (26.7%) (Dash & Niemi, 1992). In response to this growing social problem, President Clinton has instituted a national initiative on race entitled "One America in the 21st Century," appointing by Executive Order 12050 a seven-member Advisory Board on Race Relations to advise him in promoting a national dialogue on race relations (U.S. Embassy Israel Press Archives, 1997).

It would seem that teachers particularly need tolerance and understanding of gender, ability, race, and cultural differences in order to be successful in the pluralistic classroom of the future. Many colleges have made minimal curricular changes to address these issues by requiring multicultural, women's studies, and/or world music classes. Research has not yet shown resultant changes in tolerance or acceptance of diversity among prospective teachers. Demonstrating this point, Stanley (1996) recently reported that preservice physical education majors were overwhelmingly negative about the ability to teach academics to lower socioeconomic groups and those of another race; 72% reported being uncomfortable around students from an ethnic heritage different from their own.

Though America is becoming more culturally diverse, the teaching pool is becoming increasingly homogeneous, with the number of white, middle-class, Euro-American females increasing dispropor-

tionately (Cartledge & Milburn, 1996, p.2). The homogenous background and attitudes of preteachers, coupled with student diversity in the classroom, both present a growing social and educational problem. Youth from cultures that are ethnically disparaged often react with maladaptive social behavior and academic failure (Cartledge & Feng, 1996, p. 30). Most educators profess the goal of accepting every child, but disparity along racial, ethnic, gender, ability, and religious lines still exists in our schools. To what extent are prospective teachers intolerant of diversity and how might such attitudes be changed?

Background

Early in the multicultural education movement, it was assumed that integrating multicultural information into the curriculum would affect students' attitudes about diversity. Research has shown this to be a fallacy. Griego (1997) tested the relationship between multicultural education in the reading program and found that reading skills and comprehension increased, self-esteem increased, but understanding of other cultures failed to increase. Likewise, in music education, simply teaching the world music subject matter did not increase multicultural understanding and tolerance (Fung, 1994). Despite these research findings, multicultural music activities continue to be a popular curriculum component for a variety of reasons (Carter, 1996; Young, 1996).

If current efforts show little benefit in multicultural perceptions in the field, how shall educators better prepare teachers for the students and classrooms of the future? Banks (1995) believes that college and university classes must be reformed to allow students from diverse racial, ethnic, and social-class groups to experience educational equality within a curriculum that moves beyond token exposure to multicultural literature. Rather, he advocates education and information

Jayne M. Standley is professor of music therapy at Florida State University in Tallahassee.

about differences in cultural perceptions, immersion and involvement with other cultures, and reduction of prejudice accompanied by compassion for and "role taking" of diverse populations' perceptions. Banks (1995) concludes that such an approach would result in increased social reform and activism.

Johnson and Darrow (1997) demonstrated the benefits of immersion and involvement on attitudes of band students regarding students with disabilities. They used videotaped models of inclusion in music education activities and positive peer and teacher affect to significantly alter acceptance of elementary, junior, and senior high band students. They advocated long-term, consistent teaching of inclusion objectives and modeling behaviors in the music education classroom.

Little research exists in music education to document how well prepared our future teachers are to model, provide, and teach equitable, inclusive relationships. To what extent are prospective music educators tolerant of individual differences that might commonly be encountered in the American classrooms of today? To what extent does college preparation affect these attitudes? Are the techniques recommended by Banks (1995), such as experiencing equitable education activities, immersion, and instruction in differences in cultural perceptions, demonstrably better at promoting tolerance? A college course and attitudinal assessment instrument were designed to answer these questions. Curricular issues included racial prejudice, cultural and ethnic perceptions, equity, ability, and prejudice against issues of personal appearance.

The Study

Participants included 104 music education majors in either a diversity class or undergraduate music education preparation class. Thirty-two participants were enrolled in a 6-week, legislatively-mandated prototype for a summer course, "Teaching Music to Diverse Populations," and were primarily senior music education majors in the final year of coursework prior to internship. Attitude assessments were also made on a second class of 36 similar participants during a second summer to determine if results were replicable. The attitudinal changes of the two diversity classes were contrasted with a comparison group of 36 undergraduate music education majors enrolled in a 6-week introductory music education course, either "Directed Observation and Foundations of Music Education" or "Choral Techniques for Non-Voice Principals." These students had not had a course in diversity within school populations.

On the first day of class, all students were asked to complete an anonymous questionnaire about their personal identity. The questions were quite personal and students were invited to complete only those items they chose to share. Table 1 shows comparative demographics for the three groups as they described themselves. The students in the diversity classes were primarily female (62% and 64%) and relatively homogeneous in ethnic and socioeconomic background, representative of the trend in America's teaching pool (Cartledge & Milburn, 1996).

Table 1
Participant Demographics

	Diversity Classes		Music
	Prototype group	Replication group	Intro Class
N	32	36	36
Music education track			
% Choral	50	15	28
% Instrumental	47	75	67
% General music	3	10	6
Mean age in years	21.4	21.3	20.1
Gender: % Female	62	64	47
Socioeconomic level			
% High	12	10	11
% Middle	88	85	89
% Low	0	5	0
Religion			
% Protestant	43	50	53
% Catholic	31	21	25
% Jewish	3	8	8
% Other	15	13	6
% None	9	8	8
% White European	81	81	81
Sexual preference			
% Heterosexual	91	97	91
% Homosexual	9	3	6
% Bi-sexual	0	0	3
% Reporting disability	9	11	0

Attitude Assessment

All students completed an anonymous, researcher-designed questionnaire concerning their attitudes about diversity before and after the 6-week courses. The Diversity Comfort Scale had 20 statements of beliefs concerning social diversity and multicultural issues, such as "It is good to have friends and acquaintances of other races" or "Cross-cultural marriage is good." Some items were specific to the music education classroom, i.e., "As a music educator, it would be good to have a drum major who utilized a wheel chair." Participants reported their personal comfort with these items on a Likert scale from 1 (very uncomfortable) to 5 (very comfortable). A second section of the questionnaire asked about 36 specific behaviors in which the person might have engaged during the last month, as "Have you invited a person of a different race to your home?" or "Have you used a racial slur?" Participants responded yes or no to these items.

Diversity Curriculum and Teaching Techniques

The diversity classes met 1 hour and 20 minutes a day, 4 or 5 days a week. The course began with confrontation of intolerant attitudes. The first day participants viewed and discussed a videotape, "The National Hate Test" originally broadcast on the USA Network on April 30, 1998, a date designated by the U.S. Senate as "National Erase the Hate and Eliminate Racism Day." This 1-hour presentation confronted prejudice by portraying real-life situations of racism, ageism, sexism, and intolerance against those who are disabled, overweight or of a different religion. A discussion followed each vignette featuring typical U.S. citizens who boldly spoke to the issues of prejudice and sought alternatives for cross-cultural understanding and acceptance.

A research-based text provided information about diverse cultural groups' perceptions and suggested effective, related teaching strategies to increase success

in the classroom (Cartledge & Milburn, 1996). Additional topics of discussion were the MENC policy on the use of religious music in the schools and the adaptation of the National Standards for Music Education for specific groups covered in the course. Transfer was emphasized, with writing tasks applying taught concepts to the classroom situation and to society in general. Additionally, observation and discussion of videotapes of multicultural students and persons with disabilities succeeding in inclusive music education settings were utilized.

Throughout the diversity course, special emphasis was placed on involvement/immersion and on equitable and cooperative group learning. Immersion was accomplished in two ways: (1) an assignment to sing once a week in a school choir consisting of secondary students with mentally handicapping conditions at the trainable level, and (2) an assignment to spend time outside class with people of differing backgrounds from the students.'

To facilitate cooperative group learning, the class was divided into three or four small discussion groups with student diversity representative of that of the class. Equity, tolerance of differences, and cooperative learning styles of problem solving were structured for every group interaction. The following group discussion rules were established by the teacher and moni-

Table 2
Pretest/Posttest Mean Ratings on Comfort Scale by Groups

	Diversity 1		Diversity 2		Introductory	
Item	Pretest	Posttest	Pretest	Posttest	Pretest	Posttest
Friends–other races	4.91	5.00	4.53	4.89	4.56	4.65
Interracial marriage	4.28	4.63	3.44	3.69	3.51	3.68
Friends–higher socioeconomic level	4.44	4.63	4.36	4.64	4.31	4.41
Friends–lower socioeconomic level	4.63	4.88	4.44	4.72	4.19	4.38
Interreligious marriage	3.37	3.94	3.44	3.63	3.31	3.26*
Friends–different religion	4.25	4.75	4.33	4.75	4.09	4.47
Friends–different sex pref.	4.28	4.66	4.08	4.50	3.92	4.12
Mus ed–gay drum major	3.72	4.28	3.33	3.81	3.17	3.38
Mus ed–gay male majorette	3.69	4.19	3.31	3.86	3.31	3.24*
Friends–overweight	4.56	4.75	4.31	4.58	3.94	4.09
Music ed–overweight majorette	3.53	4.03	2.89	3.58	3.03	3.00*
Friends–immigrants	4.69	4.72	4.33	4.58	4.09	4.21
Cross-cultural marriage	4.47	4.66	3.94	4.31	3.92	4.03
Americans should be multilingual	4.50	4.72	4.36	4.42	4.25	4.38
Friends–opposite gender	4.97	4.97	4.69	4.97	4.67	4.65*
Friends–older	4.69	4.88	4.61	4.83	4.47	4.41*
Mus ed–drum major in wheel chair	3.81	4.53	3.69	4.14	3.42	3.29*
Friends–disability	4.59	4.88	4.39	4.58	3.94	4.21
Friends–HIV positive	4.25	4.53	4.22	4.47	3.94	3.91*
Mus ed–female drum major	4.69	5.00	4.67	4.86	4.22	4.53

Notes: 1 = Very uncomfortable, 5 = Very comfortable. * = posttest decrease

Table 3
Percentage of Participants Engaging in Diversity-Related Activities

Item	Pretest	Posttest	Pretest	Posttest	Pretest	Posttest
Interracial socialization	56.8	63.4	50.3	53.0	40.3	52.9
Interreligious socialization	54.7	62.5	52.8	53.3	55.6	52.9*
Socialization with those of other sexual preferences	48.9	54.1	43.0	55.0	51.9	55.9
Multicultural socialization	76.6	71.9*	58.0	62.0	43.1	60.3
Socialization with disabled persons	13.1	19.4	10.0	9.0*	8.9	10.6
Socialization with older persons	75.0	59.4*	81.0	83.0	72.7	64.7*
Socialization with opposite gender	32.8	40.6	42.0	33.0*	33.3	35.3
Restraint from use of racial, religious, and ethnic slurs	88.4	92.8	64.0	71.0	71.4	78.5
Confrontation of those using slurs	32.2	48.4	33.0	39.8	30.0	33.1
World music concert attendance	32.2	27.8*	35.1	30.4*	37.8	24.7*

* = posttest decrease

tored by selected individuals in each discussion group:

• only one person may speak at a time with no interruption

• everyone must remain on-task to the issue being discussed

• males/females and minority/majority students must share equally in group-leadership and rule-monitoring roles

• males and females must speak an equitable amount of time

• individuals must seek permission of the person who had just spoken when disagreeing with that person's statements.

Finally, cooperative problem-solving tasks were structured to occur outside the classroom in the latter part of the course using the same discussion group structure and rules for interaction. These tasks consisted of developing and presenting group demonstrations of ethnic music competencies and music activities which demonstrated the social values taught in the class.

Comparison Course Curriculum

The comparison group was enrolled in one of two introductory music education courses. One consisted of discussion of material from three texts which focused on the National Standards for Music Education, values and choices of educators (Who shall we teach? How shall we teach?, etc.), and philosophy and history of music education. The other introductory course was a choral techniques class for non-voice principals. These courses were selected for comparison

as typical music education curriculum content. All courses met for comparable amounts of time each week and for the same number of weeks.

Results

Data were combined for the younger students into one group of comparison figures to assess change without the diversity curriculum. Data for the two diversity classes were kept separate to ascertain the effect of the curriculum on replicating attitude change. Table 2 shows the mean pretest/posttest comfort ratings for issues of diversity and multiculturalism by these groupings. It is important to note that the students in the diversity classes usually indicated higher comfort on the precourse ratings than did those in the introductory courses. This lesser degree of comfort evidenced in the younger students may be the result of having less time to mature and to complete course work in the music education and the general university curriculum.

The diversity classes increased comfort ratings on every issue postcourse except one, friends of the opposite gender, which remained at the same level for diversity 1. The diversity 1 overall mean for all items increased from 4.32 to 4.63 (gain of .31) and from 4.07 to 4.39 for diversity 2 (gain of .32). The introduction class had higher ratings on only 65% of the 20 items post course increasing from an overall mean of 3.91 to 4.02 (gain of .11). Though gains were made by all classes, statistically, both diversity classes were significantly higher on the posttest items than the nondiversity class ($F = 10.153$, $df = 2$, $p < .001$). The two diversity classes were remarkably similar on overall comfort gain and on both the pretest and posttest in the rank order of items by comfort level. The correlation between the two diversity classes for the pretest was .90 and for the posttest was .89. The highest comfort levels were expressed for friends of other races and friends of the opposite gender. The lowest comfort levels were given for interreligious marriage and for overweight majorettes in the music education program.

Data from the 36 questions concerning diversity behaviors engaged in during the prior month were grouped by category and mean percentages computed. Table 3 shows these data. Again, the younger students were generally less diverse in their social activities than seniors in the diversity classes. On the posttest report, all groups decreased social activity in three areas with only one of these in common: world music concert attendance. It is speculated that this is due to fewer summer semester offerings of concert opportunities. The students in the introductory classes increased the most in multicultural socialization, while both groups of seniors increased the most in confrontation of those using racial, ethnic, and religious slurs.

Discussion

This study measured the changes in attitude and social engagement of students exposed to a special curriculum to promote tolerance versus those enrolled in typical music education preparation courses. Results indicated that comfort levels with those from diverse populations and with differing abilities increased, the use of racial, ethnic, and religious slurs decreased, and confrontation of others who made such slurs increased. Students were extremely positive about the course content and regularly alluded to applications they saw to classroom situations. The second diversity class replicated closely the changes of the first group with mean comfort level increases and rank ordering of issues according to comfort level. These results add confidence to assumptions about the effect of the curriculum as it exists and provide a standard against which to measure the effect of trial techniques which might be added.

All students in the diversity and the introductory courses improved to some degree on the pretest/posttest attitudinal measures. It is reassuring to discover that the usual music education curriculum promotes tolerance, though perhaps not as much as we had previously assumed. It is also reassuring to document that predicted teaching techniques resulted in substantial increases in comfort and social engagement with diverse populations.

Table 4
Recommendations for National Dialogue on Race Relations

Who Should Be Involved
- Everyone in the country, with a National Race Relations Day
- Everyone via national broadcast similar to the National Hate Test video used in class, with scheduled group discussions throughout the country to follow-up, utilizing community peo ple from different races (ordinary, not famous people)
- School students through multiple projects
- Parents and other community adults

What Should Be Discussed
- Language instruction for teachers, ESOL techniques, ebonics, slang dictionaries
- Agreement in the culture on nonoffensive language
- Reduction of economic inequities in schools to increase stu dents' opportunities
- Ways to foster better race relations in personal life
- Ways to become bi-cultural, i.e., comfortable in both cultures, while retaining pride in one's personal background
- Ways to experience/benefit from multiculturalism in America
- Methodologies to discuss controversial issues without anger
- Celebrations of the history and contributions of various races and ethnic backgrounds to American culture
- Ways to curb high rate gang participation by minority youth
- Ways in which segregation by color occurs and constructive methods to achieve unity instead
- Ways to improve employment opportunity for minorities
- Ways to reduce violence due to racial differences
- Examination of the role of historical perception in shaping cul tural values, with topics such as the slave trade, civil rights movement, and so forth
- Development of society responsive to global concerns/values

How Dialogue Could Be Accomplished
- Discuss in roundtable format with trained mediators and dis cussion leaders focussed on solutions, not complaints, with ground rules that allow for speaking without interruption and asking permission to disagree, and that provide opportunities for everyone to speak. Move from statements about "my pain" to proposing solutions.
- Require all students to take a history course with a non-European/American perspective.
- Require teachers to be assessed on their racial attitudes before final certification.
- Require students to take classes on peer mediation, conflict resolution, and anger control.
- Provide Radio and TV broadcasts across America on this topic, with programming for all age levels.
- Provide opportunities to ask difficult questions, such as "How should I feel about...?" "Have you ever...?" "What offends you...?"

Obviously, our task as educators is not finished if some students on the posttest report continue to use racial, ethnic, or religious slurs. Long-term tracking and follow up of diversity beliefs of all participants and their impact on students in their classrooms is desirable. It would also be interesting after internship or classroom experience to determine whether students felt this material contributed to their success and whether they retained similar comfort levels.

One activity during the diversity class stimulated thinking about what we as citizens and educators can do at the present time to improve race relations in America. Students were asked to write a recommendation to the President's plan for a national dialogue on race relations. These recommendations were compiled and distributed to the class (Table 4). They offer a variety of suggestions for confronting racism that may be helpful to music educators.

As our society becomes more culturally diverse, world music activities can become a highly positive and participatory way to contribute to global knowledge and understanding. For this reason, it would seem wise to emphasize more specific teaching objectives and activities to effect changes in students' attitudes and relationships. This research would indicate that modeling, immersion, and discussion of issues of gender equity, ability, racial and cultural issues are also highly desirable. Obviously, there is still much that each of us can do as we continue to strive for the most effective means to promote social tolerance.

References

Banks, J. A. (1995). Multicultural education and the modification of students' racial attitudes. In W. D. Hawley and A. W. Jackson (Eds.), *Toward a Common Destiny: Improving Race and Ethnic Relations in America* (pp. 315–339). San Francisco: Jossey-Bass.

Carter, L. D. (1996). The world is welcome here: A survey of multicultural music teaching materials with annotated bibliography designed to assist the elementary classroom teacher. (Doctoral dissertation, The Claremont Graduate School, 1996). *Dissertation Abstracts International, 57–11A*, p.4681 (University Microfilms No. AAG97–14212).

Cartledge, G. & Feng, H. (1996). The relationship of culture and social behavior. In Cartledge, G. & Milburn, J. (Eds.), *Cultural Diversity and Social Skills Instruction* (pp.13–44). Champaign, Ill: Research Press.

Cartledge, G. & Milburn, J. (Eds.) (1996). *Cultural Diversity and Social Skills Instruction*. Champaign, Ill: Research Press.

Dash, S. & Niemi, R. (1992). Democratic attitudes in multicultural settings: A cross-national assessment of political socialization. *Youth & Society, 23* (3), 313–334.

Fung, C. V. (1994). Undergraduate nonmusic majors' world music preference and multicultural attitudes. *Journal of Research in Music Education, 42* (1), 45–57.

Griego, I. C. (1997). The relationship between multicultural education, reading achievement, and self-concept. (Doctoral dissertation, University of Colorado at Denver, 1997). *Dissertation Abstracts International, 58–08A*, p.2968 (University Microfilms No. AAG98–04543).

Johnson, C. & Darrow, A. (1997). The effect of positive models of inclusion on band students' attitudinal statements regarding the integration of students with disabilities. *Journal of Research in Music Education, 45* (2), 173–184.

Stanley, L. S. (1996). The development and validation of an instrument to assess attitudes toward cultural diversity and pluralism among preservice physical educators. *Educational & Psychological Measurement, 56* (5), 891–897.

U.S. Embassy Israel Press Archives (1997, June 12). Clinton names advisory commission on race relations. http://www.usis-israel.org.il/publish/press/whouse/archive/1997//june/wh60613.htm

Young, S. (1996). Music teachers' attitudes, classroom environments, and music activities in multicultural music education. (Doctoral dissertation, Ohio State, 1996). *Dissertation Abstracts International, 57–07A*, p.2934 (University Microfilms No. AAG96–39384).

This article originally appeared in the May 1995 issue of *Music Educators Journal.*

LANGUAGE BARRIERS AND TEACHING MUSIC

Jacqueline Yudkin suggests ways for instrumental music teachers to identify and teach students with limited English proficiency.

BY JACQUELINE YUDKIN

Every student in our public schools deserves an opportunity to study a musical instrument. The inability to speak English or a limited command of the English language should not prevent a student from being accepted into instrumental music class or hinder that student's progress. In the Los Angeles Unified School District, approximately one-third of the total enrollment for 1990–91 school year was identified as having Limited English Proficiency (LEP).[1] Some classrooms have a majority of English-speaking students with only one or two LEP students, while other classrooms have a majority of LEP students speaking the same foreign language, such as Spanish. Still other classrooms have LEP students who speak a variety of primary languages. Regardless of the combination of languages spoken in a classroom, music educators must be prepared to teach all students. The ability of teachers to identify LEP students and to develop effective strategies for teaching them can contribute to the success of the music program while meeting the needs of all students.

Most LEP students enroll in instrumental music instruction because they

Jacqueline Yudkin is an instrumental music teacher in the Los Angeles Unified School District.

· · · · · ·

Regardless of the combination of languages spoken in a classroom, music educators must be prepared to teach all students.

· · · · · ·

have a genuine interest and desire to play a musical instrument. However, some LEP students are encouraged to learn a musical instrument because an administrator, teacher, or counselor believes they will find success in a class that has less of an emphasis on language skills. Actually, the reverse is true. Instrumental music instruction involves more than just learning to read notes, playing rhythm patterns, or remembering fingerings. Teachers impart a musical tradition that is really

a felt experience. Verbal instructions only help guide students toward fulfilling the actual aesthetic experience for themselves. A teacher's and student's frustration is magnified when communication is itself a barrier.

Identifying LEP Students

Instrumental music teachers must identify LEP students in order to assess individual needs. This evaluation will then determine whether classroom structure and teaching strategies should be modified to meet the educational needs of all students.

In schools that routinely identify LEP students, music teachers may want to conduct an interview with each LEP student who wants to enroll in instrumental music class. This interview may help teachers understand and address a child's special needs and capabilities. The following questions help teachers organize their instrumental classes and reveal a student's ability to comprehend and respond in English: "What instrument do you want to study? Why have you selected that instrument? Do you own that instrument? Have you previously studied a musical instrument? Do any members of your family play a musical instrument?" More technical questions involving ear training may be too difficult to explain to a child with a language barrier.

Getting students to talk at some

Teachers should move around the classroom and point to lines or notes that relate to their verbal instructions.

length about their choice of instrument or their reasons for enrolling in a music class may not be easy. However, when teachers are forced to limit class size, they must make difficult decisions regarding a student's suitability for instrumental music instruction. A student's attitude, general intellectual ability, previous classroom performance, parental support, maturity, and physical attributes (hand size, finger width and length, arm length, shape of mouth, teeth, and so on) are common factors used by teachers to make these types of decisions. The ability to speak English is simply one more factor that, in some cases, should be added to this list. Its importance depends on the individual teacher, student, overall class size, and the language skills of other students.

When information regarding a student's English fluency is not available and an interview cannot be conducted, teachers can still learn to identify students through classroom observations. For example, some students may cover up a language deficiency by being too quiet in class. In an effort not to draw attention to themselves, they seldom raise their hands to ask or answer questions and appear to understand everything that transpires by

■ ■ ■ ■ ■

Teachers should try to draw out the quiet student, usually through questions, to ensure that the child fully understands the material.

■ ■ ■ ■ ■

maintaining good eye contact, being alert, and nodding their heads at the appropriate times during the lesson. A teacher, pleased to have such attentive, cooperative students, may overlook the possibility that these children are actually struggling to keep up with the class. Teachers should try to draw out the quiet student, usually through

questions, to ensure that the child fully understands the material. It is possible that the student who does not actively participate in class may be reflecting certain social or cultural behaviors rather than a lack of comprehension. In some Hispanic and Asian cultures, for example, asking a question seems to question the authority of the teacher and is considered disrespectful. In other cultures, asking questions or participating in classroom discussions may be considered argumentative and disrespectful. When these students have trouble learning, they often blame themselves. Some students will find their own solutions rather than ask a teacher for assistance.

Another way to identify LEP students is to watch for students who seek out classmates for assistance. These informal arrangements are usually mutually satisfying because bilingual students generally empathize with classmates struggling to learn English. LEP students may ask their classmates specific questions regarding basic instructions or fingerings to avoid falling behind in their class work.

A student's inability to follow simple verbal instructions may also be a clue for teachers trying to identify LEP students. Such students are usually able to participate in the class by imitating the teacher or classmates with regard to playing techniques (for example, fingerings and matching pitches); however, they may look confused when told to turn to a specific page or may fake playing a line of music because they really don't know what line they should be playing.

A teacher's frustration level may be another indication that language comprehension is hindering a group's progress. The continuous repetition of instructions for a specific page or line of music or verbal corrections that are apparently ignored are two examples of a communication breakdown. Such situations lead to a general feeling, on the part of teacher and students alike, that a class is not making sufficient progress. This seems especially true considering that there are no behavioral problems and students appear to be paying attention. The fact that students pay attention only proves that students want to learn but does not guarantee that they comprehend what is presented by the teacher.

Once a teacher knows that LEP students are enrolled in instrumental music instruction, he or she should anticipate problems and develop teaching strategies to ensure that the students are able to keep up with the class. Contacting a student's parents may prove helpful because it provides an opportunity for parents, teacher, and student to discuss specific recommendations, such as a bilingual tutor, more frequent progress reports, extra lessons, or translations of written instructions.

Classroom Structure

When only one LEP student is present in a class of English-speaking students, the question is "How can the needs of one student be met without disrupting the entire group's progress?" One option is to provide the LEP child with some individual instruction. With this option, a child demonstrates his or her willingness to make an extra effort by showing up for these special sessions. Furthermore, this approach does not force teachers to change their overall teaching style.

Another way to assist the individual student is to assign a "buddy" or student tutor to quietly translate during class. A tutorial arrangement may be more tolerable in advanced musical groups when a child already has some command of an instrument and needs only occasional assistance with instructions or teacher comments. In beginning instrumental classes, however, it may be more difficult or annoying to teachers to have a simultaneous translation going on during class time.

Instructional Modifications

When changing the structure of a classroom is neither practical nor desirable, teachers may want to consider modifying their instructional style. Changing instructional style includes, but is not limited to, speaking more slowly, repeating instructions using different words, and continually simplifying concepts. The ability to make these adjustments without "talk-ing down" to students or making them feel incapable of mastering the material is no easy task. Teachers must continue to find innovative ways to repeat the same material, to increase comprehension, and to sustain interest.

Visual aids may prove useful when words fail. Page and line numbers written on chalkboards, demonstrations along with verbal instructions for fingerings or hand positions, and moving around the classroom and pointing to lines or notes to complement verbal instructions can help LEP students.

■ ■ ■ ■ ■ ■

Once a teacher knows that LEP students are enrolled in instrumental music instruction, he or she should anticipate problems and develop teaching strategies to ensure that the students are able to keep up with the class.

■ ■ ■ ■ ■ ■

When teachers change their instructional style, their efforts are directed toward the entire group, rather than toward individual students. This is important because some students who try to hide their language deficiency may openly resist any effort by a teacher to provide special individualized attention. Encouraging all students to imitate your instruction is certainly one of the best means of addressing an entire group while reaching the LEP student. Carefully imitating a teacher's instrumental technique may be the most effective educational activity for the LEP student.

Finally, teachers should realize that it may be easier to modify their instructional style for one or two lessons than to sustain the changes over a longer period of time. However, continual use of these techniques should make implementation easier. Admittedly, the extra effort can be tiring, making it difficult to provide the same level of instruction offered in classes without LEP students.

Bilingual Music Education

Just as we hope students will learn English by immersing themselves in an English-speaking community, we hope students learn the Western music tradition in the same way. For the single LEP student in an otherwise English-speaking class, this approach may prove successful, but in a school where 99 percent of the students speak little or no English, music educators need to examine new ways to reach these students.

Bilingual education continues to emerge as an independent field with its own research journals, expertise, and terminology. Research generally focuses on the level of language acquisition in conjunction with overall scholastic ability, life skills, and sociopolitical implications for the child, family, and community. To date, there has been little or no research specifically directed at bilingual education, LEP students, and instrumental music instruction.

Bilingual education may not be an option in a school where there is a small number of LEP students. Practically speaking, David Dobson, a researcher in bilingual education, notes that when only a few LEP students exist in a class, "It is unlikely that the human and material resources ... will ever be secured" for a bilingual program and there is even evidence that "inadequately implemented native language programs sometimes reduce the quality of instructional activities to the extent that detrimental effects can be observed."[2]

When several LEP students who

The experiences of LEP instrumental students may provide pertinent information to music education researchers.

speak the same language are in a class, the question becomes "Is bilingual instruction appropriate?" The answer lies not only in a teacher's ability to speak a specific language, but also in the teacher's attitude toward bilingual education. According to Dobson, "Properly conducted immersion and full bilingual programs result in high levels of native language skills, high levels of skills in another language, normal-to-superior academic achievement, and adequate to advantageous psychosocial and cultural development."[3] A more recent study puts the controversy in perspective by noting that "in most school districts enrolling large numbers of immigrant students, the logic of necessity overwhelms either side of that debate."[4]

In a class with several LEP students fluent in the same language, teachers may choose to provide bilingual music education. In an ideal bilingual program, the progress of the class should be similar to English-only classes. Those teachers willing and able to provide bilingual music education may find it personally satisfying as well as educationally expedient. Another option is to encourage parents to volunteer their time or admin-istrators to hire teacher aides with the appropriate language skills to provide classroom or individual assistance.

■ ■ ■ ■ ■ ■

Despite these changes, our goal as music educators remains clear: to teach music.

■ ■ ■ ■ ■ ■

Multicultural Music Education

It is difficult to discuss issues regarding LEP students without being reminded of multicultural music education. Instrumental music instruction in our public schools is Western in nature; however, teachers should be encouraged to take every opportunity to broaden students' awareness of other cultural traditions. Certainly, the repertoire of Western music can and should include non-European composers who have written quality compositions in the Western tradition. Research already provides band and orchestra directors with lists of such music selections for their instrumental groups.[5]

On another level, when multi-cultural music education is discussed, it is usually from the perspective of helping Western-trained students understand other world-music cultures. With LEP students, the reverse is happening, and the results may prove useful to researchers. LEP students may provide answers to questions such as: Do specific communities that encourage their children to become bilingual encourage their children to be bimusical? Are there students studying both Western and non-Western music at the same time? Can these students help define bimusicality? Can the experiences of these students help Western music students learn a non-Western music culture?

Ensuring that LEP students receive the same music education opportunities as English-speaking students may involve changes in classroom organization and instructional style, including bilingual music education. Despite these changes, our goal as music educators remains clear: to teach music. Teachers should view any changes in their instructional style or classroom structure as an opportunity to broaden their teaching skills and better serve all students who openly choose to understand Western music tradition through performance.

Notes

1. Lorraine McConnell and Paul Hill, *Newcomers in American Schools* (Santa Monica: Rand Corporation, 1993), 13.

2. David Dobson, "Bilingualism and Scholastic Performance: The Literature Revisited," *The Journal of the National Association for Bilingual Education* 10, no. 1 (Fall 1985): 18–19.

3. Ibid., 21–22.

4. McConnell, xii.

5. Will Schmid, "World Music in the Instrumental Program," *Music Educators Journal* 78, no. 9 (May 1992): 44–45. ■

SECTION III

Teaching Special Learners

This article originally appeared in the January 2001 issue of *Music Educators Journal.*

INCLUSION AND THE LAW

Over the last twenty-five years, the role of music teachers has evolved gradually but steadily in regard to teaching children with disabilities.

BY LINDA K. DAMER

Although children with disabilities have been involved in creating, enjoying, and learning about music for centuries, it is only within the past few decades that the inclusion of these children in regular music instruction has become a matter of law and public policy. Since 1975, a series of laws has changed the way in which children with disabilities are educated. A number of these laws have important implications for music educators.

Public Law 94-142

The complexion of public school education was changed dramatically in 1975 with the passage of PL 94-142, Education of the Handicapped Act.[1] The most prominent features of the law were two provisions: (1) all handicapped children (the accepted terminology in 1975) must be provided a "free appropriate public education" (FAPE), and (2) this education must take place in the "least restrictive environment" (LRE). Today, these provi-

Since 1975, a series of laws has changed the way in which children with disabilities are educated.

sions are accepted practices. The law defined "handicapped children" to mean those children who were mentally retarded, hard of hearing, deaf, speech-impaired, visually handicapped, seriously emotionally disturbed, orthopedically impaired, deaf-blind, or multihandicapped, having other health impairments, or having specific learning disabilities and needing special education and related services because of these impairments.

The law mandated that an education should be provided to these children at public expense, under public supervision, and without charge to their families. Students aged three to twenty-one were to be included unless state law decreed otherwise. Additionally, the schooling was to be in conformity with an Individualized Educational Program (IEP).

The LRE requirement meant that students were to be educated to the maximum extent possible in the same environment as children who were not handicapped. Removal from the regular classroom environment could occur only when the nature and severity of the handicap prevented education in the regular class with the use of supplementary aides and services. This aspect of the law proved to be the most controversial, since there were no specific guidelines for determining when it was appropriate to remove students from the regular classroom.

A third provision that affected the public education system was the requirement that every student identified as needing special education was to have an IEP. The law clearly identified the contents of the IEP, the time frame for developing and/or revising it, and the participants in the case

Linda K. Damer is professor of music education at Indiana State University in Terre Haute.

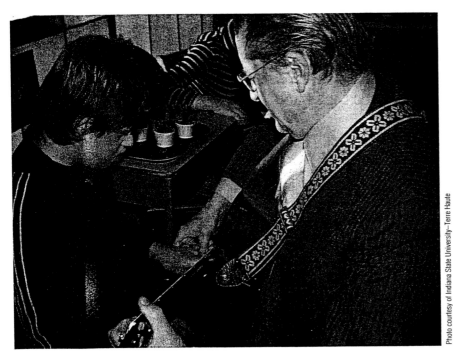

In this classroom, a student with Down's syndrome is introduced to the strings and sounds of the guitar.

conference that would be convened to develop it. In addition, the Local Education Agency (LEA) was required to document all efforts made to include parents in case conferences.

A fourth provision of PL 94-142 mandated the use of nondiscriminatory evaluation procedures to identify students with special needs. All tests or evaluation instruments were required to (1) be administered in the child's native language, (2) have been validated for the specific purpose for which they were used, and (3) be administered by trained personnel. The child was to be assessed in all areas related to the suspected disability by a multidisciplinary team that included at least one specialist in the suspected area of disability. No single measure could serve as the sole criterion for deciding the need for services.

A final provision that should be mentioned was "due process," a mechanism that parents could use to challenge the school's placement of their child.

State education agencies were given until September 1, 1978, to submit an annual plan to document their ability to meet the provisions of the law for children age three to eighteen and until September 1, 1980, to include students up to age twenty-one. How-

ever, the states were not required to include students aged three to five or eighteen to twenty-one if they could document that these inclusions were inconsistent with state law.[2]

■ ■ ■ ■ ■

For many years, music teachers have been expected to teach all children in an inclusive setting.

■ ■ ■ ■ ■

Public Law 99-457

In October 1986, Congress enacted PL 99-457, Education of the Handicapped Act Amendments of 1986.[3] Title I of this act, "Handicapped Infants and Toddlers," addressed the needs of children from birth to age two who required early intervention services because they were developmentally delayed or had diagnosed physical or mental conditions that might cause developmental delays. One goal of this law was to reduce the educational costs to "our Nation's schools, by minimizing the need for special education and related services after handicapped infants and toddlers reach school age."[4] Title II of PL 99-457 primarily addressed preschool grants for handicapped children aged three to five.

Title III, "Discretionary Programs," identified a wide range of programs for which grants could be given, including early education for handicapped children, programs for severely handicapped children, postsecondary education programs, and secondary education and transitional services for handicapped youth. Grants were also available to higher education institutions to provide stipends and scholarships to train personnel to deliver special education programs.[5]

Public Law 101-336 (ADA)

In 1990, a much more sweeping law, the Americans with Disabilities Act (PL 101-336), was passed.[6] Its purpose was to "provide a clear and comprehensive national mandate for the elimination of discrimination against individuals with disabilities and to provide clear, strong, consistent, enforceable standards addressing discrimination against individuals with disabilities," and it specifically identified the federal government as the enforcer.[7] Title I prohibited discrimination in employment practices against individuals with disabilities. Title II prohibited the exclusion of individuals with disabilities from participation in any services provided by public entities. Title III prohibited discrimination against individuals with disabilities by any organization that provides public accommodations of any kind, including nursery, elementary, secondary, undergraduate, or postgraduate private schools. Title IV addressed the area of telecommunications, requiring public carriers to provide Telecommunications Device for the Deaf (TTD) services for hearing-impaired and speech-impaired individuals. This law became effective in July 1992.[8]

PL 101-476 redefined the term "handicapped children" as "children with disabilities."

Public Law 101-476 (IDEA)

In October of 1990, amendments to PL 94-142 were passed as PL 101-476, the Education of the Handicapped Act Amendments of 1990.[9] This law redefined the term "handicapped children" as "children with disabilities," specifically identifying the following disabilities: mental retardation, hearing impairments including deafness, speech or language impairments, visual impairments including blindness, serious emotional disturbance, orthopedic impairments, autism, traumatic brain injury, other health impairments, and specific learning disabilities that require special education and related services. In addition, the law established an official mechanism for identifying, defining, and determining services needed for dealing with attention deficit disorder.

The IEP was required to include a statement of the transition services needed for eligible students beginning no later than age sixteen. The purpose of the statement was to promote a smooth, coordinated movement from school to post-school activities.

The law also addressed assistive technology devices and services.

Under "Related Services," it expanded recreation to include therapeutic recreation and social-work services and included rehabilitation counseling as part of the counseling services that should be available. A section of the law advocated improving materials for individuals with visual and hearing impairments through instructional media. The final set of amendments replaced the term "handicapped children," which was used in previous laws, with the term "children with disabilities."[10]

Mainstreaming and the Regular Education Initiative

The least restrictive environment provision of PL 94-142 gave rise to a practice labeled "mainstreaming." If students with disabilities could not be served effectively in the regular class setting for the entire day, the IEP was to identify the extent to which they would participate in the regular classroom. Typically, school systems "mainstreamed" these students into music, art, and/or physical education. Thus, for many years, music teachers were expected to teach all children in an inclusive setting. The LRE mandated that a continuum of placements would be available to students with disabilities. The goal was to provide education in a regular classroom with any needed supplementary services or aides.

In the late 1980s, a new direction in special education, the regular education initiative (REI), emerged. Betty Atterbury suggested that this initiative arose in response to two growing concerns about special education programs: (1) many special educators did not believe that the desired placement of children with disabilities in the "least restrictive environment" was being achieved, and (2) the cost of educating children with disabilities was spiraling, partially because of the continued increase in the number of children identified as needing special education.[11]

Unlike mainstreaming, which identified specific classes that students with and without disabilities were to attend together, the regular education initiative integrated students with disabilities into the regular classroom for

the entire school day, thereby making the regular classroom teacher responsible for educating all learners. This movement has been labeled "inclusion."

What are the principles upon which inclusion is based? Sandra Alper and her colleagues suggest the following:

(1) Students are more alike than not alike.

(2) Learning can occur through participation with and modeling of competent peers.

One recognized hallmark of successful inclusion programs is collaboration among all individuals.

(3) The supplementary instructional support needed to help students succeed can be provided in a regular classroom.

(4) Everyone benefits from having students with different learning styles and behavioral traits in the same classroom.[12]

Other, more pragmatic goals of inclusion mentioned in the literature include the preparation of students with disabilities for adult living, the effective use of resources on their behalf, and support of their civil rights.[13]

Debate continues among inclusion supporters. Some advocate full inclusion of all students with disabilities regardless of the severity of the problem. Others maintain that inclusion is the desired goal, but that a continuum of services must still be available to accommodate those students who cannot be successfully taught in the regular classroom.

Recent Legal Decisions

The weight of the law has more recently moved to support the practice of inclusion. Several federal district courts have issued decisions in favor of it. Affirming one of these decisions, the Third Circuit Court of Appeals stated, "Inclusion is a right, not a privilege of a select few."[14] In 1994, the U.S. Court of Appeals for the Ninth Circuit upheld the district court decision in Holland v. Sacramento Unified School District, indicating that when students with disabilities are placed in school settings, "the presumption and starting point is the mainstream."[15] In other words, these students are to be placed in regular classroom settings, with the burden of proving that the setting is inappropriate placed on the school system.

The shift away from separate special education programs toward inclusive classrooms has created a change in the role of the special education teacher. No longer providing services to students with disabilities in a separate classroom, the special education teacher becomes a team member with the regular classroom instructor, sharing the responsibility of planning the lessons, offering training and support, helping supervise paraprofessionals, and assisting with the teaching.[16]

One recognized hallmark of successful inclusion programs is collaboration among all individuals responsible for educational efforts in the school setting as well as in the home and community.[17] Dorothy Lipsky and Alan Gartner assert that "no one teacher can—or ought to—be expected to have all the expertise required to meet the educational needs of all the students in the classroom. Rather, individual teachers must have available to them the support systems that provide collaborative assistance and that enable them to engage in cooperative problem solving."[18]

If inclusive schools truly embrace and practice collaborative teamwork, guidance and assistance with planning and teaching that was not available

under the old practice of mainstreaming should be available to music teachers now. Music educators who teach in inclusive schools must become part of the collaborative process and not allow themselves to be left out of the team.

■ ■ ■ ■ ■

Music educators who teach in inclusive schools must become part of the collaborative process and not allow themselves to be left out of the team.

■ ■ ■ ■ ■

Admittedly, collaboration is not always easy to achieve. Creative scheduling of team meeting times may be necessary. The music teacher may need to be assertive, but pleasant, when indicating a desire to participate as part of the collaborative team. It may be necessary to overcome the view that music class is "fun and games." Other teachers may need help in understanding that higher-order thinking processes and discrimination skills, as well as motor skills, are necessary to a student's success in music classes. However, the effort required from the music teacher to ensure being included as part of the team will be offset by the rewards. Cooperative efforts among all school personnel will help the music teacher develop skills and strategies needed to be able to include all students in successful music experiences. This is, after all, the goal of music education.

Notes

1. See *U.S. Statutes at Large* 89 (1975): 773–96. Also see "Education of Handicapped Children Act, Implementation of Part B of the Education of the Handicapped, Part II,

Federal Register 42, no. 163 (23 August 1977).

2. Ibid.

3. See *U.S. Statutes at Large* 100 (1986): 1145–1177.

4. Ibid., p. 1145.

5. Ibid.

6. See *U.S. Statutes at Large* 104 (1990): 327–378.

7. Ibid., p. 329.

8. Ibid., p. 337.

9. See *U.S. Statutes at Large* 104 (1990): 1103–1145.

10. Ibid.

11. Betty Atterbury, "Knowing What's New Can Help You," *General Music Today* 4, no. 2 (Winter 1991): 16.

12. Sandra Alper, Patrick J. Schloss, Susan K. Etscheidt, and Christine A. Macfarlane, *Inclusion: Are We Abandoning or Helping Students?* (Thousand Oaks, CA: Corwin Press, 1995), 6.

13. Minnesota Inclusive Education Technical Assistance Program, "Inclusive Schools Communities: Ten Reasons Why" pamphlet (Minneapolis, MN: University of Minnesota, 1991).

14. Dorothy K. Lipsky and Alan G. Gartner, "Inclusive Education and School Restructuring," in *Controversial Issues Confronting Special Education: Divergent Perspectives*, 2nd ed., eds. William Stainback and Susan Stainback (Boston: Allyn & Bacon, 1996), 9, 13.

15. Richard A. Villa and Jacqueline S. Thousand, "The Rationale for Creating Inclusive Schools," in *Creating an Inclusive School*, eds. Richard Villa and Jacqueline S. Thousand. (Alexandria, VA: Association for Supervision and Curriculum Development, 1995), 35.

16. Richard Schattman and Jeff Benay, "Inclusiveness Transforms Special Education," in *Creating Inclusive Classrooms: Education for All Children* (Inclusion Resource Book) (Peterborough, NH: The Society for Developmental Education, 1994), 18.

17. Villa and Thousand, 6. Also B. Schaffner, B. Buswell, A. Summerfield, and G. Kovar, *Discover the Possibilities* (Colorado Springs, CO: PEAK Parent Center, Inc., 1988); "Collaborative Teamwork: Working Together for Full Inclusion" monograph (Minneapolis: University of Minnesota Institute on Community Integration, n.d.); Alice Udvari-Solner and Jacqueline S. Thousand, "Promising Practices that Foster Inclusive Education," in Villa and Thousand, 103–5; and Lipsky and Gartner, 3.

18. Lipsky and Gartner, 3. ■

This article originally appeared in the June 2001 issue of *Teaching Music*.

Introducing

Music

to the

Hearing-
Impaired

"How would you like to teach music to a profoundly deaf

boy?" This question set in motion one of the most challenging and rewarding projects I have yet undertaken. "Johnny," an 11-year-old boy who became profoundly deaf two years ago, had started on the vibraphone in his school's beginning band program. But because he was overwhelmed by the demands of looking at the director, his interpreter, his music, and the instrument all at the same time, it became clear that he needed more individualized attention for his special needs. After his band director contacted the music therapy instructors at the university where I was enrolled, I was asked to give Johnny private music lessons for one hour each week from October to May as part of an independent music therapy project. Though Johnny's frustration with band class increased and he later dropped out of band, he continued to spend that portion of his school day either meeting with me or catching up on other school work.

Consulting with the band director, my music therapy instructor, and Johnny's IEP (Individualized Evaluation Plan), I formulated two basic goals to ensure that Johnny could re-integrate into the band program if he wished: (1) mastery of the basics of playing an instrument, and (2) proficiency in reading notes and rhythms. I kept my plans flexible, experimenting with concepts and activities while remaining open to spontaneous opportunities that emerged during our lessons. While I did not establish formal therapy goals, I did incorporate these (e.g., encouraging him to talk, sign, and express himself creatively) into lesson activities. Brenda, an excellent interpreter who attended each session, also helped during the lessons with some ensemble playing and demonstrations. Occasionally, Johnny's best friend "Tommy" (who has hearing) would join us, which both boys enjoyed. Although Tommy needed an occasional review of some concepts, this review provided Johnny with the opportunity to teach his friend, thereby demonstrating what he himself had learned.

THE FIRST TIME JOHNNY PLAYED A paddle drum, he squealed with delight. Though he had made significant headway on the recorder, he preferred to focus on percussion because of the more direct feedback he received from those instruments. During the second semester, the band room was available during our lesson period, making it possible for us to use all the large percussion instruments. Johnny particularly liked the large paddle drums, whose vibrations he could easily feel in his hand, and the bass drum, bass bars, and timpani, whose vibrations he claimed to be able to hear as well as feel. He would often sit with his legs against the side of a drum or with a smaller drum resting in his lap. I made sure that he could touch or hear all the drums as I played them for him, because not only is "vibrotactile stimuli … a useful supplemental tool [for] music instruction," but also "tactile perception can, in part, compensate for auditory deficits" (Darrow and Schunk, "Music Therapy for Learners Who Are Deaf/Hard of Hearing," in *Models of Music Therapy Interventions in School Settings*, published by the National Association for Music Therapy, 1996, 219). Because the bass bars and timpani could be used to practice both pitch and rhythm, these instruments provided added instructional benefits for Johnny.

It was clear in the first session that Johnny was familiar with some musical terms and symbols but could not define or consistently identify them. I realized that I needed more visual aids to teach and drill these concepts. Visual and tactile aids adapted to Johnny's physical environment made better use of his "primary channels for receiving information" ("Music Therapy for Learners," 210). To the second session I brought a small dry-erase board and a homemade magnet board (consisting of an inexpensive cookie sheet with a staff drawn on it in magic marker), as well as color-coded buttons, notes, and icons cut from colored paper backed by adhesive sheet magnets; numbers or letters could be written underneath the notes with a dry-erase marker.

Strategies for Teaching Steady Beat to Hearing-Impaired Students

Marching. First, the student pretends to be the big bass drummer in a marching band, then moves on to marking time in place, and eventually alternates between quarter, half, and whole notes.

Conducting. The instructor conducts a simple 4/4 pattern while counting or saying "ta-ta-ta-ta" as the student plays quarter notes or half notes; eventually tempo and dynamic changes can be introduced.

Pointing. The instructor points to notes on the board as the student plays them in correct time.

Beating. Using a flashing metronome, the student plays a steady beat on the drums while the instructor uses a wide, even, circular motion and also plays the drumbeat.

Speeding up. The instructor introduces faster tempos (approximately M.M. = 100) because they usually make maintaining a steady beat easier for the student.

Counting games. Counting together "1, 2, 3, 4," the student plays on beats 1 and 3, while the instructor plays all four beats or just beats 2 and 4.

Drum circling. The student makes up a simple rhythm, repeating it over and over on the drum, eventually adding another pitch. The instructor "fits around" this improvised rhythm with simple patterns.

Working backwards. The student makes up a rhythm, playing it over and over until it is a unified pattern of even notes, then writes it out, and finally plays the notes again as the instructor points to them in tempo.

Substituting. After the student masters playing the rhythm ♩♩♫♩ ("ta ta tee-tee ta") evenly, the instructor writes ♩ ♫♩ ("ta-ah tee-tee ta") underneath, and the student alternates between the two rhythms until the half notes are two even beats.

These visual aids were invaluable in facilitating our communication, allowing us to manipulate notes easily, tailor each lesson to current progress, and reduce the amount of time and paper that would have been required to make endless worksheets. "Most D/HH students learn best through active participation in music making. Learning music through performing, reading, and writing music is essential for the students with a hearing loss" ("Music Therapy for Learners," 218). These aids also made direct communication much easier. Through them, along with miming and some basic signs, we could work more efficiently without waiting for interpretation. In addition, as Johnny got to know me better, his lip-reading became quite proficient.

WITHIN THE FIRST FEW LESSONS, WE had covered quarter, half, and whole notes; by the eighth lesson, the corresponding rests were added as well. Although we started counting with numbers, pronouncing them proved to be cumbersome; so we switched to "ta" ("ta-ah" for half notes, etc.). Johnny clapped or tapped the notes on a drum (moving his clasped hands or dragging the mallet across the drum to indicate the sustained beats). Then I would ask him to mix up the notes on the board to create a new pattern.

Combining notes and rhythms did not prove particularly troublesome for Johnny. By the third session, he had learned all the notes on the staff. To review note names, we wrote each other messages in "secret code," consisting of sentences in which all the letters A through G had been left out and written on the staff instead.

Dictation and imitation games formed a large part of each lesson. I would play a pattern of rhythms, pitches, or both, consisting of about five to eight notes, which he was expected to play back. As a variation, he would close his eyes and touch the base of the drums instead of watching. After performing the pattern successfully, he wrote it out on the board and then made up his own pattern for me to imitate.

MANY MUSIC EDUCATORS WOULD NOT be surprised to hear that the concept of steady beat proved to be our biggest challenge. While Johnny understood how many beats each note should receive and could count accurately while playing, these beats were usually rushed during sustained notes, with delays in between changing notes. In addition, we had some confusion about the idea of "feeling the beat"; Johnny thought I was referring to feeling the physical vibrations from the drums. Over the course of the year, we tried a wide range of activities to develop steady beat (these activities are listed in the sidebar). Through continued experimentation, modeling, and repetition of successful techniques, gradual progress was made. Playing complex rhythms with a steady beat remained a challenge at times, but that is certainly not unusual for any beginning musician and not a cause for concern.

The highlight for Johnny was his five-minute "free play" at the end of each session. This began by accident during his third lesson and consisted of his enthusiastically banging on everything around him as loudly and randomly as possible. He would remind me about this free-play time halfway through each lesson, and he made sure that we never missed it.

To help structure this improvisation, I asked him to represent different animals with the various percussion instruments. For a final project, he wrote a story and composed a different musical motif for each character; both words and music were creative and appropriate.

WHILE OTHER PROFOUNDLY DEAF children have learned to play various wind and string instruments, focusing on percussion instruments proved to be a good learning strategy in Johnny's case. The paddle drums and larger, low-pitched drums provided him with more direct stimulation and feedback.

In "Music for the Deaf," Alice-Ann Darrow concludes that "even the severely hearing-impaired child can receive sensory satisfaction and valuable auditory training from experiences with music" (February 1985 *Music Educators Journal*, 35). Johnny's progress supported Darrow's further assertions that, while "hearing is a physical process," "listening is a mental process" where "the discriminations that we make during music listening are made by the brain" ("The Role of Hearing in Understanding Music," December 1990 *Music Educators Journal*, 24, 26).

Teaching Johnny music proved a challenging, exciting, and fulfilling process in which he showed immense progress, with good retention, in the goals set for him of playing an instrument and reading music. Johnny also gained confidence and skill, finding an outlet for his energy and creativity by exploring other musical objectives, including "listening carefully" and "creating music" ("Music Therapy for Learners," 218). He reaped the benefits of some of the other "therapeutic goals supported by D/HH students' participation in music applications," including increased motivation for learning, on-task behavior, and turn-taking, as well as improved coordination, personal expression, and self-esteem ("Music Therapy for Learners," 217). And, should he choose to rejoin the school band, this training will give Johnny an added opportunity to interact and bond with his classmates.

By Elke Jahns, who recently received a master's degree in flute performance from Appalachian State University in Boone, North Carolina. She thanks Liz Rose and Cathy McKinney for their valued support and ideas and Brenda Barber for her excellent interpreting and enthusiastic participation.

This article originally appeared in the March 1990 issue of *Music Educators Journal*.

MEASURING MUSICAL GIFTEDNESS

by Carol P. Richardson

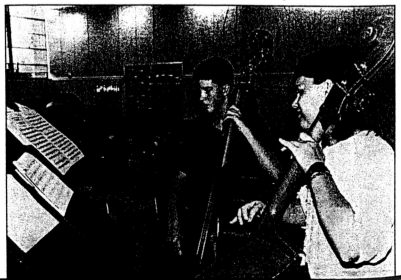

Many gifted and talented programs serve potentially gifted students as well as those with demonstrable talent. Carol Richardson, an assistant professor of music education at Northwestern University, Evanston, Illinois, presents some guidelines to help you identify students who might benefit from special programs.

If you were asked to compile a list of your twenty most gifted and talented music students so they could be placed in your district's proposed gifted program, how would you decide whom to include? This question may sound abstract, but if you teach in one of the thirty-two states whose definition of the gifted and talented student includes "advanced abilities in the fine and performing arts," you may be required to produce such a list.[1] Fortunately, music educators need not reinvent the wheel: much of the work on the identification of gifted and talented students in other academic areas has already been adapted for use in the arts.

The guidance required to develop your list of twenty is readily available through well-documented identification procedures that have been used effectively by teachers of established programs for musically gifted students. Our first task is to become familiar enough with these procedures so that we can help shape the new policies and programs that will be implemented. This article includes a short explanation of some of the issues involved in the identification process, descriptions of the various types of data and data-gathering instruments that have been developed, and some general guidelines to consider in setting up an identification procedure.

Define your terms

The first thing you need to know is how your state defines musical giftedness and talent. The terms "musically gifted" and "musically talented" can mean many things to many people, as can the term "musically gifted and talented." Before setting out to identify those students who fit the description, the meaning of each of these terms needs to be clarified. Does your state's definition focus on the student's present, demonstrable performance talent? If so, it might seem relatively easy to pick the top twenty performers from among your students by means of an audition. We are quite adept at judging the quality of student performances, and could probably explain our criteria for "goodness" in performance. If, however, your

state's definition also encompasses such factors as the student's *potential* for performance, composition, or appreciation, a number of other questions must be answered. How can you spot potential in these areas, and how can you be sure that you are not overlooking a potentially gifted music student who is *not* a star performer? One way to clarify the distinctions is to consider a definition of musical giftedness that encompasses potential as well as performance by focusing on the factors that contribute to musical giftedness.

Musical giftedness

Lloyd Schmidt, who has served as a music consultant with the Connecticut Department of Education, identified three different skills areas that need to be considered in determining musical giftedness: performance skills, creative ability such as composition, and verbal and musical-perceptual skills.[2] Schmidt proposes that by considering both demonstrable *and* potential talent in each of these three skills areas, music educators could better identify the pool of students needing special programs. To identify these students, Schmidt suggests three procedures: a performance audition, analysis of student composition, and evaluation of examples of student writing.

It is important to determine at the outset what sort of resources your district intends to commit to its gifted and talented music program. There is no point in identifying students with talent in musical composition if your program will only offer private studio instruction. Similarly, there is no reason to pinpoint talented instrumental performers if your gifted program will focus on seminars in electronic composition. There should be a direct relationship between the sorts of talents identified and the types of special services provided. You can facilitate this process by involving yourself in the initial planning sessions and by making clear your interest in developing the course offerings as well as the identification procedures.

Joseph Renzulli, an expert in the area of gifted and talented education, suggests that the best way to identify a gifted and talented stu-

dent is to formulate a case study of each student considered based on a wide array of data from five families of data: (1) preschool and developmental information, (2) psychometric information, (3) performance information, (4) motivational information, and (5) sociometric information.[3]

Developmental information

This category includes observations made by parents and preschool teachers of the student's early interests and talents, physical or intellectual precocity, and social and emotional maturity. Examples of questions in this category include "Did she/he walk, talk, read early?" "Did she/he show an advanced interest or talent in music?" Merle B. Karnes has developed a nine-point music checklist to be used by the preschool teacher to measure the preschool child's interest and participation in music as well as the quality of the child's musical performance. This checklist would also be useful in those states in which parents can nominate their children for special services. It is clear, short, and easily adaptable for identifying musically gifted and talented students in both primary and intermediate grades. According to Karnes, a musically gifted and talented child:

- shows unusually high interest in music activities.
- responds sensitively to the mood or character of music.
- repeats short rhythmic patterns with ease.
- sings in tune or very nearly in tune.
- identifies two short rhythm patterns as the same or different.
- identifies familiar songs from the rhythm alone.
- sings on the same pitch as a model (within the child's natural range).
- identifies the higher or lower of two tones.
- identifies two short melodies as the same or different.[4]

Psychometric information

This category includes data about the student's musical aptitude, creativity, interest, and performance. The sources of this type of data are varied and include standardized tests of musical aptitude, tests of musical creativity, interest inventories, self-ratings, and peer ratings. Each of these instruments can provide important pieces of information about the student that, when considered together, give a clearer picture of the student's musical abilities. None of the tests, however, can stand alone as a valid measure of musical giftedness, and these tests should not be used for such a purpose. Many states require that multiple indicators of giftedness be used in an attempt to avoid reliance on a single test score.[5]

Musical aptitude tests

Musical aptitude tests purport to measure the student's potential for success in music by focusing on particular skills such as pitch discrimination, tonal memory, rhythmic memory, chord analysis, and musical sensitivity. Four widely used tests include Bentley's *Measures of Musical Ability*[6] and Gordon's *Musical Aptitude Profile*,[7] *Primary Measures of Music Audiation*,[8] and *Intermediate Measures of Music Audiation*.[9] Teachers who routinely administer musical aptitude tests often discover that students who seem to be uninterested in music have advanced skills in one or more of the areas mentioned above. These are the very students who need to be identified as having musical potential and for whom special programs need to be devised. Musical aptitude tests are an invaluable source of information about the student that may otherwise be obscured by the student's classroom behavior.

Musical creativity tests

One of the factors of musical giftedness is the ability to think divergently in music and to produce music imaginatively. The characteristics of fluency, flexibility, and originality are usually considered when measuring musical creativity. Testing in this area is relatively new, and the tests available have not been extensively validated, nor are they available commercially. They are, however, an important source of ideas for the types of activities that are appropriate when considering musical creativity.

In Webster's *Measures of Creative Thinking in Music*, children ages six through ten, using a Nerf ball on a piano keyboard, are asked to imitate a growing rainstorm, an ascending elevator, and a frog singing; to improvise vocally "truck" and "robot" songs; and to create call-and-response patterns on temple blocks.[10] Responses are scored for musical extensiveness, flexibility, originality, and syntax.

Wang's *Measures of Creativity in Sound and Music*, for ages three through eight, asks the student to produce examples of a steady beat, to imitate six events described by the teacher, to improvise many ostinatos on a bass xylophone, and to move to six selections of recorded music.[11] Responses are scored for musical fluency and imagination. Further information about each test is available from the text author (see the "Notes" at the end of this article for addresses).

Interest inventories

Interest inventories are checklists of behavioral characteristics of musically gifted children. They are usually given to parents, teachers, or students so that they can check off the characteristics exhibited by their children, students, or peers. Two interest inventories are presented here. The first more general list is designed for grades one through twelve and requires the nominator to assign points for each of the eleven categories listed. The second, twenty-item list is intended for use in grades one through six and requires the nominator simply to determine the presence or absence of each characteristic without assigning numerical value to each response. Both are included to illustrate the varying degrees of specificity and scoring required within the same category of instruments. Elam's *Music Teacher Checklist*[12] can be used by the music teacher for grades one through twelve (see figure 1).

Meeker's *Characteristics of Musically Talented Children*,[13] intended for use by music teachers of grades one through six, is a checklist that could be filled out for each potentially musically gifted or talented student (see figure 2). It requires the teacher to check those items that he or she believes best describe the student's musical characteristics.

Performance information

This is the category of data with which music educators are probably most familiar. Included in this category are summaries and analyses of work completed, samples of highly creative products, and descriptions of outstanding performances. Although most music teachers could probably agree on the criteria for an outstanding performance, it is essential to have documented performance criteria when identifying musically gifted students. The lists in figures 3 and 4 are not meant to be exhaustive; they do not include the more aes-

Music Teacher Checklist, Grades 1–12

For each item the teacher is to respond in one of four ways: below normal expectations = 0 points; average expectations = 1 point; above normal expectations = 2 points; not observed = 0 points.

The student:
- demonstrates strong interest in music
- demonstrates understanding of the concepts of music
- discriminates pitches, dynamics, tempo, tone color, form, and harmonic changes
- creates original rhythmic and melodic patterns
- makes up songs and creates verses to songs
- expresses feelings and emotions through music creatively
- shows interest in performing
- shows confidence in performance
- is persistent in new learnings
- studies music privately and performs in recitals
- other (specify)

Figure 1. Elam's interest inventory. Adapted from the Music Teacher Checklist by Anne Elam, 1985 (available from ERIC Document Reproduction Services).

**Characteristics of
Musically Talented Children,
Grades 1–6**

- Spontaneous response to rhythm and music
- Love for singing familiar and made-up songs
- Relative or absolute pitch and strong feeling for tonality
- Highly developed ear and ability to associate pitch with visual symbols
- Interest and skill in singing descants or other harmony parts
- Remarkable memory and ever-expanding repertoire
- Ability to identify familiar melodies on tonal instruments
- Marked aptitude for playing introductions, accompaniments
- Choice of music as a means of expressing feelings and experiences
- Creative flair for improvisation and signs of ability to compose
- Special interest in musical instruments and a desire to play an instrument
- Voluntary involvement with music and a high interest in learning about music
- Notable skill in performing on one or more musical instruments
- Great enjoyment in listening to both live and recorded music
- Natural sense of aesthetic values (beauty, order, form)
- Keen power of attention, auditory discrimination, and evaluation
- Quickness in discriminating among identical, similar, and contrasting phrases in songs and sections of longer musical compositions
- Sensitivity to the communicative power of music, even to the slightest changes in tempo, dynamics, and tone color
- Ability to hear, identify, and follow two or more rhythm patterns, metric groupings, or melodic themes played simultaneously
- Perception and understanding of the subtle interrelationships within and among the constituent and expressive elements of music

Figure 2. Meeker's interest inventory. Adapted from Teaching Gifted Children Music in Grades One Through Six *by Many Meeker, 1977 (available from ERIC Document Reproduction Service).*

**Performance Criteria for
Gifted and Talented
Middle School Choral Students**

- Ability to match pitches accurately
- Ability to repeat intervals
- Ability to perform several moving notes against a second moving part
- Breathing technique sufficient to successfully sustain an average vocal phrase
- Buoyant quality to the tone
- Good melody retention
- Awareness of how written music functions
- Ability to concentrate
- Consistent and dependable (within reason for age)
- Interest in music in general

Figure 3. Criteria list for evaluating choral performance. Adapted from Project PRISM: Project Manual *by Margaret Cunnion, 1980 (available from ERIC Document Reproduction Service).*

**Performance Criteria for
Gifted and Talented
Middle School
Instrumental Students**

- Good working knowledge of the instrument (two-octave range, correct fingerings, and so forth)
- Good breathing technique
- Good sight-reading ability
- Knowledge of key signatures, accidentals (up to two sharps and two flats)
- Ability to play correctly and in correct time
- Good practice habits, attendance at lessons and rehearsals
- Not challenged by literature
- Desire to do more than is required in lessons

Figure 4. Criteria list for evaluating instrumental performance. Adapted from Project PRISM: Project Manual *by Margaret Cunnion, 1980 (available from ERIC Document Reproduction Service).*

thetic qualities of performance such as musicality and feeling. The lists can be used in two ways. First, they can be used as a starting point to help you develop a more complete checklist for identifying the pool of students whose performance record is superior. Second, they can be used to raise the interjudge reliability of the performance ratings by establishing a clear frame of reference for the audition judges.[14]

This article includes a music audition sheet meant to be used by the performance audition judges (see figure 5).[15]

Although the music audition is a relatively common occurrence in the middle and high school, it is more difficult to obtain valid performance information about elementary school students. In a recent doctoral study, Gwen Winter developed a performance audition procedure that can be used to identify students in the primary grades:

Music Audition Procedure (Grades 1–3)

Task 1: Select a simple song with which the child is already familiar (such as "I'm a Little Teapot" or "The Eency, Weency Spider") and have the child sing the song with you in the child's range. Then have the child sing the song alone, with the examiner giving the first note on piano or pitch pipe.

Task 2: Examiner and child sing or hum the song learned in task 1. Without warning, the examiner stops singing and the child must finish alone. Explain what is expected, and give the child the sign when she/he is to finish the song.

Task 3: Have the child pick the highest and/or lowest of two tones played on piano or pitch pipe. Have the child match direction of voice (or instrument) pitch to a high and/or low pitched tone played by the examiner.

Task 4: Have the child tell which of two tones is softer or louder. Have the child match the intensity of her/his voice to a loud or soft tone played by the examiner.

The examiner is to rank the student on a scale of 1–10 in the following areas: competence in performance, high interest, melodic accuracy, rhythmic accuracy, pitch discrimination.[16]

One possible problem with tasks 3 and 4 is the young child's difficulty in correctly labeling soft/loud and low/high. Although they have no trouble hearing the differences

Music Audition Sheet

Circle the appropriate number (0–5)

Tone quality and intonation	0	1	2	3	4	5
Fluency and dexterity	0	1	2	3	4	5
Rhythm and tempo	0	1	2	3	4	5
Phrasing and tonal shading	0	1	2	3	4	5
Articulation (diction for voice, pedal for piano)	0	1	2	3	4	5
Dynamics	0	1	2	3	4	5
Overall interpretation	0	1	2	3	4	5
Poise	0	1	2	3	4	5
Choice of piece (according to level)	0	1	2	3	4	5
Scales	0	1	2	3	4	5
Sight-reading	0	1	2	3	4	5

Total points (total musical effect) = _____

Figure 5. Music audition form used in judging musical performance. Adapted from ConnCeptIV, Connecticut State Department of Education, 1980 (available from ERIC Document Reproduction Service).

at this age, young children often mistakenly use the terms soft/low and loud/high interchangeably. To avoid confounding the results, the labeling portion of tasks 3 and 4 could be omitted and only the matching part of the task used.

Motivational information

This category includes the student's written or verbal expressions of musical interest and commitment, along with expressions of self-knowledge and self-concept. The first example is for use with high school students.

Describe either in writing on a separate piece of paper or on standard cassette tape what you do in the arts and in leadership activities either in or out of school. Include ideas, experiences, and ways you express and develop your talents, as well as lessons you have taken. Describe your commitment to the arts.[17]

Other interview questions can be used with students in grades one through three.[18] These questions are the type that could easily be adapted for use in the self-nomination process:

• Why do you want to be considered for the program? What opportunities would you like it to provide? How could you benefit from the program?
• In what school, family, religious, or community activities are you involved? What do you like best about school?
• Describe yourself: What do you think would tell us about your special talent? How do you go about getting help when you have a problem? How much free time do you spend on your arts activity? What is your favorite thing to do? Would you give up your favorite thing to do to practice music?

Sociometric information

This type of data is obtained from the student's peers and is a valuable source of information about the musical potential of students. The peer nomination form that follows requires the student evaluator to give responses that indicate giftedness in general as well as giftedness in music. For each item, the nominator is asked to respond with either "seldom or never," "occasionally," "frequently," or "almost always."

Peer Nomination Form

The nominee:
- tries to discover how and why
- is an alert observer: sees more and gets more than others
- looks for similarities/differences
- strives for perfection, is self-critical
- likes to organize, bring structure
- evaluates events, people, processes
- has a keen sense of humor
- expresses opinions readily
- exhibits widespread curiosity
- generates solutions and responses
- carries responsibilities well
- is self-confident
- is nonconforming, accepts disorder

In music, the nominee:
- is sensitive to rhythm
- remembers/reproduces melody
- perceives tonal differences
- can improvise music
- is aware of/identifies sounds[19]

Dealing with data

When you are asked to identify your twenty most gifted and talented music students, you can ask which of the many identification procedures are appropriate, both for the type of gifted music program your district plans to offer and for the population it is to serve. Once you have determined which types of case-study data will provide the clearest picture of your students' talents, your district must establish clear procedural guidelines for the identification process. The major problem in identifying musically gifted and talented students is not deciding which of the types of data to use but deciding how to use them.

Screening procedures need to be determined in advance, and must be politically, educationally, and financially defensible. The following types of questions must be answered before the identification process can begin: Will there be nominations? Who will be eligible to make nominations? How many times must a student be nominated to be included in the pool? Will a musical aptitude test be appropriate? Will all students at a given grade level be tested? Will there be a cutoff point for inclusion in the program? What weight will be given to the performance audition?

Who will serve on the audition panel? Who will make the final decision about inclusion/exclusion?[20] Once your district has answered these important questions, the following sequence of events could be followed in the identification procedure.

Identification procedure

Elam suggests a three-stage identification process: (1) initial screening, (2) specific screening, and (3) final screening.[21] Initial screening, used to identify the largest possible pool of candidates for the gifted/talented music program, relies on a combination of sociometric and psychometric data: nominations from faculty, parents, peers, and students themselves. Specific screening narrows the pool through two methods: a music teacher checklist and a performance audition. This second stage is the point at which preschool and developmental information might also be useful. Final screening, as described by Elam, includes a performance audition and an interview, and should be the responsibility of a committee made up of a staff member, a music teacher, and a professional musician. This committee will audition and interview the students both for admission to the program and to monitor their progress once admitted.

This three-stage procedure follows Renzulli's recommendation for a good case-study approach in that it requires a wide array of data on each student. It is up to each district, however, to use the data gathered in this procedure in the most equitable and fair manner possible. Issues such as cutoff points, weighting of nominations, and ongoing evaluation procedures must be resolved by the administrators before any identification procedure is announced to the public.

Although your school may not currently be involved in setting up a gifted music program, you can still begin to deal with the issue by thinking about how you conceive of, define, and identify the musically gifted students in your classes, and how you might explain this to your colleagues when asked for your list of twenty.

Armed with the information presented in this article, and in the rest of this special focus section, you can actively participate in implementing the inevitable changes in policy and programming that will result from the gifted and talented mandates that may already be in place in your state.

Notes

1. Woody Houseman, comp., *The 1987 State of the States Gifted and Talented Education Report* (Topeka, KS: The Council of State Directors of Programs for the Gifted, 1987), 16.
2. Lloyd Schmidt, "Gifted Programs in Music: A Nuclear Model," *Roeper Review* 3, no. 3 (February 1981), 33.
3. Joseph Renzulli, *A Reexamination of the Definition of the Gifted and Talented.* ERIC Document No. ED 177 784 (1979), 29.
4. Merle B. Karnes, *Music Checklist.* ERIC Document No. ED 160 226 (1978), 21. Further expansion of this checklist, with specific guidelines and examples, can be found in another of Karnes's works, *Nurturing Talent in the Visual and Performing Arts in Early Childhood: Art and Music,* ERIC Document No. 161 533 (1978), 26–27. Information about the ERIC Document Reproduction Service is available by calling 800–227-ERIC.
5. Houseman, 11–12.
6. Arnold Bentley, *Measures of Musical Ability* (London: George G. Garrap and Co., Ltd, 1966).
7. Edwin Gordon, *Musical Aptitude Profile* (Chicago, IL: Riverside Press, 1965).
8. Edwin Gordon, *Primary Measures of Music Audiation* (Chicago, IL: G. I. A. Publications, 1979).
9. Edwin Gordon, *Intermediate Measures of Music Audiation* (Chicago: G. I. A. Publications, 1982).
10. Peter R. Webster, *Measures of Creative Thinking in Music: Administrative Guidelines.* Unpublished manuscript (1989), 6–8. Available from Peter R. Webster, School of Music, Northwestern University, Evanston, IL 60201.
11. Cecilia Wang, *Measures of Creativity in Sound and Music.* Unpublished manuscript (1985), 2. Available from Cecilia Wang, School of Music, University of Kentucky, Lexington, KY 40506.
12. Anne Elam, *Music Teacher Checklist.* ERIC Document No. ED 267 561 (1985), 48.
13. Many Meeker, *Teaching Gifted Children Music in Grades One Through Six.* ERIC Document No. ED 152 022 (1977), 21.
14. Margaret Cunnion, *Project PRISM: Project Manual.* ERIC Document No. ED 195 071 (1980), 88.
15. Connecticut State Department of Education, *ConnCept IV.* ERIC Document No. ED 160 226 (1980), 58.
16. Gwen Winter, *Identifying Children in Grades 1–3 Who Are Gifted and Talented in Visual and Performing Arts Using Performance Rated Criterion.* ERIC Document No. ED 289 330 (1987), 138.
17. Houseman, 151.
18. Winter, 73–74.
19. Houseman, 142.
20. Cunnion, 14–16.
21. Elam, 7–8.

This article originally appeared in the September 1998 issue of *Music Educators Journal*.

RESOURCES FOR HELPING BLIND MUSIC STUDENTS

A variety of resources is available to help educators teach blind students how to read music and become part of the music classroom.

BY MARY A. SMALIGO

While literary braille is well-known as a tool that blind students can use to read text, surprisingly few people are aware that Louis Braille, a blind piano teacher, also invented music braille to help blind students learn to read and play music. The general principles of literary braille and music braille are similar. Both systems use a "cell" containing six dots in varying combinations that blind people read by touching, but music braille, which is the only internationally unified code, assigns different meanings to the dot combinations.

Music educators can help blind braille readers learn music reading skills. An entire braille music symbol system correlating to the print music system exists, and a large amount of sheet music for individual or group use is available. Taking advantage of existing resources, teachers can provide braille music so that blind students have the opportunity to learn to read music at the same time that sighted students do.[1] If the effort is successful,

■ ■ ■ ■ ■ ■

Parents of blind children may already be well on their way to locating resources.

■ ■ ■ ■ ■ ■

the braille student can read music independently and can participate in ensemble groups or perform as a soloist to the extent that his or her musical ability allows.

Blind students are a low-incidence factor in the overall population; in an entire career, a music teacher may encounter such a student only once or twice. Overwhelmed by what seems to be required, but unable to locate suitable resources, the teacher may still try to do the right thing despite having virtually no tools. A general awareness about braille music and its availability

can help to resolve this dilemma. Although this article is not a comprehensive, detailed survey of existing resources for blind music students, a number of readily available resources are discussed.

Colleagues and Parents

The assistance that local teachers of blind students can provide through their thorough knowledge of resources, specifically in educational settings, cannot be underestimated. Such a teacher, usually employed by the area's major special education office, may already teach the blind student who is entering the music class. Acquiring classroom music textbooks for the proper grade level, helping the student to braille his or her own musical compositions, determining braille music reading readiness, contacting braille music transcribers, and acting on behalf of the student's needs and school personnel are just some of the ways in which these local teachers can help music educators and their students.

Parents of blind children may already be well on their way to locating resources for their child. Collaborating with parents, especially if they are also working with the child's braille literary teacher, can be invaluable. It is advisable to consult with them frequently as to resources and progress and to explain to them how they can help advance their child's music educa-

Mary A. Smaligo, an instructor of piano and voice, has taught elementary and high school chorus, band, and strings in Pennsylvania public schools.

Access to printed braille music allows blind music students to practice away from the classroom.

tion. Parents may be able to supplement the teacher's efforts to obtain information and material and will appreciate being kept informed.

First Steps for the Youngest

Like most sighted students, blind students begin to learn to read in first grade, and like many sighted students who take music lessons, they begin learning to read music one to three years later.

A tactile music staff with various textures for notes (sandpaper, cardboard, etc.), along with verbal explanations, can provide the student with some idea of the format of printed music, the shapes of print notes and symbols, and the linear motion of notes. Much of this information will transfer to learning to read braille music when specific note and symbol reading is introduced to all students.

Beyond Recorded Music

As a music student progresses, a desperate but dedicated teacher may decide that having the student listen to recorded music and learn by memorization is the only option available for helping the student maintain progress with the rest of the class. While helpful in some aspects of music education

for all students, these methods alone are insufficient for blind students learning how to read music. Even if a sighted student already knew how to read music, a committed music educator would not permit him or her to learn music using only recorded materials and rote methods.

In combination with braille music reading, however, instrumental teachers who teach individuals, small groups, and bands/orchestras would do well to use a lesson book that comes with a play-along cassette or CD. The nature of braille music reading means memorization of each lesson after the student reads it and the teacher is confident that the student understands it. A play-along cassette, which should never be used as a substitute for braille music, can streamline memorization efforts and equalize the mechanics of braille music reading in comparison to standard printed music.

A free correspondence course for learning to read braille music notation is offered by the Hadley School for the Blind. See the Resources for Teaching Blind Students sidebar, found on page 24, for contact information for this service and other resources discussed in this article.

The National Library Service

The Music Section of the National Library Service (NLS) for the Blind and Physically Handicapped is the main source for borrowing braille music in the United States. Materials in braille make up the largest portion of the collection. The NLS holdings, which include virtually all available printed and hand-produced braille scores, recordings, and texts, offer instrumental music, vocal and choral music, some popular music, librettos, textbooks, instructional method books, and music periodicals. Recorded courses for beginning guitar, piano, organ, accordion, recorder, voice, and theory have been purchased or specifically developed for the NLS program. Anyone who is unable to read or use standard printed materials as a result of temporary or permanent visual or physical limitations may receive service. Loaned items are sent to borrowers and returned to NLS by postage-free mail. The staff also provides information about purchasing or borrowing music from other sources.

Blind or otherwise visually disabled persons can enroll in the National Library Service system upon request. A letter or call to the Music Section of NLS from the music teacher, the student's parents or guardians, or the teacher of the blind who provides services to the student will bring information about all NLS braille music resources. Loans are made in the name of the certified individual, and teachers, parents, or guardians can request materials for the student's use. (For example, while a music teacher or school would not be loaned *How to Read Braille Music*, the eligible student can borrow it in both large print and braille.) If the braille teacher, the music teacher, and the student will be working together, arrangements can be made to borrow two braille copies and one printed copy of the same book in the student's name so that each person has a book to use.

Useful Publications

A simple, concise resource is *How to Read Braille Music*, Book I, which is written on a fifth-grade reading level so that it can be used as a self-help resource for beginning through intermediate level braille-reading musicians. (The Resources for Teaching Blind Students sidebar provides publisher information for this book and other books discussed in this article.) Especially useful in the classroom, *How to Read Braille Music* includes vocal and instrumental music code peculiarities, as well as an index of music symbols.

The *Primer of Braille Music*, another possibility, contains thirty lessons, twenty-four of which cover the basic knowledge required for reading music. Lessons 25–30 cover vocal and instrumental music. Each lesson presents the same information for both sighted and blind users, with braille characters and signs on the left side of each page and text and music on the right side.

Although it was published in 1960, *Braille Music Chart,* new revised edition, available in print and braille, is still useful as a ready reference in classroom music lessons and as a guide for braille readers to music symbols written on the chalkboard for sighted students. Containing a complete list of all braille music symbols, it may also be useful to the advanced student. The *Dictionary of Braille Music Signs,* a more detailed reference work, is suitable for advanced students.

If knowledge of increasingly advanced braille music notation becomes necessary, the *New International Manual of Braille Music Notation,* published in 1996, is now available in print, braille, and CD-ROM.

The Central Catalog, published by the American Printing House (APH) for the Blind, lists volunteer-produced braille, large-print, and recorded textbooks; commercially produced large-print textbooks; and regular press braille and large-type books produced by APH. The database from which the catalog is produced daily is called APH-LOUIE and is available on the Internet by subscription through APH.

Transcription Resources

One particularly important resource from the National Library Service is an annually published circular listing braille music transcribers around the country. Because some music that the teacher wants his or her

students to learn to play may not be available in braille through the usual channels, access to transcribers is necessary for successfully mainstreaming blind students into the music class.

■ ■ ■ ■ ■ ■

The nature of braille music reading means memorization of each lesson.

■ ■ ■ ■ ■

If a music teacher uses worksheets for the class, a braille music transcriber can transfer the printed text and music to braille. Turn-around time for this sort of brailling makes it necessary to plan well ahead. While music transcribers now have the technological advantage of computer software to assist in the process, time must still be allowed for the transcriber to receive the printed worksheet, mentally convert the printed notation into braille, and then input the result. Using software similar to word processing, the transcriber can then correct, copy, move, delete, and save the data in the file. The file is then printed on a braille printer and sent back to the requestor, or a disk can be sent for printing if the requestor has access to a braille printer. Each braille music transcriber determines the cost for each page of braille.

Band and choral music otherwise unavailable can easily be sent to a braille music transcriber in the same fashion as the worksheet.

It is also possible to become trained as a certified braille music transcriber. Prerequisites include a Library of Congress certificate in literary braille

and some specialized equipment. For more information, contact the NLS.

Some newly developed software automatically converts print to braille, allowing a sighted person with no knowledge of braille music transcription to scan printed music into a database from which braille can be printed. Other software offers similar or other functions related to or supportive of computerized transcription or braille music reading. This area of software development is very new, and a number of products are being developed by private enterprises. Music educators interested in computer technology for their blind students are encouraged to contact the NLS or other advocacy organizations to obtain the latest information.

Organizations

In circumstances other than school situations, a call to a local blind association, rehabilitation agency for the blind, or chapter of the National Federation of the Blind could provide extra help, if needed. A list of state agencies that administer rehabilitation and special education services is available from NLS.

The National Braille Association assists those involved in developing and improving skills and techniques for producing materials for those who are print-handicapped. A central depository for hand-transcribed braille masters, the association offers items for sale at prices under cost, and all production is done by volunteers. The catalog, free upon request, offers brass, string, woodwind, percussion, organ, piano, and voice music materials, as well as items on harmony theory and popular music.

A source of general information is the Music Education Network for the Visually Impaired (MENVI). It describes itself as "a coalition of parents, educators, and students" who function as a network providing information and resources, including phone numbers, on music education topics concerning blind students. MENVI will send a membership application and regular newsletters in braille and print containing helpful articles upon request. Recent newsletters have addressed such topics as free

■ *Resources for Teaching Blind Students* ■

Organizations

American Council of the Blind, 1155 Fifteenth Street Street, NW, Suite 720, Washington, DC 20005. Phone 202-467-5081. Fax 202-467-5085. Web site http://www.acb.org.

Hadley School for the Blind, 700 Elm Street, Winnetka, IL 60093-0299. Phone 847-446-8111; 800-323-4238. Fax 847-446-9916. E-mail hadley@theramp.

Music Education Network for the Visually Impaired (MENVI), Southern California Conservatory of Music, MENVI Headquarters, 8711 Sunland Boulevard, Sun Valley, CA 91352. Phone 818-767-6554. Fax 818-768-6242. E-mail taeschr@ix.netcom.com.

Music Section, National Library Service for the Blind and Physically Handicapped, Library of Congress, 1291 Taylor Street, NW, Washington, DC 20542. Phone 202-707-9254; 800-424-8567. Fax 202-707-0712. E-mail nlsm@loc.gov.

Music & Arts Center for the Handicapped (MACH), National Resource Center for Blind Musicians, 600 University Avenue, Bridgeport, CT 06601. Phone 203-366-3300. Fax 203-368-2847. E-mail 1027301.163@compuserve.com.

National Braille Association, Inc. Three Townline Circle, Rochester, NY 14623-2513. Phone 716-427-8660. Fax 716-427-0263.

National Federation of the Blind, 1800 Johnson Street, Baltimore, MD 21230. Phone 410-659-9314. Fax 410-685-5653. Web site http://www.nfb.org.

Publications

Braille Music Chart, new revised edition, 1960. American Printing House for the Blind, 1839 Frankfort Avenue, PO Box 6085, Louisville, KY 40206-0085. Phone 502-895-2405; 800-223-1839. Fax 502-895-1509.

The Central Catalog: Textbooks for Students Who Are Visually Handicapped. Educational Resources Network of the American Printing House for the Blind, PO Box 6085, Louisville, KY 40206-0085. Phone 502-895-2405 or 800-223-1839. Fax 502-899-2274. Web site http://www.aph.org.

Dictionary of Braille Music Signs, Bettye Krolick. 1979. Music Section, National Library Service for the Blind and Physically Handicapped, Library of Congress, Washington, DC 20542. Phone 202-707-5100; 800-424-8567. Fax 202-707-0712. TTY/TTD 710-822-1969. E-mail nlsm@loc.gov.

How to Read Braille Music, 2nd ed., Bettye Krolick, 1998. Opus Technologies, 13333 Thunderhead Street, San Diego, CA 92129-2320. Contact Samuel O. Flores, phone 619-538-9401; or e-mail samf@opustec.com.

New International Manual of Braille Music Notation. 1996. Opus Technologies, 13333 Thunderhead Street, San Diego, CA 92129-2320. Phone/Fax 619-538-9401.

Primer of Braille Music, Compiled by Edward W. Jenkins. American Printing House for the Blind, 1839 Frankfort Avenue, PO Box 6085, Louisville, KY 40206-0085. Phone 502-895-2405; 800-223-1839. Fax 502-895-1509.

Internet services for the blind, exercises that parents can use to begin their blind child's musical education, and tips for blind children on how to learn to sing in a choir.

Located at the University of Bridgeport, with satellite locations throughout Connecticut, the Music & Arts Center for the Handicapped (MACH) offers a variety of courses and programs focused on braille music, musicianship, and using the computer as a music tool. Affiliated with MACH, the National Resource Center for Blind Musicians responds to inquiries about sources for braille music and provides advice on accessible music technology.

The National Federation of the Blind's mission is to seek "the complete integration of persons who are blind into society on a basis of equality." The organization focuses on legislative issues, publishes a monthly magazine, *Braille Monitor,* and two quarterlies, and sells additional publications and assistive devices through its Materials Center. Two divisions, the Music Division and the National Organization of Parents of Blind Children, have established the Music Education Network for the Benefit of Blind Students, which is coordinated by volunteers.

The American Council of the Blind serves as an information clearinghouse on blindness, provides advisory service on federal legislation, and acts as an advocate on a number of issues, including educational opportunities and vocational training. Among its numerous special-interest affiliates are the Council of Families with Visual Impairment and the National Alliance of Blind Students.

For College-Bound Musicians

For the past three years, the MACH Summer Music Institute has offered a three-week live-in program for blind college-bound music students. The program focuses on music, braille music, and computer skills (including composition and scoring) and helps students develop strategies for university-level academic study and on-campus living. To obtain a brochure and an application, send a request to MACH (see the sidebar).

In addition to its Preparatory and Conservatory Divisions, which address the needs of beginning and advanced students, the Southern California Conservatory of Music offers bachelor and associate degrees in music to blind students through its Braille Music Division. Its stated goals are to prepare the serious student for a professional career and to train the motivated student for a full, active cultural life and influence in society. The Conservatory can be contacted through MENVI.

While blind students may attend any college or university as long as they meet the school's requirements for all students, there are other college-level courses specifically for blind students and teachers at various locations throughout the United States. Help in locating these programs may be obtained by contacting the organizations dedicated to promoting music education for blind students.

Help Is at Hand

Those involved with music education for blind students make up a small community that is growing steadily. These highly active groups, many of whom know each other and are aware of each others' work, are generous with their information and often suggest additional resources beyond their own that may be helpful to the inquirer. Many of these are free or minimally priced. With a few phone calls, letters, or e-mail messages, music educators can obtain as much help as they need to provide the same education to blind students that sighted students receive.

Note

1. Many of the organizations cited in this article also provide services, including large-print sheet music and books, to "visually impaired" music students. The term "visually impaired" refers to people who may have partial sight or some other related disability. ■

This article originally appeared in the Spring 1999 issue of *General Music Today*.

CHALLENGES OF INCLUSION FOR THE GENERAL MUSIC TEACHER

by Keith P. Thompson

Inclusion arrived in many general music classrooms when music educators, returning to school one September, found students with varying degrees of disabilities included in general music classes. Although teachers may be experts at providing instruction for large and diverse groups of students, adapting instruction to meet the unique and sometimes extreme needs of students with disabilities has presented an enormous challenge. However, music educators have accepted the challenge with a missionary zeal and the determination to be true to the credo "Music for every child and every child for music."

Listening to general music teachers from across the country, I sense a high level of frustration and a lack of confidence about teaching students with disabilities. In this article I offer a few suggestions from my own experience, from conversations with and observations of other teachers, and from the literature in an attempt to help general music teachers attain more success with

Keith P. Thompson is professor of music education in the School of Music at The Pennsylvania State University.

■ ▪ ▪ ▪ ▪

Pedagogical issues are almost completely under teachers' control.

▪ ▪ ▪ ▪ ■

inclusion. Additional sources of information can be found in the sidebar.

Inclusion Issues

Music educators face two kinds of issues in dealing with inclusion. One is administrative, and the other is pedagogical. It is frustrating to teachers if they feel there is little they can do to control or influence administrative policies related to inclusion. Questions arising from these issues can influence educational policies that form the basis for many decisions:

• Which students are placed in which music classes?

• How many students are included in a given class?

• Are classroom aides available and willing to work with students

during music class?

• How available and willing are support personnel to consult with the general music teacher?

• What funds are available for adaptive music materials and equipment?

These issues cannot be ignored. Music educators need to become active participants in the process by which school policies are established, vigorously lobbying for supportive environments for students so that they can be successfully included in general music classes. At the same time, it must be realized that this process takes time and effort at every level and cannot always satisfy the needs of every individual.

Pedagogical issues, on the other hand, are almost completely under teachers' control. Certainly, the policies of inclusion significantly affect the degree to which teachers can provide a special music education for their students, but teachers of general music usually decide what and how to teach, and they can make changes immediately to increase the likelihood that their students will learn successfully.

A special education in music generally means *more*—more models, more hands-on activities, more multisensory experiences,

Sources for Additional Information on Inclusion

Articles

Bernstorf, Elaine D. and Betty T. Welsbacher. 1996. Helping Students in the Inclusive Classroom. *Music Educators Journal*, 82:5, 21–26.

Bulawa, Eugenia. 1993. Music Instruction and the Hearing Impaired. *Music Educators Journal*, 80:1, 42–44.

Humpal, Marcia Earl and Jacquelyn A. Dimmick. 1995. Special Learners in the Music Classroom. *Music Educators Journal*, 81:5, 21–23.

Smaligo, Mary A. Resources for Helping Blind Students. 1998. *Music Educators Journal*, 85:2, 23–26, 45.

Thompson, Keith P. How Accessible are Your Concerts? 1996. *Teaching Music*, 4:2, 33–34.

Books

Atterbury, Betty. 1990. *Mainstreaming Exceptional Learners in Music*. Englewood Cliffs, NJ: Prentice Hall.

Schaberg, Gail. 1988. *Tips: Teaching Music to Special Learners*. Reston, VA: Music Educators National Conference.

Internet Sites

Inclusive Schooling Links Projects:
www.pub.naz.edu:9000/~jwblack/inclusion.html
The Book on Inclusive Education:
ww.quasar.ualberta.ca/ddc/incl/intro.htm

more repetition, more practice, more time to learn, and more individual attention. Regardless of limitations imposed by administrative policies, teachers can examine their pedagogy to determine if they are offering learning experiences that will ensure successful music learning for all students, including those with disabilities. The remaining sections of this article offer some suggestions for pedagogy that might lead to more successful inclusion in general music.

Three Questions

Goals for music learning should be the same for all students. With very few exceptions, students with disabilities can learn to sing, play instruments, and respond to music just as other students do, though they may need different ways to learn. When preparing for classes that include students with disabilities, teachers can plan lessons as usual. Once the plan is completed, they should review it with three questions in mind:

• *Language Use:* When are students required to use language?

• *Interaction Requirements:* When are students required to interact with others?

• *Physical Involvement:* What physical activity is required?

While these questions do not address all disabilities, most students with disabilities have limited language, social, and physical abilities. Adapting music learning activities to accommodate students in these three areas is a giant step toward assuring successful music experiences for all students. Here are some suggestions for responding to each question in terms of teaching general music.

Language Use

When are students required to use language?

Many disabilities limit students' ability to speak, read, or process language. One reason that music experiences are so valuable for students with language-related difficulties is that music offers a nonverbal, yet highly communicative, means of expression. Unfortunately, however, some teachers seem to equate teaching with talking. They feel they must verbally introduce songs, give verbal directions, offer verbal explanation, and verbally describe music that is heard. To be truly helpful, teachers should ask themselves if students must be language-proficient to be successful in their general music classes. Finding ways to reduce the necessity to read, hear, and process language in general music classes could raise the likelihood of success for many students. Consider, for example:

• Greeting students with a song or instrumental fanfare

• Using only gestures to give directions for handing out books and other materials

• Modeling desired posture and instrumental accompaniments without talking about them

•Using visuals (colors, shapes, or pictures) to guide listening.

Admittedly, songs have texts that must be learned, and lyrics can be problematic for students with limited verbal skills. Try using pictures to represent parts of the text. For example, pictures of each animal mentioned in "The Old Lady Who Swallowed a Fly" can help students learn and remember this lengthy text. Perhaps giving the text of songs to classroom teachers for use as reading lessons or making tapes so students can listen to the songs between music classes for more repetition and practice would help.

Review each lesson, identify language-intensive portions, and consider how demonstration, gesture, or visuals could be substituted. As teachers of a nonverbal art, music educators have the potential to create environments in which language-limited students can find success.

Interaction Requirements

When are students required to interact with others?

Some students' disabilities limit social learning. Some may withdraw into isolation; others may display aggressive or other inappropriate behaviors when interacting with peers and adults. Most school music experiences are social experiences; students usually perform in ensemble rather than alone. Adapting lessons for inclusion should not remove social interaction, but provide sufficient structure so that disabled students' social interactions can be successful. This effort requires a teacher to plan carefully to ensure that no students are excluded from learning activities and that opportunities for inappropriate behavior are limited. For example, a teacher can plan:

• Ways students will enter the classroom and find their seats

• How books and other materials are distributed

• Procedures for selecting students to play instruments

• Procedures for selecting partners, small groups, or other social units

• How he or she moves from one part of the room to another.

Some teachers do an excellent job of planning the content of their lessons, but their effectiveness is limited when they fail to plan classroom management. Students with weak social skills need consistent, highly structured social environments. Review lesson plans and identify when students will interact with one another or with the teacher. Be certain that in those instances all students will know exactly what to do and understand the behavior that is expected of them. Insofar as is possible, provide a structure with little opportunity for behavior other than what is expected. For example:

• Many discipline problems can be prevented by assigning seats so that students prone to off-task behavior are positioned near the teacher's usual location in the classroom.

• Rather than asking for volunteers to play instruments, select students and carefully assign parts according to their ability so that all students can participate successfully in making music.

• When activities require working with partners or in small groups, assign students to groups rather than relying on student choice or chance.

Physical Involvement

What physical activity is required?

Some physical disabilities are obvious, but hearing and visual impairments, muscular weakness, and poor coordination are often not readily detected. It is important to be fully aware of each student's physical capabilities and limitations. Rather than eliminate physical involvement from music-learning opportunities, devise alternative ways for students to become physically involved. A student with a hearing impairment may be unable to hear musical sounds, but perhaps he or she can feel their vibrations by lightly touching the back of a piano or guitar. For recordings, some sounds can be felt when an inflated balloon is held in front of a good quality speaker.

A visually impaired student may not be able to see the difference between a clarinet and a trumpet, but can feel their different shapes and components when holding the instruments. The same student may not be able to read standard notation, but can learn by rote if given recordings and access to playback equipment. It is also possible that the child could learn to read music braille (see the sidebar).

A student with poor coordination may have difficulty holding a triangle and playing it with a striker. However, if the triangle is suspended from a music stand, the student's chances of success may be greatly increased. A student in a wheel chair cannot step to the beat in a circle game, but may still physically experience the sense of pulse and phrasing when his or her chair is pushed around the circle by another student or a classroom aide.

Giving Students More

When planning for classes that include students with disabilities, committed teachers can ask, "Is there another way to experience this part of the music? Is there another way to learn this aspect of the music?" In my opinion, accepting the challenge of providing "music for every child and every child for music" means accepting the responsibility for providing a special music education for those students who do not learn in ordinary ways. If a special education means *more*, I believe that it is essential to find ways to provide more musical models, more ways for them to personally experience making and responding to music, and more opportunities to practice and develop their own musical skills. In doing so, general music educators will meet the pedagogical challenges of inclusion. At the same time, I feel that teachers need to continue as activists in the process by which the policies of inclusion are formulated. When music educators have met the administrative and pedagogical challenges of inclusion, both they and their students can be more successful.

This article originally appeared in the November 2001 issue of *Music Educators Journal*.

CHORAL MAINSTREAMING:
TIPS FOR SUCCESS

By focusing in advance on the special needs of students with disabilities, music teachers can pave the way for their success in the choral ensemble.

BY KIMBERLY VanWEELDEN

More than half of the music educators responding to recent surveys about mainstreaming work with disabled students.[1] The surveys also reveal that mainstreamed music classes (those having students with special needs) are not limited to the elementary level but take place at the junior and senior high level as well. Because many high school choral programs spend a majority of time and energy working toward performance-related goals, the unique and oftentimes overwhelming demands of mainstreaming placed on the secondary choral music teacher can make success in these goals seem unobtainable. However, if approached from the right perspective, successful integration of special learners into choral performing ensembles can be achieved in ways that not only meet the necessary goals but also prove rewarding for the teacher, the student, and the rest of the ensemble.

Planning Ahead

A successful learning environment begins before the first student enters the rehearsal room. First, the choral

Kimberly VanWeelden is assistant professor of choral music education at Florida State University in Tallahassee.

Success in mainstreaming students with special needs involves careful planning in classroom set-up and procedures, as well as support from peer mentors.

Photo by Jim Kirby

teacher should find out how many students with special needs will be in his or her ensembles. Teachers often raise the question of how many students with special needs should be included in any one class or ensemble. Although no specific number is written into the law, national experts recommend that the percentage of students with special needs in any one class should not exceed the percentage of students with special needs in the total student body.[2] For example, if 10 percent of the total student body are students with special needs, then each class should comprise no more than 10 percent of students with special needs. Rather than using this recommendation to refuse mainstreamed students into their ensembles, teachers should consider it as a way to help ensure a positive learning environment for all. With this guideline, teachers can also make the necessary adaptations needed to help promote success while keeping the number of adaptations within a fairly reasonable range.

After establishing the number of students with special needs in each class, it is important to gather specific information from special education teachers, counselors, and others most familiar with each of these students' specific disabilities. This step allows the choral teacher to take preventative measures to ensure the success of the ensemble experience. If, as in some school districts, the special needs' diagnosis is confidential, this lack of information need not be a stumbling block. The descriptions and suggestions of special education teachers who have worked with these students in the classroom can provide the input that music teachers need to keep these students participating in ensemble to their highest potential.

When the special needs of these students are known, the choral teacher should formulate musical objectives for each student, making sure that these goals are added to the student's individualized education program (IEP). The teacher should also ask about assistive devices students are currently using to determine if they might be beneficial in the rehearsal setting. Examples of these include amplifiers for students who are hard of hearing, octavos written in Braille for students who are blind, and the presence of teacher paraprofessionals in the rehearsal room if they accompany these students to other classes.

Classroom Set-Up

The way choral teachers set up their classrooms can make a difference in the way students with special needs respond, act, and perform while in rehearsal. For example, colorful bulletin boards or murals in the front of the classroom, rather than arranged on the sides, could distract students who are mentally disabled or have autism,

attention deficit hyperactivity disorder, or an emotional disorder. If not told ahead of time, the student who is visually impaired or in a wheelchair could be endangered as well as embarrassed by a change in the riser set-up. Other preventative strategies that could prove helpful include the following:

■ Write the rehearsal plan on the board. This helps students who rely on visual cues, such as students with hearing impairments.

■ Keep the rehearsal room neat. This helps students who get disoriented or confused if things are not in their "proper places," such as students with autism, mental retardation, and attention deficit hyperactivity disorder. Also, excessive clutter can distract and frustrate students.

■ Be consistent with room set-up. This can create a sense of security in the students' surroundings and thus help them to feel in control of their situation. If permission sheets or fundraising forms are always turned in at the same place, students who would normally have difficulty with such tasks can learn where to hand in their materials with minimal prompting over time.

■ Clearly mark changes to classroom set-up. Prepare the students by making signs and announcements before changes take place. Give early notice of changes to students who are mentally retarded, visually impaired, or in a wheelchair. Plan the necessary logistics, especially if these changes need to take place during the course of a single rehearsal (e.g., changing from section to quartet seating).

■ Have a consistent seating arrangement. This allows students with mental retardation, autism, visual impairments, or wheelchair requirements to find their correct place within the ensemble without constant reminders from you. This will also give you time

in advance to adapt the environment for students with physical disabilities.

■ Have an alternate seat assigned for students who are prone to move. Some students with special needs have a tendency to get up and roam about the room. One solution that may minimize disruptions is to provide that student with an alternative place to sit within the ensemble.

■ Be open to other preventative measures. Nothing is guaranteed to work every day with every student. Keep this in mind and think of other ways to prepare your classroom for all students.

■ ■ ■ ■ ■ ■

Modeling and rote-singing are useful instructional techniques to help students with special needs within a chorus.

■ ■ ■ ■ ■ ■

Rehearsal Modifications

The goal to successful mainstreaming during rehearsal is to meet the individual needs of each student while conducting the rehearsal as you normally would. However, though many teachers find that they may have an opportunity to help students with special needs before and after class, it is nearly impossible to help these students during the actual rehearsal without neglecting the other members of the ensemble or stopping the flow of the rehearsal completely. One solution is to enlist the help of students without disabilities by pairing these students with those who have disabilities. The helper students then take on the role of peer mentor for students with a disability within the rehearsal setting. Specifically, they could help by answering questions, by reiterating directions, and by assisting the student with various individual tasks—remaining in the appropriate place in the score and rehearsal, handing in materials on time and in the right place, solving small logistical problems such as finding a folder or pencil, and being prepared the night of a concert with uniform and knowledge of stage entrances and exits.

Establishing a peer mentorship program within the choral ensemble has advantages for all persons involved. First, the teacher is freed from stopping rehearsal numerous times to answer questions that are specific to only one person. Second, the student with special needs has a person who answers his or her questions immediately, as well as a prompter who helps him or her make the most of each rehearsal. Peer mentors have a chance to use their leadership abilities in a positive and constructive way.

A successful peer mentorship program requires several things. First, it is essential that a teacher discuss with students with special needs whether they would like to have extra help during rehearsal. Not every student with special needs will require or want a peer mentor in the choral ensemble. If the student does elect to have help, the teacher must exercise great care in choosing the appropriate peer mentor for that student. Some potential peer mentors may display natural leadership qualities but not nurturing qualities. Do not choose students to be peer mentors who become easily frustrated with imperfection or slower-paced understanding—a potential disaster for both the peer mentor and the student with needs. Success in this effort also requires advance training

programs for peer mentors that outline their roles within the program and present different role-playing scenarios that might occur.

Another factor that teachers should take into consideration before the program begins is the importance of seating the peer mentor next to the student at all times during the rehearsal, especially if several seating arrangements are used in one rehearsal. Keeping the same peer mentor for the same individual should also be a priority. Students with disabilities may take time to become comfortable enough to ask their peer mentors questions, and mentors may need time to develop specific strategies that work well with the students they are helping.

■ ■ ■ ■ ■ ■

Students with disabilities may take time to become comfortable enough to ask their peer mentors questions, and mentors may need time to develop specific strategies that work well with the students they are helping.

■ ■ ■ ■ ■ ■

Although peer mentoring is a wonderful program, teachers can make other additions to the rehearsal to help students, including the following:

■ Adjust the time of participation. This is particularly helpful if it is known ahead of time that a particular student has difficulty concentrating and participating for the full rehearsal time. It is much better to have the student actively involved in the rehearsal

for thirty minutes and return to the self-contained classroom than to have the student conform to a time frame that does not work for him or her.

■ Have a routine rehearsal structure. To limit confusion, make rehearsals as similar as possible. Of course, it is not very practical to rehearse the same pieces during the same time at every rehearsal. However, students who need to follow a routine will benefit if, for example, physical warm-ups start immediately at the beginning of class, followed by vocal warm-ups and then the first piece of music, which is listed on the board.

■ ■ ■ ■ ■ ■

Most students with disabilities can learn what is musically expected of the ensemble. The difference is that it takes them much longer to understand and execute the concepts.

■ ■ ■ ■ ■ ■

■ Be open to other modifications. It is impossible to know and plan for every situation that might arise during rehearsal. Be prepared for this eventuality and learn to modify techniques along the way.

Promoting Quality Singing

Teaching good vocal technique to students within a choir is one of the choral teacher's primary jobs—and can be one of the most demanding experiences a teacher faces because of the individual needs of each student.

Teachers must take into consideration not only the physical differences of each student's voice, such as level of maturation, but also the differences of how each student learns new concepts. These differences are oftentimes magnified when teaching students with special needs. Therefore, instructional practices must be tailored to help these students sing to the best of their ability.

One of the first steps a teacher can take to aid the success of students with special needs is to help them learn their vocal parts for each piece of music. For some students, this may mean that their vocal line within the score be highlighted in some way so they have an easier time following along. Other students may need not only highlighted vocal lines but also rehearsal tapes of their individual parts so they can practice outside of class. While making rehearsal tapes does require advanced planning, they are particularly helpful to students who need additional prompts to learn their music.

Modeling and rote-singing are useful instructional techniques to help students with special needs within a chorus. Students, such as those with mental retardation or autism, who have a particularly hard time learning their part or a specific vocal technique will benefit from both of these approaches. A key to keep in mind when using modeling and rote-singing is to demonstrate both acceptable and unacceptable techniques so that the student can begin to see and hear the differences, as well as learn what the teacher expects.

Encouraging students to be conscious about choral blend and dynamic awareness is also a very important instructional goal. While students with special needs may have a greater difficulty demonstrating these techniques, it is important that these concepts be taught to all students. To do so successfully, it may be necessary to address persons individually within the rehearsal. Such individual attention, if not handled appropriately, could create negative feelings in the person who is singled out. Therefore, it is important for the teacher to make the situation as positive as possible. The following suggestions may help:

■ Use modeling. Teach by clearly demonstrating appropriate and inappropriate techniques.

■ Maintain a respectful environment. Students should not be allowed to criticize others within the ensemble.

■ ■ ■ ■ ■ ■

Teachers should formulate musical objectives for each student, making sure that these goals are added to the student's individualized education program.

■ ■ ■ ■ ■ ■

■ Praise students' efforts. Spontaneously praising the efforts of individuals during rehearsal can have a great effect on the climate of the class. Also, remain positive with the small gains shown by students with special needs; it may not be feasible to expect them to execute all of the vocal concepts taught for each piece of music. Having specific musical goals in the student's IEP can be helpful because it allows the teacher to focus on concepts that were thought out ahead of time. Also, by focusing on a few important concepts that remain constant for all pieces of music, the student with disabilities can become confident about his or her skills.

Other suggestions to aid students in singing to the best of their ability include the following:

■ Be consistent with terminology. Try to use the same terms and examples to label commonly used vocal pedagogical techniques. For example, "good breath" means that shoulders

should not go up when taking in air and the rib cage expands.

■ Mark the music. Students who have difficulty following along within the score may benefit from extra markings such as measure numbers, breath markings, tempo changes, and definitions of other musical terms found within the score. While a future goal may be for the student to mark his or her own music, it may be necessary for the teacher to place these markings within the student's score ahead of time until the student becomes accustomed to this practice.

■ Allow extra time to learn concepts. Most students with disabilities can learn what is musically expected of the ensemble. The difference is that it takes them much longer to understand and execute the concepts. Therefore, repetition of the concepts in various forms, such as modeling and rote-singing, can aid these students in their success.

■ Provide vocal lessons. Students with special needs can learn much more if given individual attention. Therefore, if a teacher has time to give additional instruction and students have time to take instruction, individual vocal lessons can really help students learn the music, vocal techniques, and other specific concepts.

Dealing with Disruptions

Disruptive behavior exhibited by some students with special needs, such as students with emotional or behavioral disorders, oftentimes frustrates and overwhelms teachers to the point where they no longer wish to comply with mainstream policies. Dealing with these disruptions leads to an ineffective use of time and energy for the teacher and also detracts from other students' learning. To prevent this cycle, it is important for teachers to have several management and intervention plans in place in the likelihood that such an occasion should arise, including the following suggestions:

■ Seating arrangements: Many teachers know the value of a good seating arrangement. The strategic placement of all students could prevent or reduce disputes between students in the future.

■ Secret words or signals: Students may have a specific word or signal that special education teachers are already using to let them know they are off-task. Usually chosen by the student and the special education teacher, this word or signal is usually enough to stop undesirable behavior.

■ Discipline for others: Sometimes when students with emotional or behavioral disorders are acting out or are off-task, another student may actually have provoked the action. Having an intervention plan in place for students without disabilities is as important as having a plan for students with disabilities.

■ Intervention plan: An intervention plan should be thought out in advance of need. This planning also provides opportunities for discussion of strategies with special education teachers to gain their thoughts and ideas.

Conclusions

Creating a classroom environment that promotes success for all students is a goal that all teachers share. Concerts, contests, and festivals provide a wonderful avenue to have students' achievements acknowledged in a way that most other disciplines do not offer. Yet, because of the performance aspect, teachers of music ensembles often shy away from allowing mainstreamed learners into their domain. This reluctance, however, is unnecessary. The strategies discussed within this article can give students with special needs successful experiences making music with their peers. All they need to succeed are the right tools.

Notes

1. James Frisque, Loretta Niebur, and Jere T. Humphreys, "Music Mainstreaming: Practices in Arizona," *Journal of Research in Music Education* 42 (1994): 94–104; Kate Gfeller, Alice-Ann Darrow, and Steven K. Hedden, "Perceived Effectiveness of Mainstreaming in Iowa and Kansas Schools," *Journal of Research in Music Education* 38 (1990): 90–101; Janet P. Gilbert and Edward P. Asmus, Jr., "Mainstreaming: Music Educators' Participation and Professional Needs," *Journal of Research in Music Education* 29 (1981): 31–37.

2. MENC, *Opportunity-to-Learn Standards for Music Instruction: Grades PreK–12.* (Reston, VA: MENC, 1994). ■

This article originally appeared in the January 2001 issue of *Music Educators Journal*.

INSTRUMENTAL MUSIC FOR SPECIAL LEARNERS

By making minor adaptations, instrumental music teachers can find ways to include special learners in their classes.

BY STEPHEN F. ZDZINSKI

Teaching special learners in the general music classroom is a commonly accepted concept, but the idea of teaching instrumental music to special learners is less common. The wide variety of cognitive, physical, and social abilities and disabilities possessed by "special learners" makes the task of inclusion a challenge, especially for the instrumental music teacher who must keep in mind the individual modifications and instructional goals needed to successfully teach such a student. However, instrumental music teachers can successfully teach learners with a variety of disabilities to play band and orchestral instruments by making minor modifications to traditional instrumental teaching techniques and by employing approaches used primarily in special education. With these adaptations, inclusion of students with special needs into the regular instrumental music program can take place.

Stephen F. Zdzinski is assistant professor of music education at the University of South Carolina in Columbia.

■ ■ ■ ■ ■

Students need to be individually evaluated to determine both instrument preference and instrument suitability related to their particular disability.

■ ■ ■ ■ ■

Adapting Musical Instruments

An essential step in the teaching of instrumental music to special learners is selecting appropriate instruments. Students need to be individually evaluated to determine both instrument preference and instrument suitability related to their particular disability. For students who are mentally challenged, valved brass (trumpets, baritone horns, valved trombones, and tubas), single reed woodwinds, and percussion instruments are suggested by several sources as the most appropriate choices.[1] If possible, the music teacher should confer with the special education teacher to determine the extent of any developmental limitations that may affect the student's ability to play a specific instrument.

For students with significant physical challenges, a variety of band and orchestra instruments may be appropriate if selected carefully. Consultation with the school's occupational or physical therapist before an instrument is chosen will provide useful guidance, especially in determining the physical suitability of the instrument.[2] The student's instrument preference must also be considered.[3] Modifications may be needed such as holding adaptations, mouthpiece adaptations, or, in the case of percussion instruments, beater adaptations. Donna Chadwick and Cynthia A. Clark offer numerous suggestions for these alterations.[4] The sidebar lists resources for helping teachers accommodate students with disabilities in the music classroom.

Adapting the Social Environment

An instrumental music teacher who plans to include a learner with a disability needs to take several steps in order to ensure that the learner will be accepted into the ensemble. The initial step is to prepare the class for a new "special" student and to assign a "buddy" to help the student with new rules and instructional work. In preparing the class, care should be taken to explain to the students how the learner with special needs may be like and unlike them and what accommodations might be needed for this new student. In creating a suitable social environment, the instrumental music instructor will also need to prepare the special student for the music classroom. Classroom conduct rules and routines must be explained. These include such matters as respecting others, knowing how to request assistance when needed, rules for working in groups, proper procedures for participating in class, listening to and following directions, and understanding teacher and student roles. The student must be treated in a sensitive, yet non-patronizing manner that maintains his or her dignity.

Another way to adapt the social environment for the learner with special needs is through the use of positive image-building techniques, similar to those used in the Great Expectations Band Program.[5] For example, the teacher can select goals for the student that are readily obtainable and ask the student to repeat each goal until it is mastered. Any progress towards those goals is reinforced while negative experiences are de-emphasized, so that the special learner continues to visualize positive outcomes. Comparisons with traditional students should be avoided, as their progress may be quicker and thus discourage the special learner.

Parental Involvement

One way to successfully adapt the social environment for special learners is through the informed use of parental involvement strategies. In special education settings, parental involvement is a vital part of the instructional mix. Research indicates that the following parental strategies are related to more positive student attitudes and greater achievement in music:

■ singing with the child
■ taking the child to school and nonschool concerts
■ talking to the child about his or her progress in music
■ listening to music with the child at home
■ assisting with the child's practicing
■ providing musical materials for the child
■ providing transportation to the child's musical activities
■ taping performances of the child
■ attending meetings of music parent groups.[6]

■ ■ ■ ■ ■

In special education settings, parental involvement is a vital part of the instructional mix.

■ ■ ■ ■ ■

Parents who have little aptitude in music are able to follow the above strategies. They can be given a list of these items and asked to assist in their child's instructional process in these ways.

Adapting Music

Reading written notation is troublesome for students with visual information processing difficulties. Instrumental music teachers may need to adjust their traditional method of teaching music reading skills. An aural approach to teaching notation, as outlined in Stanley L. Schleuter's book *A Sound Approach to Teaching Instrumentalists,* may be very effective in teaching special learners to read musical notation.[7] In this approach, aural

experiences start with singing songs that are familiar to the students; then notation for these songs is provided. In addition, flash cards with pitch and rhythm patterns extracted from the songs are used to reinforce music reading.

Another approach that has the potential to help learners with special needs to read music is the use of color-coded notation. George L. Rogers, in his research with traditional band students, utilized color to distinguish various note values or pitches.[8] While the results do not show statistically significant differences in achievement, students using the colored notation appear to prefer it. The use of color-coded notation may enhance the comprehension of musical notation by students with visual processing and mild mental disabilities, as they tend to learn better with information presented in multiple modalities.

When selecting music for learners with special needs, the instrumental music teacher must keep in mind the differing ability levels of the special learner and the other students in his or her program and then adapt the music accordingly. Larry Williams suggests that well-known and catchy tunes, such as "Jingle Bells," "Ode to Joy," "When the Saints Go Marching In," "Bingo," and "Row, Row, Row Your Boat," work well with developmentally disabled students.[9] When arranging music that includes learners with special needs at the beginning level, the teacher can use unison, two-part, or three-part music, as well as partner songs and rounds. The ability level of the student may require that more difficult music be simplified in one of several ways. Students may be responsible for only one or two pitches and play only when those pitches are sounded in the ensemble, much in the manner of writing used in handbell choirs. Parts may be rewritten, eliminating difficult rhythmic passages using quarter, half, and whole notes that follow the harmonic progression of the music.

Adapting Teaching Techniques

Two approaches that may be helpful in teaching instrumental music to the special learner are *task analysis* and *precision teaching.* In task analysis, teachers break down complex technical and musical tasks into their prerequisite steps, creating more manageable and more easily obtainable goals. Instrumental techniques such as embouchure, holding position, breathing, and fingerings can be broken down into subskills that can be thoroughly taught and reinforced and then combined after mastery. When teaching students with special needs various facets of instrumental technique, task analysis can provide the teacher with the means to analyze situations that have gone wrong and therefore more quickly remediate problems as they occur. Breaking instruction into smaller steps helps the special learner experience more success.

Below is an example of task analysis for teaching students to make the proper embouchure for brass instruments:

- make horse noises
- make motor noises (slow to fast)
- put fingers on each side of your nose
- put fingers on your lips and make motor noises
- buzz without the mouthpiece
- put the mouthpiece on your nose and then bring it down to your lips
- buzz with the mouthpiece (natural pitch)
- make buzzing sirens (high and low)
- buzz with the mouthpiece and the instrument.

The Great Expectations Special Education Band Program uses task analysis extensively in instrumental music instruction.[10] In addition, the program uses a teaching and measurement technique borrowed from special education called "precision teaching." Teachers using this approach set goals for each student and then continuously measure and chart the student's progress through daily testing. Error patterns are analyzed in order to modify instruction so that the learner who is developmentally disabled makes steady progress. Progress is charted and recorded on the attainment of all goals, so that the teacher can decide if any goal needs to be further subdivided through additional task analysis. If

■ Resources for Accommodating ■ Students with Disabilities in Music Classes

Birkenshaw-Fleming, Lois. *Music for All: Teaching Music to People with Special Needs.* Toronto: Gordon V. Thompson Music, 1993.

Chadwick, Donna, and Cynthia Clark. "Adapting Music Instruments for the Physically Handicapped." *Music Educators Journal* 67, no. 3 (November 1980): 56–59.

Elliott, Barbara. *Guide to the Selection of Musical Instruments with Respect to Physical Ability and Disability.* St. Louis: Magnamusic-Baton, 1982.

Rogers, George L. "Effect of Colored Rhythmic Notation on Music-Reading Skills of Elementary Students." *Journal of Research in Music Education* 44, no. 1 (Spring 1996): 15–25.

Schleuter, Stanley L. *A Sound Approach to Teaching Instrumentalists.* New York: Schirmer, 1997.

the student is not meeting his or her goal, the objective is modified so that the student is able to make progress. In this way, students can make slow but continual progress that can be documented with appropriate reinforcement provided.

Adapting Evaluation Techniques

When working in instrumental music classes with learners who have special needs, teachers may need to modify evaluation techniques. Technical goals, musical content goals, and social goals should be included in their grading criteria. Students who have unique difficulties with auditory or visual perception may require both aural and written directions. Students with shorter attention spans may need more frequent, less lengthy testing situations. Anxiety may also be a problem, especially if test objectives are too difficult. More frequent testing with less complex objectives may help.

Evaluation and grading should be used to help build positive images. Instruction will need to be adapted and segmented to show continuous progress. While progress may be slower, attainment of each objective should be documented and charted to show progress, so that students and parents will not become discouraged.

Instrumental music study goals should be included in the student's Individualized Education Plan (IEP). Grading adaptations, if appropriate, should also be included in a student's IEP, and grading should be based on the attainment of IEP objectives for instrumental music. In some cases, traditional letter grades may be less appropriate than alternative grading systems, such as pass/fail grading, mastery-level grading, or the use of portfolio assessment. In all cases, instrumental music teachers need to be involved in the development of the IEPs of special learners in their music classes.

Conclusion

Students with disabilities can be successfully included in instrumental music programs, as long as teachers are ready and willing to find ways to accommodate the needs of these students. Instrumental teachers may have to seek the assistance of parents, other students in the program, preservice music teachers, or music therapists. Instruments must be selected carefully and adapted as needed, taking into consideration physical, musical, and social factors. Classes should be prepared for the inclusion of a "special" student. Additional self-esteem enhancement and parental involvement strategies may prove useful. Once the student is mainstreamed into the instrumental class, complex tasks may need to be broken down into simpler subtasks, and music may need to be simplified for the student. Grading may also need to be modified and should include both musical and social objectives. These strategies will take time and additional resources for the instrumental teacher. With a little effort, however, teachers can include learners with special needs in their instrumental classrooms and can help them include instrumental music in their lives.

Notes

1. Lois Birkenshaw-Fleming, *Music for All: Teaching Music to People with Special Needs* (Toronto: Gordon V. Thompson Music, 1993); Larry D. Williams, "A Band That Exceeds all Expectations," *Music Educators Journal* 71, no. 6 (February 1985): 26.

2. Barbara Elliot, *Guide to the Selection of Musical Instruments with Respect to Physical Ability and Disability* (St. Louis: Magnamusic-Baton, 1982).

3. A measure such as Gordon's *Instrumental Timbre Preference Test* (Chicago: GIA, 1984) may be used.

4. Donna Chadwick and Cynthia A. Clark, "Adapting Music Instruments for the Physically Handicapped," *Music Educators Journal* 67, no. 3 (November 1980): 56.

5. Williams, "A Band That Exceeds All Expectations."

6. James Shelton, "The Influence of Home Musical Environment upon Musical Response of First-Grade Children" *Dissertation Abstracts International* 26 (1966): 6765–6766; Manny Brand, "Relationships between Home Musical Environment and Selected Musical Attributes of Second-Grade Children, *Journal of Research in Music Education* 34, no. 2 (Summer 1986): 101–110; Stephen F. Zdzinski, "Relationships among Parental Involvement, Selected Student Attributes, and Learning Outcomes in Instrumental Music," *Journal of Research in Music Education* 44, no. 1 (Spring 1996): 34–48.

7. Stanley L. Schleuter, *A Sound Approach to Teaching Instrumentalists* (New York: Schirmer, 1997).

8. George L. Rogers, "Effect of Colored Rhythmic Notation on Music-Reading Skills of Elementary Students," *Journal of Research in Music Education* 44, no. 1 (Spring 1996): 15–25; Birkenshaw-Fleming, *Music for All.*

9. Williams, "A Band That Exceeds All Expectations."

10. Ibid. (The Great Expectations Program has been incorporated into the special education curriculum of the Great Falls, Montana, Public Schools.) ∎

SECTION IV

Teaching Beyond the School Years

This article originally appeared in the July 2001 issue of *Music Educators Journal*.

MUSIC FOR LIFE

Music educators can help meet the musical, social, and health needs of adults by creating new communities of music makers.

BY ROY ERNST

The Grand Masters Series is an ongoing feature offering the opportunity for MEJ readers to learn more from or become acquainted for the first time with those special individuals who have led our profession with distinction during their music careers. It is also an opportunity for senior members of our profession to share their insights relative to what they have seen and experienced in music education.

This month's article, "Music for Life," was prompted by a nomination that included the following words, "Although it is the rage to push for music education at the earliest moments of a person's life, due to the pioneering efforts of Roy Ernst, successful attempts at music making are also being extended well beyond a person's retirement years."

Roy Ernst is a professor of music education at the Eastman School of Music of the University of Rochester, where he has taught for twenty-five years and chaired the music education department for twelve years. He teaches courses in curriculum and instrumental methods. Ernst began his career teaching instrumental music in elementary and secondary schools in Michigan, and he was a member of the applied faculty at Wayne State University in Detroit. He received his B.S. and M.S. degrees from Wayne State University and Ph.D. from the University of Michigan. He received the President's Arts Achievement Award from Wayne State University in 1994. Ernst was also on faculties at Georgia State University and the Sydney Conservatorium of Music in Sydney, Australia.

Publications by Ernst include books and articles on conducting, flute performance, and music education. He is the founding director of the Aesthetic Education Institute in Rochester, New York. Sometimes called the "Pied Piper of music for senior citizens," he conducts frequently at New Horizons Institutes, which are national and international events for New Horizons Band members.

—*Mark Fonder, series editor*

O ne of the frontiers of music education is service to people outside traditional K–12 school settings. I'm going to focus on the need to create new programs for adults of all ages, since this is the goal of a new project I direct called Music for Life,[1]

Roy Ernst

Roy Ernst is professor of music education at the Eastman School of Music at the University of Rochester in Rochester, New York.

funded by the National Association of Band Instrument Manufacturers and the National Association of Music Merchants. The New Horizons Band project, which has the goal of creating entry and reentry points to music for older adults, continues under the larger umbrella of Music for Life. My own interest in beginning instruction for adults was influenced especially by Mary Hoffman, who made "Lifelong Learning" the theme of her MENC presidency, and by John Burley for his research in the late 1970s on instrumental music education for adults.

Photo by Williams & Williams Creative Photography

The leading edge of the Baby Boomer generation (with seventy-four million people) is just now reaching retirement age, increasing a population in which the number of people over sixty-five is already greater than the number of people under eighteen.[2] This demographic shift will be even more pronounced in the future.

Music education programs that create appropriate entry points for adult beginners and "returnees" have a good record of success. These programs include intergenerational choral and instrumental ensembles, group keyboard classes, Weekend Warriors (a program to reinvolve adult rock musicians), Tri-Tone jazz camps for adult amateurs, parent bands, faculty bands, chamber music, jazz bands, and New Horizons Bands and Orchestras (for people age fifty and above). In most locations, however, the opportunities are limited at best.

Quality of Life

Numerous retired adults have ideal conditions for learning music. Most have time that they can devote to new interests, and many can afford to pay for instruction and purchase instruments. A full schedule of music activities often helps to fill the void left after leaving careers. Retirees in the well-elderly category can look forward to many years of good health, and most want challenging and rewarding activities. For many people, their new music activities become one of the most important aspects of their lives.

The intrinsic qualities of making music have a high priority for most adults, who tend to be motivated by the music itself. Grades, chairs, festival ratings, competitions, and so forth are not factors in any situation that I know of.

Adults also value the social aspect of group music making. Gerontologists generally feel that when social opportunities decrease and people feel more isolated, their health declines. Music can provide an opportunity to meet new friends who already share common interests and goals, such as preparing for a concert or going to a music camp for adult amateurs.

A recent medical study at the University of Miami School of Medicine and six other universities found that older adults who made music enjoyed measurable health benefits.[3] Participants in the study experienced decreased feelings of loneliness and isolation, an increased sense of well-being, and improvements in their immune systems. Although much more research is needed, the conclusions of this study agree with a great deal of anecdotal evidence. In addition, there is abundant evidence that the "use it or lose it" principle applies to our minds as well as to our bodies. The constant intellectual challenge of music supports good mental abilities.

The human qualities of music also provide a good counterbalance to the world of technology. As people spend more and more time isolated at their computers and alone in office cubicles, the need to come together with other people for a significant reason becomes greater than ever.

■ ■ ■ ■ ■ ■

Most adults report that they love to practice, and they do so regularly.

■ ■ ■ ■ ■ ■

Entry and Reentry Points to Music Education

We see many adults who sing and play in community groups getting a lot of enjoyment from making and sharing music. The vast majority of these people are continuing music participation that they started when they were in school. But what about all those who did not have a substantial music education in school (about 90 percent of the population) and all those who did have substantial music education but put it aside for many years? I would venture that these two groups together probably constitute about 99 percent of the population.

Imagine a middle-aged adult who would like to learn clarinet and play in an ensemble. In almost all cases, the last entry point for doing that was elementary school. Yes, it would be possible to find a good private teacher and take lessons, but most people would need an ensemble experience to sustain their interest. Theoretically, this person could take lessons and then join his or her local community band, but in many cases this is not realistic. Community bands are often too advanced to serve as entry points for novice ensemble players. In many bands, almost everyone has a music degree, and auditions are required when openings occur.

Let's compare music making to playing golf. Most golfers don't start playing until they are well beyond their early adult years. If playing golf were limited mostly to people who began in school, the whole golf culture would be a very small part of what it now is. The substantial audience for professional golf is not a product of people taking golf appreciation classes or golf history classes—it's a byproduct of people playing golf. Adults of any age feel that they can start golf, and beginning instruction is easily found. Similar conditions in music would create a much larger and more vital musical culture in which support for music education of all kinds would increase.

Model Programs

I believe that modeling is the most effective way of influencing change in music education. It may explain why there are so many successful bands, orchestras, and choruses. There is an almost endless supply of good models, and they receive a lot of visibility. There aren't as many models of successful adult music education programs, and they are often not known beyond the school or community they serve. We need to find those that do exist and give them national visibility so that others can use them as models for starting their own programs.

In 1991, I started the first New Horizons Band.[4] The goal was to create a model program emphasizing entry and reentry points for adults aged fifty and above. Part of the band's purpose was to gain some visibility for the concept and gather information that would help others create their own version of the model. Nine years later, there are more than fifty similar programs in the United States and Canada, and the number continues to grow. Through our new program, Music for Life, we will create a similar process for other kinds of models. When good models are found, Music for Life will give them national visibility and will provide information that will help in starting similar programs. Where the need for a type of program is identified and no model exists, we will create a model, evaluate it, and then provide information about it.

■ ■ ■ ■ ■ ■

The common factor in successful programs for adults is group instruction.

■ ■ ■ ■ ■ ■

The first new Music for Life model program started in Hot Springs, Arkansas, last year, where the community band started offering beginning classes and added a New Horizons Band to create entry and reentry points for adults in its community. The main innovation of the Music for Life model is that a community band explored the various ways in which it and a New Horizons Band could support each other. A very successful program involving parents, teachers, administrators, secretaries, cooks, and the custodial staff was founded at the Northwestern Middle School in Fulton County, where teacher Marcia Laird includes them all in an annual "flashback" concert that is the hit of the year.

Adult Learners

Both aging and the way adults learn are very individual. Some adults at the age of eighty have very active and independent lives, while others need assisted care. Still, there are some patterns. A very small number of adults with arthritis or other similar conditions may need to make small changes in how instruments are held. I found, surprisingly, that denture problems for wind players are not very common. The most frequent problem for senior adults is hearing loss—a problem that will probably show up at younger ages because of the increasing frequency of loud sounds, both musical and nonmusical. Placing players with hearing problems closer to the front of an ensemble helps them to hear instructions and other performers. Closed-loop audio systems of the type sometimes provided in professional performance venues may also help.

Sometimes it's difficult for adults to share music parts, especially if one person has bifocals and the other doesn't. The solution is simply to provide separate parts for each person. Some adults enlarge their parts by photocopying them if the notation is too small.

Adults have many special strengths. Most adults report that they love to practice, and they do so regularly. Singing in a group is comfortable and enjoyable for most adults; so singing can become a main mode of instruction. The band leader can simply say, "Let's all sing it. Now let's play it." Adults have many years of music in their memories. That becomes a point of reference for sensing how music should sound. When music that they already know is included in their classes, they move ahead in leaps.

Adults are involved because they choose to be. Serious discipline problems are nonexistent, although there is plenty of humor that can cause short disruptions—with everyone enjoying a good laugh. Like everyone else, adults want to learn in a situation that is comfortable, nurturing, and enjoyable. They want their conductor to be a positive person with a good sense of humor, and they don't want to be intimidated or embarrassed. A good

general rule for adults (and children) is "Your best is always good enough."

Creating an inclusive rather than an exclusive ensemble provides opportunities for many more people and has its own satisfactions. Making inclusiveness a high priority may require adjusting some performance goals, but by no means rules out satisfying and even exciting performances. Audiences like a relaxed performance style with some informal talk. Controlling the obsession to be perfect can be liberating for everyone, especially the conductor, and can make music more enjoyable for all concerned. The difference between china dishes and pottery dishes is an apt analogy. China is usually more perfect, but pottery is also beautiful, and the imperfections are part of its charm. For most conductors at any level, it's important to be able to make a musically convincing and satisfying whole out of parts that are not perfect.

■ ■ ■ ■ ■ ■

Creating a new ensemble is a personal legacy from teacher to community.

■ ■ ■ ■ ■ ■

Group Instruction

The common factor in successful programs for adults is group instruction. Most interested adults want to learn music in groups, and they want to perform with ensembles. Many adults who start with group instruction also take private lessons to increase their progress and enjoyment.

Group music education in K–12 schools is a great success story. Many music teachers probably don't really appreciate how unique and important it is. Adults want music education that is very much like school music programs, and many features of school music can be adapted to create new opportunities for adults. Public school music educators already know most of what is needed to create successful programs for adults.

Group instruction is a specialty of the music education profession—we generally do it much better than other musicians. We learn, practice, and evaluate methods for group instruction, and we observe and emulate other teachers who successfully use group instruction. One of the important skills of group instruction is dealing with a wide range of abilities in one ensemble. Some of the repertoire needs to be appropriate for the advanced players or singers. When that is being performed, those who are less advanced can learn by taking small, gradual steps, such as the following:

■ Just listen to the music. Being able to hear it is the most important step in being able to perform it.

■ Listen, keep a beat, and feel the meter.

■ Listen, keep a beat, and say rhythm syllables or pitch names.

■ Listen, say syllables, and put your fingers over the notes on the instrument without actually playing it.

■ Listen, keep a beat, and play or sing what you can.

■ Playing or singing incorrectly is not progress. It is impossible to hear it right at the same time that you are performing it wrong.

This step-by-step approach can keep everyone involved and learning at his or her own rate, while the ensemble is able to play music that is interesting for the more advanced participants.

Some composers and arrangers include a very easy part for each instrument so that beginners can play with more advanced players. Some teachers create their own easy parts. The demand for such publications will grow, and I hope that publishers will respond.

When performing music that is most appropriate for beginning players, the more advanced players can be challenged to do the following:

■ Make the best sound you've ever made.

■ Feel the meter and tonality and express it in the music.

■ Focus on precision—long notes that are exactly the right length. Feel the subdivision of the beats.

■ Examine every aspect of breath support, posture, hand position, and tone production.

■ Shape phrases with feeling and conviction.

■ Play by memory.

Playing a simple piece beautifully is always a great challenge—one that can bring a lot of satisfaction to all players and improve important aspects of their musicianship.

■ ■ ■ ■ ■ ■

We need to define the special strengths of older singers and then create new arrangements, compositions, and methods that take advantage of what they can do.

■ ■ ■ ■ ■ ■

There are some special challenges for adult choral groups. One choral conductor told me, "I think bands and orchestras for senior adults are great, but senior choruses can never be successful because voices worsen as they age." I don't believe that. I believe voices become *different* with age. We need to define the special strengths of older singers and then create new arrangements, compositions, and methods that take advantage of what they can do. In many cultures, the oldest singers are the most revered because of the wisdom and years of life experience that they bring to making music. A seniors'

choral group in Iowa City alludes to that by calling itself "The Voices of Experience." I love hearing this group sing because they really do offer something special.

Teacher Education and Benefits

Music teacher education schools that offer a wide range of classes and ensembles for adults can give their preservice students an opportunity for firsthand experience in serving the adult population in new ways. Some music students may want to teach, but they don't want to teach children in schools. For them, new models of adult education create new career options. Many teachers, having had a good experience teaching adult amateurs in college, go on to start similar programs wherever they teach.

People who become involved in adult ensembles support music education in the schools by their example of choosing to be active music makers. They tend to admire and support music teachers. One senior adult musician told me, "I heard the elementary concert in my district. Wow! Those kids are good, and the teacher is wonderful!"

Adult ensembles sometimes share concerts with elementary and secondary school ensembles, and in intergenerational models the sharing is ongoing, leading to rich personal and musical experiences for everyone. Sharing concerts brings out the best in both younger and older musicians. The presence of musicians on stage ranging from school age to old age gives the community the strongest possible message about the lifelong value of music making.

Getting Involved

There are many ways to get involved in Music for Life. If you have a program that creates entry or reentry points for adults or if you know of such a program in your area, send information about it to me at New Horizons, 201 Pine Street, Corning, New York 14830, or e-mail me at royernst@aol.com. Also contact me if you would like to start a New Horizons band or orchestra or create and evaluate a new model.

Many opportunities exist for research and development in music education for adults. We need additional research about musical and nonmusical outcomes. We need to know more about how adults learn music. Leadership is needed to create new professional organizations and networks. Instruction books geared to adults. Events are needed that bring adults together for music making such as music camps, Elderhostel programs, and classes in collegiate settings are needed. Many adults who sing or play an instrument want to go on to study other subjects, such as music theory, music history, and composition. These classes need to be adapted to serve adult amateurs.

■ ■ ■ ■ ■ ■

Events are needed that bring adults together for music making such as music camps, Elderhostel programs, and classes in collegiate settings.

■ ■ ■ ■ ■ ■

Starting an ensemble that creates a new entry point brings a special satisfaction. As it grows and brings happiness to many people, the teacher who started it will know that none of it would be happening without his or her initiative. Creating a new ensemble is a personal legacy from teacher to community.

I teach and conduct senior adults on a regular basis and help others start new programs for senior adults. My career satisfaction has never been greater, and the power of music has never been more clear to me. I also have memorable moments. One

occurred when the New Horizons Band (more than a hundred players) of the Eastman School of Music played its annual spring concert. When a mom or dad has recently taken up music and is playing a concert, their children make a big effort to be there—with the grandchildren. About 1,500 people were in attendance, many of them from out of state. It was during a moment of silence between sections of a piece that we all heard a young voice from the audience shout, "Yeah, Grandma!"

Notes

1. The term "Music for Life" was registered and put in the public domain by R. Gabe Ireland, president of Jupiter Band Instruments, Inc.

2. Annual Population Estimates by Age Group and Sex, Selected Years from 1990 to 2000, United States Census Bureau, May 26, 2000 (www.cache.census.gov/population/estimates/nation/intfile2-1.txtl).

3. "Scientific Findings Show That Music Making Helps Make Active Older Americans Healthier," American Music Conference, press release, April 27, 1999.

4. The New Horizons Band project was supported by the National Association of Music Merchants, the National Association of Band Instrument Manufacturers, the University of Rochester's Eastman School of Music, and the University of Rochester's School of Medicine and Dentistry. ■

This article originally appeared in the Spring 1999 issue of *General Music Today*.

EARLY MUSIC EXPERIENCE AND MUSICAL DEVELOPMENT

by Moira Szabo

Music educators and researchers agree that humans are innately musical (Blacking, 1973; Elliott, 1995; Gordon, 1993; Serafine, 1987). Blacking makes the point that musical tradition could not continue to exist if the majority of humankind was not musical. It has been argued that humans are endowed with internal cognitive processes that make it possible for them to acquire both language and musical understanding from a very young age (Aiello, 1995; Blacking, 1973; Gordon, 1993; Serafine, 1987). Blacking believes that "It is reasonable to suppose that music, like language and possibly religion, is a species specific trait." (7)

A number of renowned pedagogues base their philosophy on the premise that music education, like language acquisition, should begin as early as possible. Kodály believed that as children learn their mother tongue, so should they learn their musical mother tongue (Kodály, 1974), and Suzuki (1969) believed that musical ability can be developed in any child. Since the onset of Suzuki's "Talent Education" program, thousands of children, many as young as three years old, have learned to play the violin. Orff (1978), too, emphasized the importance of building on the natural musical ability of every child beginning at the preschool age. Gordon (1990) recommended appropriate music instruction at an early age as an important aspect of a child's developmental music aptitude or potential for musical achievement.

Given the overwhelming agreement that the vast majority of children are musical, questions regarding the most effective means of developing a child's musical ability remain to be addressed. The purpose of this article is to investigate the influence of early musical experiences on musical development in the hope that the information gleaned may help primary music teachers furnish musically underdeveloped children with remedial musical experiences. This information could also be used to inform parents of young children about the role they might play in stimulating their children's musical development. The pertinent questions are:

- How does the home environment affect a child's musical development?
- Are there similarities between musical development and language acquisition?
- What might parents and teachers do to develop young children's musical development?

The Home Environment

Researchers believe that a rich musical environment has an optimal effect on a child's development of music aptitude, thus laying a foundation for future success and involvement with music (Doxey and Wright, 1990; Moore, 1990; Pond, 1981; Simons, 1986). A strong relationship has been found to exist between kindergarten children's musical responses and the home environment (Atterbury and Silcox, 1993; Kirkpatrick, 1962; Moore, 1973; Shelton, 1965). In each of these studies, kindergartners were tested, and their responses were correlated with the results of interviews with their parents on the amount of music

Moira Szabo is a visiting lecturer in the Arts Education Department at the University of Victoria on Vancouver Island in British Columbia.

to which the children were exposed at home. Researchers found that in homes in which parents sang to their children, played instruments, or listened to music regularly, the majority of children had acquired singing competency by the time they reached kindergarten. Shelton (1965) reported that seventy-five per cent of musical homes produced musical children, and seventy-three per cent of nonmusical homes produced nonmusical children. Brand (1986) found that overall parental attitudes toward music and music involvement with the child in the home had a strong effect on the musical achievement of second graders but not on musical aptitude as measured by Gordon's *Primary Measures of Musical Audiation: Test Manual* (1979). During interviews of accomplished pianists, Sosniak (1985) discovered that music had been an integral part of their early home life and was highly valued by their parents, especially in the early years of three to seven. Similar results were found by Sloboda (1990), who collected seventy adults' musical memories of the first ten years of their lives. Those who were highly involved with music as adults had positive memories of childhood musical events. Events such as attending concerts, listening to music in the home, experiencing music with family and friends, and similar events evoked strong positive responses.

Language Development

Language development and music development have many similarities (Aiello, 1995; Gordon, 1993). Both are communicative modes, aurally and orally transmitted; contain phonetic, syntactic, and semantic components; develop early in life; and

are socially interactive mediums. North American child-rearing practices, however, assign more importance to the acquisition of language skills than to the acquisition of musical skills. It is a fact that children's early active musical experiences are dwarfed in comparison to the amount of language experience they receive. A *Newsweek* poll of parents with children under the age of four (Begley, 1997) revealed that only fifty-five per cent of them sang to their children or played music for them every day. Conversely, most parents spent time talking to their babies and encouraging them to respond with language babble.

■ ■ ■ ■ ■

Those who were highly involved with music as adults had positive memories of childhood musical events.

■ ■ ■ ■ ■

Mothers use a specific type of language termed "motherese" that consists of higher pitched sounds with carefully enunciated slow and repetitive speech (Taggart and Gouzouasis, 1995, 10). It is believed that this preverbal form of speech is an important link to the verbal speech development of children between twelve months and five years of age.

Moog (1976) makes the distinction between babbling as a precursor to speech and babbling as an early form of singing. Tonal babbling, which may begin as early as six months, occurs only in response to music that the child hears, either recorded music or a

parent singing to the child. Tonal babbling consists of sounds of varied high pitches, usually produced on a single vowel or a few syllables. Gordon (1993) claims that the majority of children entering kindergarten have not yet emerged from the tonal babble stage. He suggests that "a kindergarten child who has had the benefit of informal music guidance during the music babble stage, regardless of her level of developmental music aptitude, will emerge from the babble stage sooner than a kindergarten child who has not received such guidance" (1993, 307). The significance of this rather commonsensical conclusion is that children whose parents play an active part in their early musical development will achieve a greater developmental music aptitude quotient by age nine that those children without early guidance (Gordon, 1990). After age nine, the potential for musical development (music aptitude) stabilizes.

Adult Involvement

The frequency and quality of tonal babble experiences of the young child are directly related to early emergent singing ability (Gordon, 1990; Gouzouasis, 1992). Early childhood and primary teachers need to be aware that children's lack of singing ability at this stage is not an indicator of low musical aptitude. Rather, these presingers have most likely had limited musical experiences in their early development. Gordon (1993) believes that the more tonal babble a young child has engaged in, the sooner he or she will learn to audiate (to hear the sound internally after it is no longer present). Audiation is fundamental to in-tune singing and musical behavior in general. A teacher will recognize that a child has emerged from the tonal babble stage when that child is able to sing one or more short phrases of a song in tune. Until such time, music instruction should be of an informal nature.

Informal music activities should have neither directed instruction nor required responses. Teachers should spend time singing with and singing to children frequently throughout the day, as well as provide them with many opportunities to move their bodies freely in response to music. Classroom teachers can support the efforts of music specialists by integrating singing into any subject of the curriculum, for example, by singing instructions to children and encouraging them to sing back.

Parents and caregivers can make a very significant contribution to infants' musical development by singing to them routinely and encouraging their tonal babbling response. I speculate that a significant number of parents are unaware that tonal babbling is an important part of their children's musical development. I have spoken to a number of mothers of grown children about their memories of their children's early singing (tonal babbling). Very few recall singing to their children. It seems that the reason mothers do not sing to children is because singing for them is not a natural response; what may have been natural in their own childhoods may have been discouraged later in life.

Educating parents regarding how they can musically stimulate their children from the time they are born is essential. Mothers and fathers need to know that just as the child who is read to regularly is more likely to become a reader, so too the child who is sung to will more likely become a singer and hence, ultimately, a more developmentally advanced musical child.

Literature Cited

Aiello, R. 1995. Music and language: Parallels and contrasts. In R. Aiello, ed., *Musical perceptions.* 40–63. New York: Oxford University Press.

Atterbury, B. W., and L. Silcox. 1993. A comparison of home musical environment and musical aptitude in kindergarten students. *Update: Applications of Research in Music Education* 11(2):18–22.

Begley, S. 1997. How to build a baby's brain. *Newsweek,* Spr/Sum special edition, 28–32.

Blacking. J. 1973. *How musical is man?* London: Faber & Faber.

Brand, M. 1986. Relationship between home musical environment and selected musical attributes of second-grade children. *Journal of Research in Music Education* 34(2):111–20.

Doxey, C., and C. Wright. 1990. An exploratory study of children's musical ability. *Early Childhood Research Quarterly* 59(3) 425–40.

Elliott, D. 1995. *Music matters.* New York: Oxford University Press.

Gordon, E. 1993. *Learning sequences in music.* Chicago: GIA Publications.

Gordon, E. 1990. *A music learning theory for newborn and young children.* Chicago: GIA Publications.

Gordon, E. 1979. *Primary measures of music audiation: Test manual.* Chicago: GIA Publications.

Gouzouasis, P. 1992. An organismic model of music learning for young children. *Update: Applications of Research in Music Education* 11(1):13–18.

Kirkpatrick W. C. 1962. Relationship between the singing ability of pre-kindergarten children and their home musical environment. Doctoral diss., University of Southern California. *Dissertation Abstracts International* 23:886.

Kodály, Z. 1974. *The selected writings of Zolton Kodály.* London: Boosey & Hawkes.

Moog. H. 1976. *The musical experience of the pre-school child.* Trans. C. Clarke. London: Schott.

Moore, D. L. 1973. A study of pitch and rhythm responses of five-year-old children in relation to their early music experiences. Doctoral diss., Florida State University. *Dissertation Abstracts International* 34:6689.

Moore J. L. S. 1990. Towards a theory of developmental musical aptitude. *Research Perspectives in Music Education* 1(1):19–23.

Orff, C. 1978. *The Schulwerk.* New York: Schott Music.

Pond, D. 1981. A composer's study of young children's innate musicality. *Bulletin of the Council for Research in Music Education,* no.1, 1–12.

Serafine, M. L. 1987. *Music as cognition.* New York: Columbia University Press.

Shelton, J. S. 1965. The influence of home musical environment upon musical response of first grade children. Doctoral diss., George Peabody College for Teachers. *Dissertation Abstracts International* 26:6765.

Simons, G. 1986. Early childhood music development: A survey of selected research. *Bulletin of the Council for Research in Music Education,* no. 86:36–52.

Sloboda, J. A. 1990. Music as language. In F. R. Wilson and F. L. Roehmann, eds., *Music and child development,* 28–43. St. Louis: MMB Music.

Sosniak, L. 1985. Learning to be a concert pianist. In B. Bloom, ed., *Developing talent in young people.* 19–67. New York: Ballantine.

Suzuki, S. 1969. *Nurtured by love.* New York: Exposition Press.

Taggart, C. and Gouzouasis, P. 1995. Music learning and language learning. *Update: Applications of Research in Music Education* 13(2):9–13.

APPENDIX

The Housewright Declaration

Whenever and wherever humans have existed music has existed also. Since music occurs only when people choose to create and share it, and since they always have done so and no doubt always will, music clearly must have important value for people.

Music makes a difference in people's lives. It exalts the human spirit; it enhances the quality of life. Indeed, meaningful music activity should be experienced throughout one's life toward the goal of continuing involvement.

Music is a basic way of knowing and doing because of its own nature and because of the relationship of that nature to the human condition, including mind, body, and feeling. It is worth studying because it represents a basic mode of thought and action, and because in itself, it is one of the primary ways human beings create and share meanings. It must be studied fully to access this richness.

Societal and technological changes will have an enormous impact for the future of music education. Changing demographics and increased technological advancements are inexorable and will have profound influences on the ways that music is experienced for both students and teachers.

Music educators must build on the strengths of current practice to take responsibility for charting the future of music education to insure that the best of the Western art tradition and other musical traditions are transmitted to future generations.

We agree on the following:

1. All persons, regardless of age, cultural heritage, ability, venue, or financial circumstance deserve to participate fully in the best music experiences possible.

2. The integrity of music study must be preserved. Music educators must lead the development of meaningful music instruction and experience.

3. Time must be allotted for formal music study at all levels of instruction such that a comprehensive, sequential and standards-based program of music instruction is made available.

4. All music has a place in the curriculum. Not only does the Western art tradition need to be preserved and disseminated, music educators also need to be aware of other music that people experience and be able to integrate it into classroom music instruction.

5. Music educators need to be profi-

cient and knowledgeable concerning technological changes and advancements and be prepared to use all appropriate tools in advancing music study while recognizing the importance of people coming together to make and share music.

6. Music educators should involve the music industry, other agencies, individuals, and music institutions in improving the quality and quantity of music instruction. This should start within each local community by defining the appropriate role of these resources in teaching and learning.

7. The currently defined role of the music educator will expand as settings for music instruction proliferate. Professional music educators must provide a leadership role in coordinating music activities beyond the school setting to insure formal and informal curricular integration.

8. Recruiting prospective music teachers is a responsibility of many, including music educators. Potential teachers need to be drawn from diverse backgrounds, identified early, led to develop both teaching and musical abilities, and sustained through ongoing professional development. Also, alternative licensing should be explored in order to expand the number and variety of teachers available to those seeking music instruction.

9. Continuing research addressing all aspects of music activity needs to be supported including intellectual, emotional, and physical responses to music. Ancillary social results of music study also need exploration as well as specific studies to increase meaningful music listening.

10. Music making is an essential way in which learners come to know and understand music and music traditions. Music making should be broadly interpreted to be performing, composing, improvising, listening, and interpreting music notation.

11. Music educators must join with others in providing opportunities for meaningful music instruction for all people beginning at the earliest possible age and continuing throughout life.

12. Music educators must identify the barriers that impede the full actualization of any of the above and work to overcome them.

Diversity and Inclusion

SOCIAL ISSUES, CHANGING DEMOGRAPHIC PATTERNS, AND INCLUSION of special learners in the music classroom present significant challenges for music education. The fact that today's music educator must be prepared to teach diverse and underserved populations underscores the need for examining the best methodologies, techniques, conditions, and materials for bringing music to the entire student population in the nation's classrooms.

The profession's best thinking is needed to explore questions such as the following:

- How may different learning characteristics be approached successfully in music instruction? Under what conditions are adaptations necessary in ensemble or classroom instruction? What types of adaptations are the least intrusive and allow for maintaining high musical standards within the inclusive setting?
- What classroom environments are most conducive to the inclusion of children with disabilities, and what strategies can best facilitate successful inclusion?
- How can music facilitate interaction and communication among children with different learning abilities and cultural backgrounds?
- What principles should guide the selection of repertoire and materials for children in various settings (urban, rural, suburban, regional) and groupings (multicultural, multiethnic, homogeneous)?
- What techniques and materials are available to ensure that American and international students whose first language is not English are involved in school music programs?
- What are some strategies for including other significant persons (parents, other teachers, classroom aides, other music professionals) in the development, implementation, and evaluation of individualized programs for children with different learning abilities and cultural backgrounds?
- What techniques are available to ensure that learning in the classroom will transfer to environments outside the school setting?

School and Community

I N THE FUTURE, WE CAN EXPECT THAT THE ROLE OF THE CERTIFIED AND qualified music specialist will grow, expanding to that of a facilitator who works with others who are involved with students' music education, including parents, other teachers, and the community. To be most effective, music educators will need to promote lifelong learning in music, becoming involved with music programs for both preschool children and older adults. Such efforts will require contributions and cooperation from the community, other school personnel, the media, and the music industry.

The profession's best thinking is needed to explore questions such as the following:

- How do school music programs contribute to community life? What contributions can music organizations and musicians in the community make to the school music program?
- What types of outreach programs can be developed between school and community that will provide lifelong music learning and involvement?
- How can music programs be extended to young children and older adults? What opportunities exist for intergenerational music participation?
- How can school personnel more actively engage parents and other caregivers in their children's music education? How can music teachers assist parents in helping their children reach long-term goals?
- How can local and national news media contribute to music education by working with schools and professional organizations on programmatic initiatives?
- How can the music industry and professional arts organizations contribute to music education?

Music Education for New, Diverse, and Underserved Populations

BECAUSE OF CHANGES IN SOCIAL IDEALS AND public policy, today's music educators must be prepared to include students of diverse backgrounds, abilities, and interests in their classes and ensembles. Initiatives in music in early childhood and in later adulthood are increasingly common. The expansion of music education services to diverse populations was voiced as a priority for research by many MENC members. Questions related to Music Education for New, Diverse, and Underserved Populations fall into two broad categories: Diversity and Inclusion, and School and Community.